A SPECIES ON THE BRINK

We have come now to a more telling and a more powerful view of mass extinction. Cruelly, the way to this revelation has been paved by our own depravations. Our interactions with other species—as we have overkilled, deforested, acidified, polluted, threatened the ozone layer, started the greenhouse effect, and even considered unleashing a nuclear winter—have brought home to us the possibility of global disaster that previous generations could blissfully ignore. We have brought our living planet to the brink in the course of pursuing competitive rights which we believed derived from nature's law, the survival of the fittest.

Therefore we have to ask: Is Darwinism science? As we ponder the full significance of death from the sky, does our new perception destroy the scientific validity of social Darwinism and give us reason to shun it?

D0712048

Also by Kenneth J. Hsü:

THE MEDITERRANEAN WAS A DESERT:
A VOYAGE OF THE GLOMAN CHALLENGER

PALEOCEANOGRAPHY OF THE MESOZOIC
ALPINE TETHYS

THE GREAT DYING

Kenneth J. Hsü

BALLANTINE BOOKS • NEW YORK

Copyright © 1986 by Kenneth J. Hsü

All rights reserved under International and Pan-American Copyright Conventions. Published in the United States of America by Ballantine Books, a division of Random House, Inc., New York, and simultaneously in Canada by Random House of Canada Limited, Toronto.

No part of this publication may be reproduced or transmitted in any form or by any means, electronic or mechanical, including photocopy, recording, or any information storage and retrieval system, without permission in writing from the publisher.

Library of Congress Catalog Card Number: 86-9979

ISBN 0-345-34490-1

This edition published by arrangement with Harcourt Brace Jovanovich, Inc.

Manufactured in the United States of America

First Ballantine Books Edition: March 1988

This work is dedicated to the memory of my mother, Su-Lan Huang, who died in China during the Great Hunger of 1961 with a picture of her first grandson in her hands and dry tears in her eyes. She accepted the fate of her life with love and humility.

I would like to express my indebtedness to Barbara Das Gupta, who typed four drafts of this manuscript over the last three and a half years. I thank Uel Briegel, Markus Baumann, and Peter Jordan for their assistance when Barbara and I failed to communicate with our Macintoshes. I appreciate the forbearance of my wife, Christine, and my son, Peter, for enduring weeks and months of silence at the dinner table when I was immersed in my thoughts about *The Great Dying*. Finally, I have a deep gratitude to Sara Stein, my editor. Her insistence on perfection necessitated repeated revisions of the production schedule, but, as she admonished me in my impatience, the race is not to the swift. Her rewrite during the long incubation helped create the manuscript in its final form.

KENNETH J. HSÜ
February 18, 1986

Contents

THE GREAT
DYING

1

The Question
of Fitness

MY ADOLESCENCE WAS MARRED BY CONTRADICTION.
I lived then in Chungking, the provisional capital
of China, during the nine years of the Sino-Japanese War
which ended with the World War II defeat of Japan in
1945. At home, Mother extolled the Confucian virtues of
moderation and forgiveness and taught me the Taoist essence of accepting one's fate in love and resignation. At
school, we were instilled with radical patriotism. Every
morning we lined up for half an hour of gymnastic exercises to make our bodies strong. Then, for the remainder
of the hour before breakfast, we were harangued by the
rector. We had to steel our will to fight in the struggle for
existence, he told us. The weak would perish; only the
strong would survive. We were to acquire strength not
through the acceptance Mother prescribed, but through
hatred.

At the same time on the other side of the battlefront a
teenage German boy listened to Goebbels's polemics and
was inducted into the *Hitler Jugend*. According to both
our teachers, one or the other of us should have pre-

1

vailed, yet it would not have surprised my mother to discover that we are now colleagues, neighbors, and friends.

Though both of us survived the war, we were victims of a cruel social ideology that assumes that competition among individuals, classes, nations, or races is the natural condition of life, and that it is also natural for the superior to dispossess the inferior. For the last century and more this ideology has been thought to be a natural law of science, the mechanism of evolution which was formulated most powerfully by Charles Darwin in 1859 in his *On the Origin of Species by Means of Natural Selection, or the Preservation of Favored Races in the Struggle for Life*.

Three decades have passed since I was marched into the schoolyard to hear the rector contradict my family's wisdom with his Darwinian claim to superiority. In light of all that happened in the war, and that has happened since, and that may happen most catastrophically in the future, I must question what sort of fitness is demonstrated by the outcome of such struggles. As a scientist, I must especially examine the scientific validity of a notion that can do such damage.

DARWIN WAS A GEOLOGIST AND A NATURALIST, A STUdent of the history of life. The study of the history of life on our planet leads immediately to a paradox: There are millions of living species, yet virtually all species that have ever lived are now extinct. This is so because although the total number of species living at any one time has not changed very much in the last half billion years, the average longevity of a species is about as ephemeral in the history of life as an individual's life span in the history of mankind. Living species represent only a fraction of 1 percent of all the kinds of organisms there have ever been.

Viewed in this perspective a theory of evolution must not only account for species' arising, it must also account for species' expiring. To Darwin, the mechanism for extinction was one and the same with the mechanism for creation. Each individual organism differs in some degree from all other organisms, and its unique characteristics are inheritable. Nature works creatively among this infinite variety of individuals. Those whose characteristics best fit them for their way of life tend to survive, reproduce, and pass their superior traits to their offspring. Those less fit die, and their inferior traits are thus lost from the population. When such a continually changing population is isolated from the mainstream of its kind in such a way that interbreeding does not occur, it may become so different as to constitute a separate species. When next it meets its close relatives, one or the other will prevail and will exterminate its competitor in the struggle for life. As Darwin explained this consequence of the natural law of survival of the fittest:

> I think it inevitably follows, that as new species in the course of time are formed through natural selection, others will become rarer and finally extinct. It is the most closely allied forms, varieties of the same species, and species of the same genus or of related genera, which, from having nearly the same structure, constitution, and habits, generally come into severest competition with each other. Consequently each new variety or species, during the progress of its formation, will generally press hardest on its nearest kindred, and tends to exterminate them.

Strangely enough to our generation so familiar with dinosaurs and other amazing creations of former times, the fact of extinction was still news in Darwin's day. Fossils, particularly fossil shells, had been known since antiquity, but it seemed possible to many that although they were clearly different from present species, they might represent only an earlier form in a continual transformation from one species to another. In this view, it would be as incorrect to call the disappearance of an earlier form an extinction as it would be to claim that a child has become extinct in the process of its transformation into an adult. The first fossil skeleton of a giant reptile was unearthed in 1770, about forty years before Darwin's birth. It was certainly like no living creature that had ever been seen.

The fossil jaw, a meter and a third long with dagger-like teeth, was chipped from a chalk deposit in a quarry on St. Peter's Mount near Maastricht, Holland. A father-and-son team of anatomists was summoned to identify it. Impressed by its size and by the fact that it had been embedded among marine shells, the father declared it to be from an ancient whale. The son, who must either have been a better anatomist or a more acute observer, thought otherwise. The jaw looked like that of a lizard. But who had ever seen such a gigantic specimen, or any lizard that swam the sea? A more likely explanation was that the monstrous beast had lived before the biblical deluge and was, perhaps, its victim.

A local priest who owned the pasture above the quarry invoked feudal rights to acquire the find. The relic was promptly housed in a glass shrine at his chateau. The news of the discovery of an antediluvian dragon spread far and wide, soon reaching Georges Cuvier, the foremost anatomist of his time. Napoleon Bonaparte, who had sponsored Cuvier's collecting expeditions, ordered his general leading a campaign to "liberate" Holland in 1795 to bring the precious fossil back intact. The victorious army entered Maastricht, occupied the chateau, but found the glass case empty. The relic had been stolen.

The general offered six hundred bottles of vintage wine for the missing jaw, and soon marauding soldiers were able to claim the reward. The booty of victory was shipped to Cuvier in Paris.

Then only twenty-six years old, Cuvier had just completed a study of mastodon bones that convinced him that these ancient elephants were not an early form of the modern species but had become extinct—dead, gone, without descendents of any sort. He was beginning to make inroads in convincing his contemporaries that such extinct animals existed; the great beast of Maastricht was the proof he needed. Although bearing considerable resemblance to the terrestrial monitors of the tropics, *Mosasaurus*, as the lizard came to be called, was a marine reptile more than twice as large.

That sensation was followed by the first find of dinosaur fossils in 1822, when Darwin was a boy of thirteen. They were only fragments—a piece of thigh bone, some giant teeth—dug up by the wife of Gideon Mantell, an avid fossil collector who lived in the south of England. She thought the remains were those of a reptile, but the reptiles most were familiar with were carnivores with the sharp teeth typical of meat eaters. The crown of the teeth Mrs. Mantell found had been worn down flat, suggesting that their owner had been a vegetarian.

Again, Cuvier the expert was asked for his opinion. He confirmed that the teeth were those of a herbivorous reptile. Mr. Mantell eventually came upon a skeleton of an iguana stored away in the Hunterian Museum of the Royal College of Surgeons in London that bore a striking resemblance to the dinosaur teeth except for the vast difference in size. He therefore named his find *Iguanodon* (iguana teeth), and the discovery together with its new name was formally announced in 1825.

Using the tooth size of living iguanas as a scale, an Oxford professor, Richard Owen, came to the amazing conclusion that *Iguanodon* had measured somewhere between 30 and 60 meters, or about half the length of a football field. Continued feverish searching by Mantell and other amateurs turned up ribs, vertebrae, and other bones during the next decade and a half. Their size forced Owen to reduce his original exaggerated estimate to about 7 meters. The fossil bones showed that these ancient saurians were of heavier build than modern lizards, as well as much larger size. He further perceived that *Iguanodon* had the same chest structure as crocodiles, whose four-chambered heart is far advanced compared to the three-chambered heart of other reptiles. He suggested that the animal may have had a heart and circulatory system approaching that of warm-blooded vertebrates.

Owen named these animals Dinosauria—terrible lizards. A sculptor of wildlife was commissioned by Queen Victoria to make a reconstruction of this terrible lizard based on Owen's description for the Great Exhibition of 1851, and *Iguanodon* took on the appearance of a huge, cumbersome quadruped gazing fiercely at visiting dignitaries that included the queen and her prince consort.

Meanwhile Ferdinand Hayden, later to head the geological survey of the United States, was collecting more dinosaur teeth in the wild west country near Judith River, Montana. His collection was donated to the Academy of Natural Sciences in Philadelphia, where they were studied by its director, Joseph Leidy. These teeth were of other dinosaur genera: a herbivore Leidy named *Trachodon* (rugged teeth), and a carnivore he named *Deinodon* (terror teeth).

The teeth proved to be only an appetizer. Leidy was soon able to procure an almost complete skeleton exhumed at Haddonfield, New Jersey, and named *Hadrosaurus*. The teeth, lower jaw, and vertebrae, as well as the humerus, radius, and ulna bones of arms and legs, all belonged to one individual. A comparison of *Hadrosaurus* teeth with those of *Iguanodon* suggested that the two dinosaur specimens were closely related, yet the skeleton of the Haddonfield specimen bore little resemblance to the one reconstructed according to Owen's interpretation. Its front and hind legs were radically different in size. Hadrosaurs and Iguanodons were not quadrupeds at all; they must, Leidy supposed, have stood on their hind legs and bounced along like kangaroos.

Over the next decades competing teams, often sponsored by industrial magnates and sometimes resorting to skullduggery to satisfy their sponsors' greed for bones, excavated a bewildering array of monsters. Their trophies were assembled and presented as tributes to monarchs and presidents and displayed in their royal or national museums for the enjoyment of a gaping public.

Some were supergiants: *Brontosaurus* and *Brachiosaurus*, at about 55 tons or the weight of eight elephants together, were thought to be too heavy to support their bulk on land. They were depicted mired in swamps with their long necks delicately curved to reach for aquatic weeds, or immersed in water right up to the nostrils on the top of the head. Gigantism among carnivores reached a peak with *Tyrannosaurus rex*, the largest predator that ever existed, with teeth the size of a pickaxe. When that skeleton was restored in an upright posture, its heavy tail dragging along the ground, viewers were flabbergasted to discover that a person of average height reached only to the beast's knee.

Other dinosaurs proved to have exotic ornament or armament: The huge frilled bone that crests the neck of ceratopsian dinosaurs; the various spine plates, tail spikes, and maces of stegosaurs; the oddly shaped head crests of hadrosaurs; and the thumb spikes that *Iguanodon* eventually possessed and that could have been useful only for gouging out the eyes of its otherwise invulnerable predators.

There also turned up, as the scramble for fossils continued, diminutive toothsome creatures with clawed wings and long feathers that made them resemble mythical griffins; they were thought to be primitive birds and were therefore named *Archaeopteryx* (ancient bird). There also emerged from the bowels of ancient sediments reptiles—not dinosaurs—as wonderful as anything invented in fairy tales. *Elasmosaurus* was a sea dragon, whose image may have inspired the legend of the Loch Ness Monster. Pterosaurs were winged reptiles, some crow size or smaller, others the size of eagles. One, the oceangoing *Pteranodon* with a wingspan of 15 meters, had reached the probable ultimate size limit for an airborne animal. Apparently too heavy or weak to flap, pterosaurs were thought to be gliders that could soar aloft only by launching themselves from treetops or cliffs.

According to Darwin, this remarkable bestiary that lived prior to 65 million years ago became extinct because it lost the competitive struggle for existence. Darwin compared the arena to "a yielding surface, with ten thousand sharp wedges packed close together and driven inwards by incessant blows, sometimes one wedge being struck, and then another with greater force." Each wedge in his analogy corresponds to a variety or a species, and the blows each receives represent the driving force of natural selection. Since there is a finite area of surface into which each wedge can be pushed, one that manages to dig in will force out a previously stuck wedge. Thus does a more fit species force out a less fit one. "The boat is full," as the Swiss said in justifying the closing of their borders to refugees during the last war.

Darwin owed his idea of a spatial limit to the number of species to Malthus's similar idea about the spatial limit to population growth. In his autobiography, he wrote:

> In October 1838, that is, fifteen months after I had begun my systematic inquiry, I happened to read for amusement Malthus on *Population*, and being well prepared to appreciate the struggle for existence which everywhere goes on from long-continued observation of the habits of animals and plants, it at once struck me that under these circumstances favorable variations would tend to be preserved, and unfavorable ones to be destroyed. The result of this would be the formation of new species. Here, then, I had at last got a theory by which to work.

Darwin did not commit this brainstorm to publication until twenty years later and then was galvanized into action only because a young colleague, Alfred Wallace, had come up with the same idea. Incredibly Wallace, two decades after Darwin's reading of Malthus "for amusement" and half a globe away on an island near New Guinea, had the same idea inspired by the same reading:

> I was then [February 1858] living at Ternate in the Moluccas, and was suffering from a rather severe attack of intermittent fever, which prostrated me

for several hours every day during the cold and succeeding hot fits. During one of these fits, while again considering the origin of species, something led me to think of Malthus's *Essay on Population* (which I had read ten years before), and the "positive checks"—war, disease, famine, accidents, etc.—which he adduced as keeping all savage populations nearly stationary. It then occurred to me that these checks must also act upon animals, and keep down their numbers. While vaguely thinking how this would affect any species, there suddenly flashed upon me the idea of survival of the fittest—that the individuals removed by these checks must be, on the whole, inferior to those that survived. Then, considering the variations continually occurring in every fresh generation of animals or plants, and the change of climate, of food, of enemies always in progress, the whole method of specific [species] modification became clear to me, and in the two hours of my fit I had thought out the main points of the theory.

Thomas Robert Malthus's *Essay on the Principle of Population* was first published in 1798 during the ferment years of the industrial revolution and is still required reading in many social science courses. Its tenet is illustrated by the recent experience of China. The Chinese population had remained stable during a century of foreign and civil wars, which ended in 1949. In the following three decades, the population doubled from 500 million to a billion. At this rate of increase, there would be 2 billion Chinese in the year 2110, 4 billion in 2140, and 1,000 billion in 2410, when there would be standing room only. This horrifying prospect, according to Malthus, can never come to be because the struggle among people for the wherewithal to survive provides a check to continual increase in their numbers.

The public outcry that greeted Darwin's *Origin* was never directed at his belief in the struggle for existence, or survival of the fittest. What offended some was the theory of common descent: that all organisms share at some fork in their family tree a common ancestor with one or more related organisms, and that if the entire tree of life were to be drawn, it would show at its very root a single life form from which all others have descended. As to the mechanism by which life forms continually branch into new forms, that seemed axiomatic to the robust doers of the industrial revolution.

Survival of the fittest was immediately embraced as a natural law that justified for capitalists ruthless competition. Andrew Carnegie wrote that "the law of competition, be it benign or not, is here; we cannot evade it; no substitutes for it have been found; and while the law may be sometimes hard for the individual, it is best for the race, because it ensures the survival of the fittest in every department." John D. Rockefeller grandiosely maintained that "the growth of a large business is merely a survival of the fittest. It is merely the working out of a law of nature and a law of God."

Enthusiasm for this newly revealed working of nature was not confined to capitalists. The Italian socialist Enrico Ferri, in fact, turned the law against capitalism. He noted that natural selection cannot be expected to function under the unnatural conditions of a class system. The fit would prevail if inequities of wealth and privilege were righted. Karl Marx turned the idea yet again. He wrote in 1861, "Darwin's book is very important and it suits me well that it supports the class struggle in history from the point of view of natural science." Friedrich Engels understandably revered both these masters, Darwin for discovering the law's workings in biology, Marx for discovering its mechanism in human history. He added his own interpretation: The proletariat was destined to win the struggle for existence because its members were superior breeders compared to the bourgeoisie.

While politicians interpreted natural selection to their own right- or left-leaning purposes, racists wasted no time justifying theirs. The subtitle of Darwin's book, *The Preservation of Races in the Struggle for Life*, was inviting; Darwin even explained that "races differ from each other in the same manner as...do closely allied species." Within two decades of the publication of *Origin* a British commentator, Alfred Marshall, was able unabashedly to voice the opinion of many of his contemporaries:

> There can be no doubt that this extension of the English race has been a benefit to the world. [But] if the lower classes of Englishmen multiply more rapidly than those which are morally and physically superior, not only will the population of England deteriorate, but also that part of the population of America and Australia which descends from Englishmen will be less intelligent than it otherwise would be. Again, if Englishmen multiply less rapidly than the Chinese, this spiritless race will overrun portions of the earth that otherwise would have been peopled by English vigour.

Racism was only one step away from eugenics, a school of applied Darwinism founded by Francis Galton with the aim of improving the fitness of the human race by applying the "theory of heredity, of variations, and the principle of natural selection." From eugenics, it was no large leap to genocide.

The intellectual history of the Nazi justification for genocide has been traced to Ernst Haeckel, a biologist and a philosopher who introduced Darwin's ideas in Germany and used them to give German racism the illusion of scientific validity. Haeckel is best remembered for an apparently benign postulate that young biology students were formerly taught: Ontogeny recapitulates phylogeny. He thought he saw evidence that ontogeny, the development of an individual animal from embryo to adult, repeats phylogeny, the development of the species from a primitive to an advanced form. For example, in a baby's flat nose and lack of body hair he detected a primitive stage of human evolution represented by the "lower"

Mongoloid (Asiatic) race. As a Caucasian baby grows, he recapitulates the evolution that ultimately resulted in the typically European features of his superior race. Noting the characteristic features of children suffering from Down's syndrome, the Haeckelians surmised that they were regressions to an even earlier stage of evolution, referring to them as "Mongolian idiots" or "Mongoloids."

Haeckel had much to say about "savages," too. Their skull, he maintained, resembled the skull of Neanderthal. "The difference between the reason of a Goethe, a Kant, a Lamarck, or a Darwin and that of the lowest savage is much greater than the difference between the reason of the latter and that of the anthropoid apes." The Jews, especially the Russian Jews, belonged to such a "filthy and outlandish" race that Haeckel could hardly consider them human at all.

Satisfied as to both the naturalness and the rightness of racism, Haeckel formalized his ideas in the monist school of philosophy. A premise of monism was the superiority of the German "race," which was to become manifest by unleashing the powerful forces of selection in open struggle with the inferior races. Hitler, heir to monism, chose simply to exterminate those races.

Social Darwinism as taught by the monists may have sown wickedness elsewhere than in Nazi Germany or among neofascists elsewhere in the Western world today. Theo Sumner, accompanying Helmut Schmidt on a visit to China, was admitted to an audience with Mao Tse-Tung. He was astonished to hear from Mao the indebtedness he felt to Haeckel's ideas. Convinced by the monist philosophy that human nature would degenerate without the continual pressure of natural selection, Mao had been inspired to advocate the ceaseless revolution that brought my homeland to the brink of ruin.

Darwin, of course, cannot be held responsible for wickedness done in his name. As George Bernard Shaw wisecracked, Darwin merely "had the luck to please everybody who had an axe to grind." Darwin himself was aware that his ideas were subject to misuse. In a letter to a colleague shortly after the publication of the *Origin of Species*, he good humoredly complained: "I have received, in a Manchester newspaper, rather a good squib, showing that I have proved might is right, and therefore that Napoleon is right, and every cheating tradesman is also right."

BUT ANYONE CAN, AND SCIENTISTS SHOULD, QUESTION whether the law of the survival of the fittest is really a law, or is even science.

The generally accepted test of whether an idea is science or ideology is that to be science, a theory must be falsifiable: That is, one can devise an experiment, investigation, or observation that, if its results fail to correspond to those predicted by the theory, would prove it to be wrong.

This test was used in the Arkansas trial in 1982 in which Judge William Overton ruled that creationism, or "creation science," as its disciples call it, is not science. For a year, Arkansas's Balanced Treatment Act of 1981 had allowed schools in the state to give the teaching of the creationist theory of the origin of species equal time with the Darwinian version. Creationism teaches that "the Bible is the written Word of God, and because we believe it to be inspired throughout, all of its assertions are historically and scientifically true in all the original autographs. To the student of nature, this means that the account of origins in Genesis is a factual presentation of simple historical truth."

The American Civil Liberties Union took the issue to court on the basis of the constitutional separation of church and state. Judge Overton therefore had to decide whether creation science was science or religion.

Ironically, the defense was undermined by its own witnesses. One supporter of creationism as science claimed that "it is impossible to devise a scientific experiment to describe the creation process, or even to maintain whether such a process can take place." Another stated that "We cannot discover by scientific investigation anything about the creative processes used by the

Creator." That is because, another defense witness added, "He used processes which are not now operating anywhere in the universe."

Because the creationists had hoisted themselves on their own petard by claiming there was no way to prove their theory false, Judge Overton had no choice but to declare that creation science is not science. However, the issue of whether Darwin's theory of natural selection is science did not arise at the trial. Can evolution theory be proved wrong?

Karl Popper, the philosopher of science whose test was used to unseat the creationist claim, did not think so. He said that Darwin's theory is an attempt to interpret a historical process—the history of life on earth. Since history is not repeatable (we cannot, for example, perform an experiment to see whether Rome fell for a theorized reason), Popper felt that all attempts to discriminate between historical truth and falsehood are a matter of judgment or of faith.

But in fact there are quite a few tests that can and have been used to judge the possible falsity of Darwin's theories. The hypothesis that has emerged triumphant from these tests is that of common descent.

The most powerful test of a theory is its predictive value. Popper was right to insist that a theory that explains only already known facts is nothing more than a historical interpretation. But most scientists agree that a theory that predicts something that has not yet been observed is science. Such a theory is falsifiable because it may predict something that then cannot be found, or is shown not to exist, or when found does not accord with the prediction. On the other hand, its approximation of truth increases with each new discovery that confirms the prediction.

Darwin, much to the annoyance of many of his contemporaries, postulated that humans and apes had descended from a common ancestor. At the time he first jotted down his ideas on descent in 1833, no skeleton in any way different from *Homo sapiens*, modern man, had been found. His theory thus predicted something novel, if not shocking: When such fossils were found, they would be more apelike than modern man. The first "missing link" was discovered in 1857, two years before Darwin's theories were published. This previously unknown subspecies, *Homo sapiens neanderthalensis*, or Neanderthal man, was indeed somewhat apelike; when the skull and parts of the skeleton were exhibited at a German scientific meeting at Bonn that year, some expressed doubts that it was truly human. Others thought it was an aberration. Geologist Charles Lyell, however, perceived that "the newly observed deviation from a normal standard of human structure is not a casual or random monstrosity, but just what might have been anticipated if the laws of variation were such as the transmutationists [such as Darwin] require."

If the word *experiment* is defined as a procedure adopted for testing a hypothesis, then a project or an expedition for the purpose of verifying a prediction is an experiment. From the discovery of Neanderthal until now, many purposeful searches for human and prehuman fossils have been made in Europe, Asia, and Africa. The results, including the latest find of "Lucy," the most primitive hominid yet uncovered, have been nothing less than sensational. Moreover, they have amply confirmed Darwin's prediction, for each older fossil also more closely resembles an ape in its anatomy. Lucy represents a diminutive hominid named *Australopithecus afarensis* that lived some 3 million years ago and walked upright as we do; her skull could easily be mistaken for that of a chimpanzee.

These confirmations were made in the same way they were in Darwin's time, through comparing skeletons. In the last few decades other experiments using sophisticated technology have been devised to test the theory of common descent. Evolution is conducted through changes in the genes, the functional portions of deoxyribonucleic acid (DNA) that are manifested in biochemical and morphological differences among species. Tissue typing, the technique doctors use to match donor to recipient for organ transplants, provides one measure of gene difference: The more closely two species are related, the more alike the immunological "profile" of their cells. Molecular biology, in which DNA itself can be examined, yields not only an estimate of the degree of relatedness between species, but also a measure of how much time has passed since each of two species began its evolution from a common ancestor.

By using both immunological and molecular analysis, the relationships among humans, apes, and monkeys have been clarified. Chimpanzees are our closest relative; we two species began to evolve our separate ways from a common ancestor 7 million years ago. Two million years before that, gorillas had begun to branch off from the same ancestor. The other apes are more distant both in time and kinship, and the monkeys even more so.

The same pattern predicted by Darwin's theory of common descent has emerged from countless other investigations of myriad life forms. Comparative anatomy has been used to discover in a group of bipedal and possibly warm-blooded reptiles that lived 200 million years ago the common ancestor of dinosaurs and birds, and reptiles have been linked in turn to mammals via mammallike reptiles called therapsids that dominated the earth some 250 million years ago. The linkage of groups continues back into the very distant past all the way to bacteria, the oldest fossils known, whose microscopic remains are found in rock fully 3 billion years old. The descent of all life forms that have ever existed from a single original life form is demonstrated most dramatically in DNA itself, for the chemical language by which it instructs life processes is identical in all organisms.

Extraordinarily, Darwin could guess no mechanism by which traits are inherited, nor imagine what it was that changed traits over time, for he knew nothing of genes or DNA. Yet when Gregor Mendel's work in genetics was rediscovered in the twentieth century, and Crick and Watson decoded the universal language of the DNA molecule in the 1950s, his century-old prediction of common descent was stunningly confirmed.

* * *

HAS NATURAL SELECTION BEEN THAT CLEARLY DEMON-
strated? Some aspects have. Selection implies choice
among multiple alternatives: Its raw material is variation
in genetic makeup among individuals. The same work
that has confirmed common descent has also confirmed
that each individual organism is unique.

Natural selection also implies adaptation: The organisms that survive to pass their genes to their offspring are
those whose unique combination of genes best suits
them to their way of life in their environment, or the
"profession" that biologists call a niche. Knowing an animal's niche allows one to predict the traits that that species might be expected to exhibit. If, for example, both
male and female of a bird species cooperate in the rear-
ing of young, and the species is subject to predation,
both sexes should exhibit dull or mottled plumage to
camouflage them from predators while they are performing such dangerous tasks as incubating eggs. Those with
showy plumage should be more subject to predation during breeding season and thus produce fewer young.
Therefore either a species with showy plumage should
prove to have few predators, or those individuals that
are brightly colored should not participate in the more
vulnerable childrearing tasks. Field studies have confirmed such predictions for birds and many other organisms over and over again.

IF NATURAL SELECTION IS THE DRIVING FORCE OF EVOLU-
tion, then adaptation should be responsive to changes in
the environment. The most well-known case history of
adaptation to a changing environment is the peppered
moth of England. Individuals of the species vary in the
genes that determine wing color. Some years ago, most
individuals were pale, matching in color the bark of trees
on which they rested. A few were dark; their numbers
were limited by the circumstance that their dark color
made them highly visible to the birds who preyed on
them. As soot from factories darkened tree bark, the
proportion of dark to light moths changed. Now, almost

all peppered moths are dark; the few that are white are seen and eaten. One would think such case histories—and there are many of them—would close the case on natural selection: Clearly the fit survive.

But do they become new species? Darwin realized that in a population such as that of peppered moths, adaptation is not analogous to speciation, for characteristics of the species merely shift in response to environmental changes over time. For the species to branch into new forms, as gorillas and hominids branched from a common ancestor, some individuals who among them contain variations not crucial to survival in the population as a whole must be reproductively isolated from their fellows under circumstances in which those variations are crucial to survival. Darwin saw in the Galápagos Islands an obvious opportunity for speciation: Each island is separated from the others by large expanses of water, and each island differs in the habitats it offers. Refugees from the mainland population—storm-tossed survivors, for instance—were reproductively isolated. Whatever useful genes they brought with them, and whatever useful changes to their genes occurred thereafter, would contribute to adaptations selected by the vicissitudes of their new environment. The Galápagos Islands are, in fact, inhabited by numerous species of Darwin's finches, each uniquely adapted to its unique niche, and all evolved from a single mainland species.

Since that original study in speciation other mechanisms for reproductive isolation have been identified, the most important being, perhaps, sexual selection, or the refusal of females to breed with just any male. These confirmations of the mechanisms of speciation have, however, raised new questions. Darwin's and Wallace's Malthusian brainstorms both involved a leap from the mathematics of a population explosion to the mathematics of speciation. Although organisms overproduce offspring, and therefore increase continually if not limited by their mortality rate, species spawn new species only under rather special conditions. Moreover, where speciation appears to have been prolific, as in the tropical rain forests of the Amazon, each novel version of an organism creates for itself a novel niche. Contrary to Darwin's prediction, the "wedge" of its adaptation appears not to have dislodged its kin; the total resources of the environment are continually divided up in different ways.

An analogy is the capitalist economy that Carnegie and Rockefeller thought so amply illustrated the truth of the law of the survival of the fittest in the struggle for existence. The burgeoning of the automobile industry not only created its own niche within the economy, but also created niches for the rubber, steel, and oil industries. So, too, does speciation within one group create opportunities for speciation among other groups—novel plants that can be exploited only through novel adaptations among herbivores, novel herbivores that can be captured only through the novel adaptations of predators. The phenomenon of coevolution—a new species of fly that pollinates a new species of orchid—appears to be very common. Competition—two species of fly that fight for the nectar in a single species of flower, or two flowers that battle for a single species of pollinator—appears to be quite rare. Rather, the struggle in which an individual finds itself is a struggle with nature. Those English moths have no argument with one another; their relative fitness is associated with the color of bark and with the eyesight of birds.

On the basis of such investigations, many scientists believe that a kingpin of Darwin's theory of natural selection has been falsified. The agent of evolution may be natural selection, but the selector is not a competitor, and the birth of a new species is not paramount to a death sentence for the old.

That makes the problem of extinction more problematical by far than Darwin suspected. Take the dinosaurs: If Darwin's postulate of competition for identical or very similar niches were true, then the rate of speciation would be, as he predicted, perfectly balanced with the rate of extinction. But the dinosaurs all disappeared at once; none of their fossils has ever been found in sediments younger than the chalk at Maastricht. Did mammals do them in? Few have seriously suggested that. The small mammals of that day, whose niches were unlikely to have overlapped those of a tyrannosaur or a ceratopsian, could hardly have felled such giants.

We must look instead to where the struggle for existence seems actually to occur, at the interface between an organism and its environment. Darwin knew well from both the fossil record and selective breeding of domestic plants and animals that evolution occurs very slowly. Change cannot be accomplished by the individual in its lifetime: An organism cannot decide, say, that climate is becoming drier, and therefore it had best become a camel. Change occurs only over many generations of drying during which individuals that can tolerate a degree of dehydration (or have a means to avoid it) have a reproductive advantage over individuals that cannot. Some extinction undoubtedly occurs at all times, because even the slow changes that all earthly environments continually undergo are at times too rapid for the rate at which a species is capable of adapting.

But, in fact, the geological record shows two quite different rates of evolution. There are quiescent times, when most species remain unchanged and the number that evolve into new species really are balanced by the number that become extinct. There are other times when speciation is very rapid, and times of even more rapid extinction. Those events are not simultaneous. First, there is a massive extinction such as that which claimed the dinosaurs. Then there is a pause during which the survivors do just as Malthus predicted: They multiply like rabbits. Then, they speciate, sometimes so rapidly that their evolution is described as "explosive."

If one looks at the way environmental change might relate to such a pattern, an interesting link becomes apparent. Very rapid change must increase the extinction rate way beyond the speciation rate because there is a limit to how quickly any organism can evolve to suit its evolving environment. Under such circumstances, the extinction of old species has nothing to do with competition from arising new species. Rather, it indicates an inability to adapt to changes in the physical environment, and Darwin was mistaken when he emphasized the role of biotic interactions.

The rate of environmental change thus deserves a central position in the formula for extinction: The faster the rate of change, the greater the extinction rate. Thinking along these lines, it seems possible that something drastic happened to the environment to cause the mass extinction of all the wonderful beasts paleontologists have been digging from the earth this last century or so. Were a catastrophe to prove the explanation for this or other extinctions, the very root of Darwin's "law" becomes suspect. What is fitness if we cannot, examining the remains of past life or the circumstances of present species, predict which will survive and which will become extinct?

This is the final test of the law of the survival of the fittest. We can say that fitness is the criterion for survival, we can define fitness as the degree to which an individual is adapted to its present niche, and, looking at individuals, we may predict which have the better chance of surviving a temporary drought. But can we say which has the capacity to adapt rapidly enough to carve for itself a new niche should circumstances change catastrophically? Even if we were able to guess the nature of a future catastrophe, could we predict the nature of the niche that might be created as a result? There is now no niche for herbivorous snakes because there are no herbivorous snakes. Should we hypothesize a catastrophe in which rodents and insects became drastically scarce, we would be hard put to predict on the basis of any snake's fitness its chances of being able to survive on algae at a moment's notice, or even the chance of a thousand snake generations' being able to create that niche in time to avoid extinction.

The law of the survival of the fittest may be, therefore, a tautology in which fitness is defined by the fact of survival, not by independent criteria that would form the basis for prediction. The "natural law" that has given a "scientific" basis for so much wickedness may also be falsified: If most extinctions are caused by catastrophes, then chance, not superiority, presides over who shall live and who shall die. Indeed, the whole course of evolution may be governed by chance, and not reflect at all the slow march from inferior to superior forms so beloved of Victorians, and so deeply embedded in Western thought.

I THINK AGAIN OF THE CONTRADICTIONS OF MY CHILD-hood, and of my life which has been, at the time of this writing, equally divided among three nations. The first nineteen years of my life were spent in China; for the next nineteen years I studied and worked in America, and since then, I have lived for nineteen years in Switzerland. Each of these nations has a favorite card game, and it has occurred to me that in these games may be reflected the national character or folk wisdom of the players.

The Chinese play mah-jongg, a game of adaptation. One who is too headstrong to bow to inevitability finds himself in ruin, lamenting lost opportunities. One wins by taking advantage of what luck falls to him. Luck, say the Chinese, does not smile twice, yet it may come to anyone and, consistent with the Taoist and Buddhist philosophies which see intrinsic worth in every form and way of life, anyone may benefit from the chances that fall to him.

Americans play poker, a game of power. One can win by bluffing, but one can only bluff with the chips to back the bluff. The game is won by strength, the American way. I learned to play poker in my student days, when Americans' faith in their superiority was severely tested. The Western philosophy represented by Darwin's per-spective of competition among individuals and "races" of varying worth was then under siege, but neither faith in power nor love of poker has gone away.

The national game of Switzerland is jass. I will always remember the jass game we played August 23, 1968, as the Russians marched into Prague. A Swiss jass master and I teamed up against my wife and an American, who were both rank beginners. We played jass in our hotel room all evening while bullets whistled by in the streets outside. As luck would have it, the beginners won decisively. Jass is so dependent on luck that its outcome cannot be predicted on the basis of the players' skill. Some say a person is lucky to be a Swiss, but I rather think it is the other way around: If one is Swiss, one had better be lucky, for there is little chance to get ahead there unless one happens to be born into the right social position.

So I have gotten equal doses of three ways of perceiving success: That success comes to those who take destiny into their own hands and overpower their competitors; that success is luck and is out of our hands altogether; and that success comes to those who can tolerate misfortune while taking advantage of whatever good luck falls to them. So, too, one might see evolutionary success as poker, jass, or mah-jongg: strength, chance, or flexibility. I like to think that those thrice-nineteen years of differing perspectives have broadened my ability to judge whether such value systems have distorted the way we see the history of life.

I do not wish to choose among those three nations any more than I wish to decide whether I or my neighbor deserved to survive the war, or wish to predict whose present fitness guarantees survival in a nuclear holocaust. As a scientist, I see instead an opportunity to pull from beneath any such judgments the justification of science. The law of natural selection is not, I will maintain, science. It is an ideology, and a wicked one, and it has as much interfered with our ability to perceive the history of life with clarity as it has interfered with our ability to see one another with tolerance.

This book will discuss the evidence for the best investigated episode of terrestrial catastrophe and of mass extinction in earth's history. In order to seek out defective stones in the foundation of our science, I have adopted a historical approach, retracing especially the discoveries made by geologists, paleontologists, and physicists, and the impact of those discoveries on our thinking about biological evolution. Did struggle for a place in the sun decide the fate of dinosaurs, or did events extrinsic to the ways they earned their living cause their extinction? If a catastrophe cut the thread of their continued evolution, what enabled the survival of others? Were those survivors the fittest? Or were they, simply, the luckiest?

2

Boundless Seas, Mulberry Trees

"**B**OUNDLESS SEAS, MULBERRY TREES" WAS AN EXpression I heard often as a child at the conclusion of long stories narrated by my elders lamenting the relentless changes wrought by time. I do not know the source of this piece of Chinese wisdom, but to a modern geologist it summons to mind the very essence of his profession: Time is long. Our planet is more than 4.5 billion years old; with the passage of time mountains are worn down to plains, plains sink into the sea, the sea bottom rises to become land, and where once there was ocean, mulberry trees grow.

When I left my homeland to study geology at university I soon came upon a quotation by Chevalier de Lamarck that gave me a modern version of my relatives' ancient wisdom:

In this globe which we inhabit everything is subject to continual and inevitable change. These arise from the essential order of things and are effected with more or less rapidity or slowness, according

to the varying nature or position of objects implicated in them. Nevertheless they are accomplished
within a certain period of time. For Nature, time is
nothing, and is never a difficulty; she always has it
at her disposal, and it is for her a means without
bounds, wherewith she accomplishes the greatest
as well as the least of her tasks.

Larmarck wrote toward the end of the eighteenth century when the Western concept of time was undergoing a
revolution as profound as Darwin's concept of speciation, whose roots are also to be found in the closing decades of the Age of Enlightenment. The realization of the
depth of time that is recorded in the fossils and formations of Earth's crust was to enable science to wrench
itself from the hold of biblical revelation.

It is difficult now to appreciate the pervasiveness of
Christian doctrine at that time, or the emotional commitment (sometimes the fear of persecution) that held people to a belief in the literal truth of Earth history as
depicted in Genesis. For about a century the Christian
world's version of liberal biblical interpretation had been
that the Earth dated from 9:00 A.M. on October 26 in the
year 4004 B.C. By extending that calculation by painstak-
ing study of the generations since Adam and Eve,
Noah's Flood was claimed to have begun on November
18, 2349 B.C. To most of his contemporaries who thus
perceived time as reaching back a mere six thousand
years, Larmarck's concept of time as "a means without
bounds" was incredible.

Chevalier de Lamarck had crowned his successful career in botany with an appointment by the French National Convention of 1793 as professor of zoology, of
insects, of worms, and of microscopic animals. Two
years later, in 1795, James Hutton, a Scottish physician
who never had time to examine patients because he was
too busy examining rocks, published the startling conclusion he had reached after years of observing the outcrops around Edinburgh, which became the basis for
Lamarck's musings. The processes at work eroding old

rock and creating new rock had been so many times repeated that he saw "no vestige of a beginning, no prospect of an end." His mind, he admitted, grew "giddy by
looking so far into the abyss of time."

The ability to comprehend geological time does not
come easily. We tend to appreciate time in terms of our
own experience of its passage. One of the very first
memories I have of my childhood was my confusion
about the significance of the term *some time ago*.

I STARTED MY EDUCATION AT TOO EARLY AN AGE, FOR MY
parents wished me to be in the same class as my sister,
who was two years my senior. I was not ready for
school. I was scared by the tales our teacher told us,
especially by her recounting of the Manchu invasion of
South China. Despite a valiant defense by the people of
Yangchou, my hometown, those barbarians had broken
into our city and plundered, raped, and killed for three
days and three nights. Very few of the residents had survived. The Manchu invasion was enacted in a school
play. My sister and I did not see the conclusion, because
our rickshaw man came to fetch us just as a messenger
appeared on stage with the tiding that the Manchus had
taken the city of Hwaiyin (where my father was staying
at that time) "some time ago." When I got home, I ran to
my mother and, though I refused to confide to her my
fear that my father had been killed, begged her to help
me write a letter:

Dear Father:

How are you? We are fine. It rained the day before
yesterday, and the roof had a leak. Did you see the
Manchus?

Yours, Jinghwa

I was overjoyed a week later when my mother gave
me a letter from Father. He was naturally pleased to
have heard from me, but puzzled by the reference to the

Manchus. No, he had not seen them. They had come some time ago, to be exact, 289 years before.

MOST EIGHTEENTH-CENTURY SCIENTISTS WERE AS BLIND to geological time as a child is to historical time. George Bellas Greenough, the founder and first president of the Geological Society of London, declared in a rage during a scientific dispute over the way rivers cut deep valleys, "No river has deepened its channel one foot; no amount of time could enable Nature to work wonders." The old man had lived by the Thames for more than half a century, yet he had never seen a deepening of its channel by erosion. He could not appreciate that our lifetime is only a split second in the immense flow of geological time that does, indeed, allow nature to work wonders.

Larmarck did appreciate it. The botanist had had little knowledge of animals, and less of rocks, but it was not too late for the fifty-year-old to master a new science or to pick up on the revolution that was occurring in geology. He studied the shell collections of the University of Paris and found differences between fossil specimens and modern ones. The distinctions were regular enough that he could classify them on the basis of their lesser or greater resemblance to living mollusks and to one another. The results were sequences of shells in which Larmarck thought he could detect relatedness. He proposed, therefore, a theory on the transmutability of species, the forerunner of the evolution theory, that envisioned populations originally belonging to one species becoming at length transformed into others distinct from the first. The change had to be very slow, and Lamarck, functioning in a Huttonian rather than a biblical time scale, could imagine a very long succession of generations before the transformation was accomplished.

Both Hutton as a geologist and Lamarck as a zoologist committed themselves to what has since come to be called a uniformitarian view. Even the vast, sweeping changes that have overtaken the world, turning ocean bottom to blooming orchard and alien shells to modern mussels, are the result of nearly imperceptible increments directed by processes still occurring. To both, this uniformity of causes was the very foundation of science. As Hutton put it, "If a stone which fell today were to rise tomorrow, there would be an end of natural philosophy, our principles would fail, and we would be no longer investigating the rules of nature from our observations."

That the "rules of nature," or natural laws as we would call them today, had directed change through all time was not so obvious to Hutton's and Lamarck's colleagues. Georges Cuvier, elected to the Chair of Comparative Anatomy of the College of France in 1795, soon after Lamarck's appointment in zoology and the same year in which Hutton's work was first published, saw a different meaning in the fossils he examined. One day workmen brought him mastodon bones from a gravel pit of the Seine valley in a geological formation around Paris. He saw at once that the ancient elephant belonged to a different species from either of the two living forms, the African and the Asian. Found together with the giant mammal were bones of hippopotamus, rhinoceros, and tapir—all extinct in France, although still extant in tropical Africa and Asia. Some years later, in reconstructing mammalian skeletons unearthed from a gypsum quarry at Montmartre in a different layer in the same general area, he found that all differed from any known creatures of the modern world. Because the gypsum deposit was older than the gravels, those extinct mammals must have lived in an earlier epoch. Eventually Cuvier found in still older rocks on the periphery of the Paris Basin the really bizarre skeletons of dinosaurs. With this evidence, he was able to delineate four faunal dynasties for the region of Paris: the Dinosaurian, the Extinct Mammalian, the Mastodon, and the present assemblage of land animals.

The apparent extinction of the older forms was hard for this doctrinaire believer to integrate with church dogma. Cuvier had studied mummified plants and animals discovered in ancient Egyptian tombs and had found no difference between the mummified and living specimens. Working within the traditional time scale, in which Egypt was a superpower not many generations after the Creation, he saw no reason to assume that the original organisms God had created had ever changed if they had not changed a whit in the millenia since Exodus. The fossils from the Paris Basin must, therefore, have lived prior to Genesis and must have been destroyed by catastrophes outside the natural laws that now govern God's Creation. These revolutions were so stupendous, Cuvier imagined, "that the thread of Nature's operations was broken by them, that her progress was altered, and that none of the agents which she employs today could have sufficed for the accomplishment of ancient works." This school of natural philosophy came to be called cataclysm or catastrophism.

The biological debate between catastrophists and uniformitarians was mirrored in the geological debate between Neptunists and Vulcanists. Neptunists postulated a catastrophe, the biblical Deluge, to explain the origin of rock. Vulcanists observed that one kind of rock, at least, was of volcanic origin; as followers of Hutton, they looked to ongoing, normal processes to explain geological formations.

DILUVIAL THEORY FIT IN WELL WITH AN OBSERVATION often made by those who grow up in the Alps. Hiking is a Swiss national sport, but, as I found out one day when I drove my family above the timberline for an ascent of Mont Vendôme in southern France, small children do not always share their parents' enthusiasm. The sun was hot, the landscape bare, and my nine-year-old boy went on a sitdown strike. The idea of a treasure hunt occurred to me: Peter was to get a nickel for every fossil shell he found, and a dime if the shell were an ammonite, a beautiful and ancient relative of the chambered nautilus. Motivated by monetary gain, the enterprising young man was soon to empty my pockets, for the limestones of Provence are stuffed with marine fossils.

SEASHELL REMAINS CLEARLY INDICATE THEIR MARINE origin. They had provided the foundation of diluvial theory since the seventeenth-century cleric and would-be naturalist Thomas Burnet proposed that when God in His anger had split open Earth's crust and let the "central waters" burst forth upon an unrepentant mankind, fossil shells and stratified rock had settled with great rapidity from the "chaotic sediments" of the Flood. To many eighteenth-century naturalists, marine fossils residing in such unlikely places as the Alps remained dramatic evidence of the reality of the Deluge. A most able proponent of that catastrophist theory was John Woodward, professor of natural history at Oxford during the first decades of the eighteenth century. His impressive collection of fossils from England were, he declared, authentic relics of Noah's Flood. The zenith of the folly was reached in 1726 when Jakob Scheuchzer, a Swiss friend and devout follower of Woodward, communicated excitedly to the Royal Society of London that he had found the bones of "one of the infamous men who brought about the calamity of the Flood." His *Homo diluvii testis* seemed to have had a stature about the same as his own, or 58½ Paris inches. (It was, in fact, as Cuvier was to discover, a giant salamander.)

Abraham Gottlob Werner, a professor of mineralogy at Freiburg in Saxony and a contemporary of Cuvier and Lamarck, taught diluvial theory in the less biblical version that became the credo of the Neptunists. Werner reasoned that rocks were laid down in what had originally been a Universal Ocean. The first to form were the Primitive Series of precipitates that included granites and other crystalline rocks. These were succeeded by the Transitional Series of graywackes, marbles, and slates, followed by flat-lying strata of limestones, sandstones, chalks, shales, gypsum, and coal. On top of all was the Alluvial Series of gravels, sands, and clays.

That particular succession of rocks was, as it happened, typical of the area near Freiburg, and Professor Werner never traveled far from his hometown. He had implicit faith that the succession there was the Universal Formation over the entire globe. The master elaborated his system through three decades of informal lectures, and his ideas were spread far and wide by his influential disciples.

The black rock called basalt proved Werner's downfall. Found sandwiched between layered sediments on many hills near Freiburg, basalt was, Werner asserted categorically, of aqueous origin. Nicholas Desmaret, an amateur naturalist of Auvergne, France, was more favorably situated for understanding the phenomenon. He found that the basalt rocks in his neighborhood were as full of holes as Swiss cheese. It seemed that gases must have been bubbling out of molten rock that then hardened. Furthermore, the ground below the basalt had been scorched, giving additional testimony that the rock had originally been hot lava. Tracing the basalt flows to their source, Desmaret found an extinct volcano, one of many in the plateau country of central France. Although he had never seen an eruption in action, his careful observation and his logical deduction on the basis of comparison with a known process led him to the correct conclusion: Basalt is a volcanic rock. The followers of Desmaret were hence known as *Vulcanists*.

Werner himself never accepted the truth, but when one of his students, Citizen Jean François D'Aubuisson de Voisin, brought the master's Neptunist theory to France in 1803, he was invited to come to Auverge to see for himself. D'Aubuison came and was staggered by what he saw. The courageous Wernerian read his humble recantation a year later before the College of France: "The facts which I saw spoke too plainly to be mistaken; the truth revealed itself too clearly before my eyes, so that I must either have absolutely refused the testimony of my senses in not seeing the truth, or that of my conscience in not straightway making it known. There can be no question that basalts of volcanic origin occur in Auvergne."

Over the ensuing and increasingly pragmatic decades of the nineteenth century uniformitarianism continued to gain ascendancy over catastrophism. The leading proponent of the philosophy was Charles Lyell.

* * *

LYELL WAS BORN ON A MANOR. HIS FATHER HAD GREAT plans for him. The young Lyell was elected a fellow of the Linnean Society when he was a boy of fifteen, and entered Oxford three years later as a gentleman commoner—a privileged student who lived apart from the poorer scholars. William Buckland, English divine and geologist, read mineralogy at the university. He was a diehard Diluvialist and peppered his lectures with exciting and fascinating geological "proofs" of Noah's Flood. Because the Bible did not mention the extinction of any creatures, Buckland, like Cuvier, assumed that fossil skeletons of ancient animals were relics of a former world whose existence preceded the Creation described in Genesis. The pre-Creation world had been utterly destroyed, and processes now acting were not the same as those that had prevailed in that distant past.

Lyell attended Buckland's geology lectures, was soon befriended by his teacher, and was introduced to leading geologists of the time, all catastrophists. When young Lyell went to Paris as an amateur geologist, he was armed with copies of Buckland's *Reliquiae diluvianae*, as well as letters of introduction to prominent French naturalists. However, he was soon invited on a geological excursion with the relatively unknown Louis Constant Prevost, an event which radically altered the course of his thinking.

Prevost was a pupil of the uniformitarian Lamarck. He, like Cuvier before him, had studied the strata of the Paris Basin, which are alternating layers of freshwater and saltwater deposits laid down during successive retreats and incursions of the sea. But whereas Cuvier the catastrophist had thought the sea's behavior to have been of unknown cause and on a catastrophic scale, Prevost thought that the layered deposits could have been formed by ordinary geological processes, and in a gradual manner. The basin had been alternately an inlet of the sea—a bay—and then, cut off from the sea, a lake; then again a bay, a lake, and a bay again. The only drama in such a view is the greatness of the changes that can occur by the cumulative effects of ordinary processes over the long reach of time.

The excursion with Prevost to study rock outcrops in the Fontainebleau Forest within the basin converted Lyell from a catastrophist to a uniformitarian. He rejected his teacher Buckland's perspective and began on his own to discover analogies between processes occurring now and those that resulted in the geological formations of the past. He did not have to look far. On his father's estate at Kinnordy in Scotland was the loch of Bakie. It had been drained to give access to the bottom deposits of marl, a mixture of clay and calcium carbonate that was used to neutralize acid soils to make them suitable for agriculture. He compared the recent limestone of the Bakie loch with the ancient limestone of the Paris Basin and found them to be the same. Cuvier had thought that the ancient rock had no counterpart in modern lakes; Lyell had found it in his own backyard.

Now utterly convinced that modern geological processes were identical to those of the distant past and could explain geological features of any age, Lyell embraced uniformitarianism with all the fervor of a convert. Hutton had postulated that geological processes in the past and present are governed by the same physical laws. He had not claimed that the processes themselves had always remained exactly the same. Quite the contrary, he noted that if the process of erosion had always gone on in Scotland as it was in his day, the land would long since have been washed away into the ocean. Therefore other processes, ones that raised land up out of the sea or created new rock, must have been at work at other times to replace rock lost through continual erosion.

Lyell, in his overzealous conversion, added to Hutton's uniformity of physical laws the requirement that processes at work in the past must be those at work now, and that there was also uniformity in state and in rate throughout time.

* * *

GEOLOGICAL PROCESSES INCLUDE SEDIMENTATION, SUCH as the accumulation of calcium carbonate in lake bottoms that formed the limestones in Loch Bakie and the Paris Basin, and also less sedate events such as earthquakes, landslides, and volcanic eruptions. *State* refers to conditions, such as the distribution of subterranean forces that raise mountains, or the chemical composition of the atmosphere, or global climate. Rate is the magnitude of an event, the degree of energy with which it occurs. Lyell taught that geological change throughout Earth's history had been a matter of ceaseless alteration in details through processes now continuing at the same magnitude they had always had on a planet whose internal forces, chemistry, and climate had been the same since its beginning.

His ideas were immediately challenged. Louis Agassiz, a young Swiss colleague working at about the time of Lyell's conversion, had found evidence that central Europe and half of North America had been covered by ice caps during a not too distant past. Buckland, of course, was thrilled with the idea of a catastrophic global chill and visited his former pupil Lyell at Kinnordy to point out "a beautiful cluster of moraines within two miles of his father's house." Lyell was familiar with recent moraines, the mounded debris deposited at the leading edge of mountain glaciers; he had to admit the former existence of continental glaciers in Europe and North America, where permanent ice cannot form in our present climate. Still violently opposed to the idea of catastrophe, however, he minimized the significance of the Ice Age by speaking of regional shifts in climate caused by "local changes in the external configuration of our planet" that were in keeping with his uniformitarian doctrine.

Uncomfortable about revolutions in Earth history, Lyell was at first equally suspicious of the "transformations" Lamarck had suggested in the history of life forms. As late as 1832, in the first edition of his *Princi-*

ples of Geology, he wrote: "Variation, whether taking place in the course of nature, or assisted artificially by the breeder and horticulturalist, has never yet gone so far as to produce two races sufficiently remote from each other in physiological constitution as to be sterile when intermarried, or if fertile, only capable of producing sterile hybrids."

Yet Lyell was puzzled by the difference between fossil and modern species and was no doubt relieved to read in the work of Giovanni Brocchi on fossil shells in ancient formations of coastal Italy that this naturalist had discovered a striking resemblance between the fossil and living faunas of the Mediterranean Sea. In order to examine such resemblances for himself Lyell set out for Calabria in 1824. On the way, he stopped off at Turin to view a fossil shell collection from the nearby Superga Hills. To Lyell's surprise and disappointment, the curator of the museum in which the collection was housed informed him that the Turin fossils differed very much from the recent shells of coastal Italy. More puzzled than ever, Lyell continued on to Calabria and Sicily to unearth a collection of his own.

THE DATING OF FOSSILS WAS AT THAT TIME IN ITS INfancy. Cuvier had been able to assign relative ages to the four faunal dynasties of the Paris Basin on the basis of the law of superposition: Each sedimentary layer, or stratum, has been laid down on top of a lower layer; the upper stratum is, therefore, younger than the lower one. Examining the undisturbed sequence of deposits in the Paris Basin, he had no difficulty discerning that the mastodon remains found in a higher stratum must be younger than the remains of other extinct mammals from strata below, and that the dinosaur remains from the lowermost stratum were the oldest of all.

That was workable because basins such as the one that underlies Paris and the similar one that underlies London are situated atop large, coherent formations where layers are continuous over long distances. But elsewhere sediments have been disturbed to varying degrees. The uppermost layer, or any other stratum, might have eroded away, so there is no way of telling whether, say, the twelfth from the top in one outcrop is of the same age as the twelfth from the top in any other. There is also no guarantee that rocks of the same age are of the same type: While limestone was being laid down in a lake at one place, shale may have been forming on a flood plain at another. Further, various geological processes warp and tilt strata, break them, push them over one another, or even turn them topsy-turvy. They are more like a manuscript that has been tossed to the winds than like a book whose pages can be read in order from cover to cover.

A jumbled manuscript can be correctly sequenced if its pages have been numbered. A surveyor named William Smith found that fossils could be used as page numbers to identify the proper chronological position of a stratum even if the sediments in which it occurred had been disturbed. As a young man just finished with his apprenticeship, Smith had been hired to do the surveying for a network of inland waterways to be built by the British government for the transport of coal. He joined the Somerset Canal Project in 1794 and for the next six years surveyed every segment of its course and supervised construction.

Excavation laid bare outcrops on both sides of the newly dug channel, but almost no two sections showed exactly identical sequences of strata. Limestones, shales, sandstones, chalks, and clays, like strange faces in a crowd, seemed to possess no distinctive features by which they could be easily identified. Yet, after six years of growing familiarity, Smith realized that each stratum contained its own peculiar fossil remains, and that the sequential relation of the fossil faunas along the excavated channel is everywhere the same. He became so adept at recognizing fossil sequences that on a visit to one Rev. Benjamin Richardson of Bath, who collected fossils as a hobby, Smith was able to tell where each of the hotchpotch of specimens had come from. He was further able to predict what kinds of fossils the reverend was likely to find on various hilltops in the region.

Smith's geological map delineating the strata of England and Wales was published in 1815, followed a year later by *Strata Identified by Organized Fossils*. Thus was born the science of stratigraphy on which geological chronology was to be based. It awaited only a formal classification scheme, and that was what Lyell was about to introduce.

Lyell was no expert in fossil shells. An amateur collector, Gerard Deshayes of Paris, was. The eccentric Frenchman, while ruining his medical practice because of his passion for fossils, had acquired a reputation for his ability to tell the ages of shells. Lamarck had based his classification scheme on the degree of resemblance between extinct and modern species; Smith had deduced chronology based on his empirical knowledge of the sequence in which those mollusks had become extinct. Deshayes, working with more recent fossils than had either Lamarck or Smith, distinguished those of greater antiquity from those of lesser age by comparing the degree of resemblance of a whole assemblage of shells to a present assemblage. The more species within a fossil assemblage were still represented among a living assemblage, the younger the fossil group must be. Fossil assemblages containing fewer extant species must be of greater age.

Upon his return to Paris, Lyell sent the bankrupt physician £100 sterling to study the shells he had brought back from Turin, Calabria, and Sicily. Deshayes submitted a report to his employer a year later. Brocchi had been right: Most of the Calabrian and Sicilian fossil faunas were living forms; the assemblage was practically the same as a shell collection that could be gathered from a modern beach. Apparently those fossils were very young. But Deshayes further reported that the museum curator from Turin had also been right. Only 20 percent of the Superga Hills collection was of living forms; the other 80 percent belonged to extinct species. Deshayes had also compared the Turin collection with a French collection from the Bordeaux region; both, he judged, belonged to a fossil group of intermediate age. In an assemblage from the Paris and London basins, Deshayes had been able to identify as species still living only 38 out of a total of 1,112, or 3.5 percent. All others were extinct, demonstrating that that assemblage was the oldest of all.

Deshayes's report prompted Lyell to propose that geological chronology could be classified in terms of the percentage of extant species in a fossil assemblage. He called the group identified by Deshayes as the oldest Eocene, meaning the dawn of recent time; his intermediate group Miocene, or less recent; and his youngest Pliocene, or more recent.

The three names introduced by Lyell are still used, but the time spans they represent have changed as further study of fossil assemblages has required finer distinctions among their relative ages. The "dawn" of the Eocene is now preceded by the Paleocene, or remotely recent, and followed by the Oligocene, the slightly recent. Then come the less recent Miocene, the more recent Pliocene, followed by two more subdivisions—the Pleistocene, or most recent, and the Holocene, the wholly recent epoch in which we live now.

With this expanded epochal vocabulary, the Ice Age could be placed in the Pleistocene, a most recent epoch. Cuvier's bone beds in the Paris area could also be dated. The Mastodon fauna lived during the Ice Age in the Pleistocene and the extinct mammals from the Montmartre quarry belonged to the Oligocene, much earlier in time. But the dinosaurian fauna is older, older than any of the epochs Lyell named.

Lyell's classification of geological time could depend on the percentage of living species in fossil faunas because all the collections Deshayes studied were obtained from strata of the Cenozoic era, or the era of recent life forms that extends from the extinction of the dinosaurs 65 million years ago to the present. William Smith's collections excavated from the Somerset Canal in England contain, in contrast, practically no living species. They must be older than even the remotely recent, Paleocene epoch. The law of superposition gives confirmation to this deduction, for the strata revealed in the Somerset Canal underlie the Paleocene formations of the London Basin. Nevertheless, there was enough resemblance between the extinct and living species for Smith to use Lamarck's classification to identify his fossils. The term Mesozoic is used to designate this intermediate age of life forms on Earth. Fossils collected from still older rocks proved to bear little resemblance to recent faunas. The time during which they lived eventually came to be called the Paleozoic era, the era of ancient life.

As geologists and paleontologists unearthed and classified more and more fossils, a hierarchy of subdivisions was superimposed on the three eras, Paleozoic, Mesozoic, and Cenozoic. The largest subdivisions within eras are periods, which in turn are divided into epochs such as those that describe recent time. Because a veritable rash of naming had to cope with nomenclature that had already been in use before this modern scheme evolved, some names became logically disconnected from their sources. Thus the first period of the Cenozoic era, comprising the Paleocene, Eocene, Oligocene, Miocene, and Pliocene epochs, is called the Tertiary, although primary and secondary periods have dropped out of the geologist's vocabulary. The final period of the Mesozoic era is called the Cretaceous period after the chalk (creta in Latin) in which the identifying fossil assemblage was found on both sides of the English Channel.

Epochs are further broken down into stages. The final stage in the Cretaceous period was named the Maastrichtian stage after the town of Maastricht in Holland where the first fossil of a giant reptile was found. The first stage of the Paleocene epoch was named the Danian, after the land of Denmark. The dinosaurs died out at the end of the Maastrichtian, before the Danian stage began. The smallest time unit of all is a fossil zone—a typical assemblage of fossils—of which there may be many in each stage.

* * *

BY THE TIME I STUDIED AT UCLA DURING THE 1950s, over a hundred years after Lyell inaugurated this formalized chronology, my field of geology was presented to me all tied up in a neat package. Uniformitarianism had triumphed. Indeed, catastrophism had become so firmly associated with Christian dogma, with an ideological rather than an observational approach, that it had been totally discredited in scientific circles. Its last remnant in the twentieth century is creationism, whose disciples still believe in a diluvial explanation of fossil life forms. To scientists, the notion of an unusual, catastrophic event to explain phenomena in Earth history had become paramount to invoking the supernatural. My beloved teacher, Ed Spiecker of Ohio State, went so far as to exclaim that the very word revolution should be expunged from all geology textbooks.

Evolution, in geology as in biology, was the concept drilled into us then. After all, we had not only Lyell's doctrine of uniformity in processes, states, and rates to guide us, but also the exquisitely detailed and almost unimaginably long chronological sequence of geological time going back to Earth's beginning more than 4.5 billion years ago. Given uniformity and enough time, there was no phenomenon, no matter how extreme, that could not be explained. The ordinary events that we could see with our own eyes had, over the immensity of time, slowly written the entire book of Earth history as it is revealed in the geological record.

Having been trained by those worshippers of Lyell, I was to be surprised in 1954 when I took up my first assignment as a professional geologist. Working for Shell Research Laboratory in Texas, I joined a project to study the modern sediments of rivers and beaches. I often went to a sandbank along the Brazos River near Houston to gather samples. The Brazos is a mere creek most of the time; its gentle flow is incapable of carrying anything heavier than fine silt. Yet great heaps of heavy sand are deposited along its bank. One day a spring flood came.

When I returned to collect samples again at my usual spot I could hardly recognize the place. A new deposit of sand, many meters thick, had been dumped ashore by raging currents. I realized with a start that sediments are not necessarily deposited gradually by the everyday action of water, but can be heaped up all at once by the torrents of a spring rain.

My friend Robert Ginsburg was then investigating the coral reefs of Florida. Behind the living reefs were shallow shoals of broken coral rubble, yet the daily tides were far too weak to move big dead coral heads. The puzzle was not resolved until Hurricane Donna visited the reef in September 1960. Donna was the biggest storm in a quarter of a century: Winds reached 300 kilometers per hour and tides rose 3 ½ meters, or almost ten times higher than normal. No one was around to measure current velocity, but the water must have flowed fast enough to move boulders. A new layer of coral rubble was piled behind the reef. Perhaps, I thought, Lyell meant to include in "processes now acting" not only those observed every day, but also occasional disasters.

My second research project for Shell was to investigate the oil-bearing sands of Ventura, California. The sands there contain minute shells of animals that ordinarily live on the deep-sea floor known as the abyss. The idea that the Ventura sands had been deposited in the abyss (and later raised up to continent height) had been suggested but had been ridiculed because all experts knew that deep-sea sediments are fine clays and oozes. Coarse terrigenous debris—the sands and gravels eroded off continents—are too heavy to be transported by waves and currents to the distant depths beyond the shallow continental shelf. But powerful currents caused by underwater avalanches do occur on very rare occasions. Racing down an oversteepened slope at the edge of the continental shelf at a speed of 50 or 100 kilometers per hour such avalanches could conceivably generate catastrophic currents that would carry sands and gravels to abyssal depths. The idea, ignored by generations of scientists mesmerized by the Lyellian tradition, had finally been revived in 1950, and my own study at Ventura convinced me that rare and unusual submarine processes or ones of drastically extreme magnitude did exist.

I was learning, but I still did not fully realize the fallacy of the Lyellian dogma until my colleagues and I discovered a rock salt formation under the deep blue waters of the Mediterranean Sea. Salt is ordinarily deposited in shallow areas, small lagoons or salinas where evaporation concentrates the brine, causing it to precipitate as salt crystals. But the evidence was unmistakable that the Mediterranean rock salts are the residue of evaporation when the whole sea, down to a depth of 5,000 meters and over an area 2.5 million square kilometers in extent, dried up. When, in spite of the evidence, our theory was refuted by the argument that the desiccation of the Mediterranean is not a process now operating, I finally became aware that some of my fellow scientists are possessed by a mentality not much different from that of a fundamentalist in religion. A theory cannot be valid, I seemed to be hearing, if it is contrary to the gospel according to Charles Lyell.

What ridicule I suffered was nothing compared to the utter humiliation endured by two twentieth-century scientists who had earlier proposed processes or events that were contrary to orthodox uniformitarianism to explain observed phenomena.

Alfred Wegener, a meteorologist active in the first decades of this century, was inspired to his idea by a map of the globe. Like others before him, he noticed that the bulge of Brazil on the east coast of South America can be fitted neatly into the underbelly of Africa on its west coast below Nigeria, as though the two continents had once been joined together and had since drifted apart. There were also similarities between the fossil faunas of South America and Africa. Clinging to the concept that continental positions had been fixed for all time, paleontologists had postulated "land bridges" across the Atlantic across which animals had once migrated until these bridges sank without a trace beneath the ocean.

More peculiar even than the similarity of fossil fauna

was the similarity of geologic formations among several continents: Sediments deposited by ice sheets in South America seemed to Wegener continuous with glacial sediments in Africa, India, and southern Australia, as though all had suffered simultaneously the same episode of continental glaciation.

After careful study, he proposed that those continents had once all been joined in a supercontinent, for which he used the exotic name Gondwana, situated at the South Pole. He could offer no mechanism by which a continent might "drift"; he was, as a meteorologist, considered an amateur; and he had done his research outside the trodden fields of geology in North America and Western Europe. He was certainly beyond the pale of orthodoxy: The continents did not appear to be presently in motion, and therefore Wegener seemed to be proposing a "process not now operating." He was laughed out of court. The idea of continental drift, under its modern name of plate tectonics, was not accepted until fifty years later, when it was finally discovered that continents are now, and presumably always have been, on the move.

Geologist J. Harlan Bretz of the University of Chicago committed an even more grave offense when he actually invoked cataclysm to explain the scabland of the American West. He spent years studying the bizarrely carved and denuded landscape and came to the conclusion that it must have been sculpted by a catastrophic flood.

That heresy was vindicated only recently when it was found that a rim of debris damming a vast glacial lake, larger than all the Great Lakes put together, had given way about ten thousand years ago, sending a wall of billions of tons of water traveling at a speed of hundreds of kilometers an hour over the western plateau that stood between it and the sea. The carving of the scabland from that plateau is now considered to have taken only days. Harland was awarded the Penrose Medal, the Geological

Society of America's highest award, in 1983. He was then ninety-seven years old.

The trouble with Lyell was that he failed to distinguish the improbable from the impossible. The impossible is that which violates a natural law—a stone that rises instead of falls under the force of gravity. Improbable events are merely those which do not happen very often.

We Chinese have a tradition of patience. We do not hasten to avenge an injustice done to us. We tend to be philosophical and to say, Just wait; you may escape justice now, but in time your descendants will pay for the wrong you have done. Small misfortunes happen to everyone all the time; given enough time, the greatest misfortune, too, will surely overtake even the mightiest.

This folk wisdom is an expression of the statistical rule of the inverse correlation between the magnitude and the frequency of natural events. Small landslides are reported in Switzerland every year. Larger ones burying whole villages have happened only once or twice during the last few centuries. Still larger avalanches, whose debris buries the countryside over dozens of kilometers, have occurred only a few times in the last million years, and never within recorded history. Lyell was certainly wrong to claim that "natural processes have never acted with a different degree of energy from what they now exert."

His claim that states are uniform was also too adamant. For an ice age to begin, the state of our planet— its reflectivity and its position in regard to the sun—must be anything but the same as it has been at other times in its history, for climate has cooled drastically enough to trigger continental glaciation during only three periods in the last billion years, and probably only one other ice age was as great as the Great Ice Age that, one hopes, came to an end ten thousand years ago. Whatever state allowed the Mediterranean to dry up was certainly not the present state of affairs. For the Mediterranean to become an inland sea subject to desiccation either the Strait of Gibraltar had to rise, or sea level had to sink.

If Lyell erred in insisting on uniformity of rate and state, did he also err in claiming that processes have been always those acting today? In a sense, he did. An ordinary process, raised to a higher energy or rate, may unleash novel processes that would otherwise not occur. There is a well-known Chinese story that involves an old fool, Yukung, who was so simpleminded he thought mountains could be moved, taken away wheelbarrow by wheelbarrow, day after day. Lyell would have agreed with Yukung: Rocks will slide down a mountain's side and come to rest at its base, and gradually, over great periods of time, mountains are disassembled by erosion. But nature does not always work this way. Fifty million years ago the ancestral Rocky Mountains in western Wyoming collapsed suddenly, not rock by rock but all at once, spreading their debris like a carpet over the high plains of the state in a matter of hours. Mountains do not race across the plains today; no such process is now acting. But those mountains did come crashing down during the Eocene.

Time is a double-edged sword, and Lyell perceived only one side of its blade. He correctly saw that given enough time the ordinary gentle rubbing of grit off even the mightiest mountains will wear them down to the sea. He did not see that given enough time the rare and catastrophic must also happen. We are hit each day by numerous particles of cosmic dust originating in outer space. Each century, one person or so may be expected to be hit by a rock-size piece of cosmic debris, as was a woman in Canada several years ago. Once in approximately a billion years, our planet can be expected to bump into something truly gigantic. Such a disaster breaks no natural law: If something can happen, it will— given enough time. With the perspective of probability theory, catastrophism loses the religious overtones that for so long banned it from science. Catastrophes can happen, may have happened, and almost certainly will happen given enough time.

WHEN DARWIN WROTE HIS *ORIGIN OF SPECIES* HE WAS very much influenced by his friend Lyell's adamant uniformitarianism. He invoked slow and gradual processes to explain evolutionary changes. He postulated a single process, the biotic struggle of natural selection, that was uniform over all the time of life on Earth, proceeded always at the same rate, on a planet that ceaselessly changed in detail but never abruptly changed state. Curiously, there was a lot of evidence that had to be ignored to arrive at so gentle a perception of evolution.

The shortest units of geological time—zones and stages—are discernible to the expert because a species that is present or abundant at one time becomes extinct or rare as time passes, or a new species that is found in no sediments of older age arises. Therefore the composition of species in a fossil assemblage varies according to the age of the sediment in which it is found, and sediments of like ages have a like composition of fossils. These shifts are gradual.

The major divisions of geological time, however, were discerned because there is a radical change in typical life forms across the boundary. The giant reptile discovered at Maastricht, and the increasingly amazing bestiary of pterosaurs, icthyosaurs, and dinosaurs that continued to be discovered over the following century and more, never appear in sediments younger than those of the Mesozoic era. Many life forms that had been the dominant species in their environments also disappeared from the geological record at that time. The ammonites that Peter found on Mont Vendôme are all from the Mesozoic. Many other mollusks, including those that had been very numerous, such as belemnites and rudistid clams, became extinct along with ammonites. Even very tiny, but astronomically numerous, life forms—single-celled flora and fauna collectively called plankton—all but disappear at the boundary where Mesozoic sediments give way to the first Cenozoic ones. Such a fact might be explained by a sudden and drastic jump in extinction rate caused by an equally sudden and drastic change in the environment.

Although Lyell did not know of the mass extinction of plankton at the close of the Mesozoic, he did know of the more visible mass extinctions. Remarking on the faunas in the chalk at Maastricht, he wrote: "M. Deshayes, after a careful comparison, and after making drawings of more than 200 species of Maastricht shells, has been unable to identify any one of them with the numerous Tertiary shells in his collection. The belemnite, one of the cephalopods not found in any Tertiary formation, occurs in the Maastricht beds; an ammonite has also been discovered in this group."

The investigation of fossil shells by Lyell and Deshayes thus confirmed the great dying at the end of the Mesozoic era which had been recognized by Cuvier a few decades earlier. Yet Lyell could not give up his abhorrence of violence and revolution. In order to hold onto his passionate belief in slow and gradual evolution despite evidence of an abrupt and devastating extinction, Lyell assumed a gap in the fossil record. Writing in his *Principles*, and using the chronological terms he invented and that had not yet been revised, he stated: "There appears, then, to be a greater chasm between the organic remains of the Eocene and Maastricht beds, than between the Eocene and Recent strata; for there are some living shells in the Eocene formations, while no Eocene fossils are in the newest Secondary Group. It is not improbable that a great interval of time may be indicated by this dissimilarity in fossil remains."

Darwin, writing more than twenty years later, also explained the discontinuity of life forms at the boundary between the Mesozoic and Cenozoic as a chasm in time, an erosion of at least 100 or 200 million years from the sediments of the geological record, or longer than the whole Cenozoic era. In fact, Darwin devoted little space in his *Origin* to extinction; he assumed that the appear-

ance of a new species sufficed to pronounce the death
sentence of the old:

> As each selected and favoured form increases in
> number, so will the less favoured forms decrease
> and become rare. Rarity, as geology tells us, is the
> precursor to extinction. But we may go further
> than this; for as new forms are continually and
> slowly being produced, unless we believe that the
> number of specific forms goes on perpetually and
> almost indefinitely increasing, numbers inevitably
> must become extinct.

He thus took for granted that slow losses of older species were inescapable: Every unfit species of the old
faunas and floras was destined for oblivion in the struggle for life.

In the century since Darwin's ideas became generally
known, others have expanded on this "natural" theory of
extinction. Some have seen a tendency for species to
evolve increasingly specialized forms that make them
vulnerable to extinction, as the giant panda, which is
specialized for eating only a single species of bamboo, is
vulnerable to extinction now that its food has become
scarce. Pointing particularly to some of the most recent
dinosaurs—the tremendous *Tyrannosaurus rex* or the
elaborately armored stegosaurs—they claim that extreme adaptations such as gigantism or bizarrely exaggerated forms are per se a liability. Generalists of more
modest proportions and habits are by nature more fit,
more likely to have reserve capacity for further adaptation. Embedded in this idea is the quantitative notion
that there is only so much "stuff" available for evolution,
and if it is squandered in exotica there will be no reserve
for use when it is most needed.

A second, but related, theory is that species age, become senile, and die a natural death. Dinosaurs dominated most terrestrial environments for 165 million
years. After so long a time, they had lost their "evolutionary vigor." Naturally, they became extinct.

There is some truth to both of these hypotheses of extinction. Once birds had undergone the radical transformation that fused fingers into wingtips, there was no going back to the five digits of their reptile origins, whereas it is perhaps still possible for a five-toed mammal to lose toes and grow fingernails into hoofs, as did horses and pigs, or to lengthen fingers to support a wing, as did bats. Also, we have many examples besides pandas that demonstrate the dangers of overspecialization.

On the other hand, innumerable forms of life are so specialized as to make even the most experienced biologist gasp in wonder, and many are among the most successful of life forms. Even the lowly turtle has performed the astonishing feat, not yet understood by biologists, of moving its shoulder blades from outside its rib cage to inside its rib cage (presumably while continuing to walk through evolutionary history) in order to accommodate its extremely specialized armor. Turtles survived the Mesozoic, as they had survived for many millions of years before.

The senility theory is supported by evidence that species do have average life expectancies. The average life expectancy for a mammalian species is, for example, about a million years. However, opossums that were the direct ancestor of North American opossums today lived in the Mesozoic; cockroaches, those most vigorous of present pests, have been around for more than 300 million years, and *Lingula*, a small lampshell, has been with us since the very dawn of multicellular life at the beginning of the Paleozoic 600 million years ago.

Whole groups may also decline over time, represented, as Darwin pointed out, by fewer and fewer species and a declining population of individuals in any particular species. Some paleontologists think they see such a decline in diversity and number in fossil ammonites well before their final extinction at the end of the Mesozoic. Pterosaurs were certainly on a downhill slide, and by the end of the era few were left to suffer the ultimate blow to their kind.

Dinosaurs, however, put the lie to both the "monstrosity" and the senility theories, at least as far as they were concerned. Robert T. Bakker, of Johns Hopkins University, has led a revisionist faction of paleontologists who have repainted the old Victorian canvasses of dinosaurian life (amid, it is to be admitted, raging controversy).

Dinosaurs, like mammals today, varied from gigantic to chicken size, though none was as large as a blue whale or as small as a house mouse. According to Bakker's anatomical reconstructions the ceratopsians that survived to the bitter end of their era were made monstrous by the way they were originally restored in museum exhibits; reexamination of their fossils indicates that the thick frill of bone that crowned the rear of the skull was not exposed. It was beneath the skin and served as an attachment for the massive cheek muscles that enabled the animal to chew wood, and for the thick neck muscles that held up its heavy head. Various ceratopsian species had various arrangements of horns neither more nor less outlandish than rhinoceros horns today.

Hadrosaurs, best known to the public as "duckbilled" dinosaurs depicted half submerged in swamps and plucking mouthfuls of slimy weeds, have also proved to be far less bizarre than the imaginations of those who first reconstructed them. Cheek muscles covered most of the long hadrosaur jaw; they looked like antelopes. Some hadrosaur remains have been found mummified, complete with remnants of their leathery skin. Such mummification occurs only in very dry conditions, and the desiccated stomach contents also found are leaves and twigs of dry upland brush, not soft swamp weeds. These animals browsed in herds and sported head ornamentation that might have served as antelope horns do today —as a species recognition device and as courtship display. They had hoofs, too.

The wallowing habits of *Brontosaurus* and *Brachiosaurus* have also been put into doubt. Their bones were constructed like trusses; their weight hung from the pillar of their rear legs and hips like the span of a suspension bridge. They did walk on land; indeed, they browsed on conifer needles.

Some small dinosaurs, notably *Archaeopteryx*, the fossil which was for a long time considered to be the first bird, had feathers. They have been found to have an anatomical structure nearly identical to other small dinosaurs, and there is evidence that feathers evolved originally from scales for dinosaurian insulation, not for avian flight. All these diminutive dinosaurs were probably insect eaters.

Fossil footprints and nesting sites demonstrate a degree of social organization among some dinosaurs. Communal nesting sites of herbivorous species have been discovered, along with evidence in some cases that the hatchlings were raised in creches, or nurseries, guarded by one or more adults. Young old enough to accompany a herd have left their smaller footprints to the center of the larger ones left by their elders, a position modern herd animals utilize for the protection of their offspring. Tyrannosaurs may have hunted in pairs; smaller carnivores have left footprints that show them traveling in packs.

As for the lumbering, tail-dragging gait favored by late-night, sci-fi thrillers, both the skeletons and tracks of bipedal dinosaurs show animals balanced on powerful legs with the tail held high and rigid, racing as fast as a man in a sprint. There is no reason to believe that even the heaviest four-footed ceratopsian could not run like a rhino.

Perhaps the most terrible of the "terrible lizards" was *Stenonychosaurus inequalis*, whose large braincase, stereovision, and opposable thumb hint at the potential for becoming a race of intelligent beings. As Bakker pointed out in his *Scientific American* article "Dinosaur Renaissance," "When the dinosaurs fell at the end of the Cretaceous, they were not a senile, moribund group that had played out its evolutionary options. Rather they were vigorous, still diversifying into new orders and producing a variety of big-brained carnivores with the highest grade of intelligence yet present on land."

In short, the dinosaurs were the most advanced animals of their day, variously and cleverly adapted as insectivores, herbivores, and carnivores; generalists and specialists; of many sizes and habitats, who had flourished for 165 million years and showed no signs of a readiness to lay down their splendid lives.

Ammonites, belemnites, and rudistid clams were also holding their own right up to the dawn of the Cenozoic. Ammonites had been around throughout the Mesozoic, for roughly 200 million years. They were free-swimming cephalopods—relatives of squids and octopi—whose tentacles propelled them through the water from the stronghold of a coiled shell that ranged from a size no larger than that of a coin to that of a truck tire. The fossils of these cosmopolitan predators are found in ocean sediments everywhere.

Compared to the venerable age of ammonites, belemnites were kindergartners, an up-and-coming group that had arisen only in the Cretaceous. They were restricted in their habitat, so that fossils are found in only a few places, yet where conditions were to their liking, in every sea that is now a chalk deposit, their pen-shaped shells are very numerous.

Rudistid clams were, beyond anyone's doubt, at the zenith of their development. They were bivalves that included an astonishing diversity of species and huge numbers that lived their lives like oysters attached to the bottom in vast beds. Rudistids were the reef builders of their time, dominating that tropical environment as corals do today. Such communities bred uninterrupted for millions of years in the same location, building the reef through the accumulation of their shells to depths of dozens of meters. With a rise in sea level that community might die, only to be replaced by a new community when the water became shallow again. By these repeated occupations in the same location over spans as long as 50 million years, rudistid reef formations grew to several hundred meters thick. They are a prime reservoir of petroleum deposits today.

As for plankton, they had never been so diverse and

such wonders of reproduction as they were at the end of the Mesozoic. Their fossils from the latest Cretaceous sediments are counted in the millions or billions per cubic centimeter in such marine strata as those of the Paris Basin. For whatever reasons, plankton had never had it so good as they did just before their nearly total destruction, nor have their descendents since.

Lyell and Darwin, and generations of scientists to follow, did not have the advantage of the many and more precise studies that have mostly been made in the latter half of this century. Therefore they can be excused if they thought of "fossil lizards" as lumbering dunderheads in the twilight of their senescence, or perceived a dwindling in ammonities, or failed to think about plankton at all. Indeed, even with our advancing knowledge the issue of whether ammonites and dinosaurs were thriving or declining is still debatable. But the issue is irrelevant to the facts scientists now are sure of: that a total of 75 percent of all species existing at the end of the Mesozoic never appear again in the fossil record; that they included the great as well as the small, plants as well as animals, those that lived on land as well as those that lived in the sea, and ones that had survived for hundreds of millions of years until that time, as well as new, fresh species that represented the pinnacle of evolution as the Mesozoic era drew to a close.

The enormity of this fact calls for an explanation equally enormous, for there is nothing in particular that relates all these thousands of diverse species save the coincidence of their extinction. Ironically, the easiest explanation remains the one that Lyell and Darwin suggested, and that all uniformitarian geologists since have fervently proposed: a chasm in time lasting at least 100 million years during which, if its record had not been eroded away, we would surely find the separate, slow, and ordinary reasons for the extinction of so many organisms.

But is there a chasm in the geological record?

3

No Chasm
at Gubbio

I FINISHED MY DOCTORAL DISSERTATION AT UCLA IN
1953 and went to work for Shell Research Laboratory
at Houston in the spring of 1954. Shortly after I arrived,
a friend from the University of Houston invited me to
lunch. The place was expanding, he told me; there were
applicants for new staff positions to discuss, and, he
added proudly, "Doc Stenzel will chair our geology department."

Heinrich Stenzel was born in Stettin, Germany, and
went to work for the Texas Bureau of Economic Geology
during the Great Depression years. He became an outstanding paleontologist, a specialist on marine inverte-
brate faunas of the late Mesozoic and early Cenozoic,
and he had been elected president of the Paleontological
Society of America. My friend had reason, indeed, to be
proud that such an illustrious scientist was willing to
oversee the growth of his department.

The honeymoon was short. A lifelong civil servant
with a Prussian upbringing, Stenzel was used to order
and to ordering. That style of administration did not res-

onate well in an institution where academic freedom, with its disorder and autonomy, was the highest ideal. There was a coup, a palace revolution by the young Turks of the department, and Doc had to step down as the chairman. His friends at Shell, upset about what they saw as the raw deal Stenzel had been given by the university, invited him to join us as a consultant, and that is how I came to learn how hotly the issue of the Cretaceous-Tertiary boundary was debated.

My work with Shell at that time was to trace the origin of sand grains on the Texas beaches. Although to the casual observer it may seem that sand is washed up onto beaches from the ocean, it in fact erodes off the continent and is washed down to the coast. Therefore a grain of sand may have originated far inland, and from rock of varying ages. Much of the sand on the Galveston Beach was derived from Cretaceous and Tertiary outcrops inland. My boss decided, therefore, that I should go on a field trip with Doc Stenzel to east Texas.

It was a long drive from Houston, but we never had a dull moment. Doc was a great conversationalist, and he never missed a chance for an argument. The theme he chose was the controversial dispute on the Cretaceous-Tertiary boundary, the horizon marking the end of the Mesozoic era, when the dinosaurs lived, and the Cenozoic era, when mammals became the dominant life on land.

Argument about the exact placement of geological boundaries has been a favorite pastime for geologists. T. C. Chamberlain, a renowned professor from the University of Chicago around the turn of the century, believed that Earth history had been punctuated by revolutions, which he perceived as the natural divisions of geological periods. The Mesozoic, it seemed to him, ended with a big bang when all dinosaurs and all ammonites were killed off. Ed Spieker held the opposite viewpoint. A devout Lyellian, he taught us that ideas such as "catastrophe" and "revolution" have done so much harm to geology that they should be expunged from all geology textbooks. He claimed that outstanding change in successions, the assemblages of plant and animal life that follow one another in the fossil record, had taken place at three different horizons in what seemed to him the long transition from the Mesozoic to the Cenozoic. The ammonites, those large and beautiful mollusks related to the chambered nautilus, had become extinct first, toward the close of the Maastrichtian stage, whereas the other two changes, in floral assemblages and in vertebrate faunas, had come later. Freshwater mollusks, meanwhile, had undergone no significant evolution at all. Spieker maintained, based on this view of the matter, that all geological time units are purely artificial. In a gift copy of his lifelong work on the *Late Mesozoic and Early Cenozoic History of Central Utah*, Spieker underlined the following passage for my attention: "The boundary between the Cretaceous and Tertiary placed on the basis of any sort of pronounced change in the fossil succession cannot escape real possibility of fallacy, and it might perhaps best be regarded frankly as an arbitrary device."

I was such a good pupil and faithful follower of my teacher's philosophy that I was able to cite the essence of that pronouncement in my discussion with Stenzel. It was like waving a red cloth in front of a bull; Doc was furious.

"You know nothing about fossils, young man," he roared, "nor has your venerated teacher learned much paleontology." Results of an exhaustive survey recently completed left no room for doubt, he informed me. Whereas Spieker had claimed that ammonites had become extinct well before dinosaurs, Stenzel assured me they had become extinct simultaneously. He explained that Spieker had made a common mistake when he placed the dinosaurs' disappearance at the end of the later Danian stage.

If there had been such a natural end to the Mesozoic era, I inquired, why should there be so much controversy about the placement of the Cretaceous-Tertiary boundary?

"I have to give you a lecture on the history of geology," Doc replied, "It was all the fault of a Frenchman called Desor."

Lyell correctly identified the chalk beds near the town of Maastricht, Holland, as the youngest, or final, sediment of the Cretaceous; the top of this chalk signifies the termination of the Mesozoic era, and the time represented by its deposition has come to be called the Maastrichtian stage, the last stage of the last epoch of the Cretaceous period. Here the matter might have rested but for an excursion in 1846 by Eduard Desor—who incidentally was not a Frenchman but a Swiss born in Germany—to the seacoast south of Copenhagen near the village of Stevn's Klint. The sedimentary succession there includes four units: a bottom layer of chalk, two top layers of limestone, and sandwiched in between the white chalk and the white limestone a thin dark gray layer of clay called the Fish Clay after fossil fish bones that were found in it. Both chalk and limestone are sediments that originate in the calcium carbonate shells and skeletons of marine organisms that drift to the bottom as they die. Clay, however, is nonorganic in origin. It is made up of very fine particles of dust that come from continents and even from outer space.

The four sediments at Stevn's Klint had been studied by Johann Georg Forchhammer, a Danish expert in mollusks, two decades before. On the basis of the fossil mollusks in the lower and older of the two limestone layers, he expressed the opinion that it was of Tertiary age, that is, belonging to the Cenozoic. Desor was, however, a specialist on echinoids, the group that includes sea urchins, sand dollars, sea lilies, starfish, and other animals with a fivefold symmetry. He recognized that a number of the echinoid species in the lower limestone are similar to Cretaceous species, from the Mesozoic, not from the Cenozoic. He proposed the term Danian for the time interval represented by that sediment, and the Fish Clay and chalk below it, and considered the Danian to be the last stage of the Mesozoic. In fact, although the genera Desor identified did in fact live in the Cretaceous, they were not the same species. Most paleontologists have since recognized a sharp change in the echinoid fauna across the Fish Clay boundary: they consider the fauna below the clay Cretaceous, and that above it typically Tertiary. Desor had made an unfortunate mistake when he grouped the white chalk, the Fish Clay, and the limestone above it all into one Danian formation. The Fish Clay itself is largely devoid of faunal remains except for the broken fish skeletons after which it was named. The chalk below it contains a fauna that is almost totally different from that of the limestones above. Ammonites, belemnites, rudistid clams, and other typically Mesozoic shells occur in the white chalk as they do in Maastrichtian sediments elsewhere: they are completely absent in the Danian limestones above the Fish Clay.

It was well known to expert paleontologists such as Heinrich Stenzel that Desor had erred. The white chalk below the Fish Clay is Maastrichtian. The revised Danian stage, sensu stricto, is characterized by the oldest Tertiary faunas. Had Desor been an ammonite specialist; or had he been knowledgeable about mollusks, microfossils, or nannofossils; or even had he looked to species rather than genera of echinoids, he would never have put together such an assortment of strange bedfellows into a single faunal dynasty. The Danian stage is now considered to be the time interval represented by the Fish Clay and the overlying limestones. The change in life that occurred between the white chalk, the last of the Maastrichtian, and the Fish Clay, the first of the Danian, represents one of the most profound in Earth's history. Nevertheless, the confusion lingered, causing Spieker, among others, to place the ammonite extinction in the Maastrichtian and the death of dinosaurs in the Danian.

Spieker was also a believer in the "imperfection of the geologic record." Almost a century after the publication of Darwin's *Origin of Species*, he wrote: "The absence of known ancestral stock for so many important animal groups that appear suddenly, well developed, in the fossil succession should be more convincing than it seems to be of the incompleteness of the geologic record, and in recognition of this incompleteness it is impossible to sustain in theory any significant variation in the rate of evolution."

I cited that teaching of my venerated professor only to receive one lecture more from Doc Stenzel: "Yes, many groups appeared suddenly, not because of the incompleteness of the geologic record, but because they *did* appear suddenly."

Stenzel admitted that the preservation of fossils involves an element of chance; very few of all the organisms that ever lived have left their imprint behind. But the record of microfossils is far from being imperfect. Each cubic centimeter of a deep-sea sediment contains thousands and thousands of minute skeletons of one-celled animals called *foraminifera*. Stenzel's colleague Helen Jeanne Plummer of the Bureau at Austin had discovered decades before, in 1931, that all foraminiferal species belonging to the genus *Globotruncana* had become suddenly extinct at the end of the Maastrichtian epoch. The first Danian sediments contain an entirely new foraminiferal assemblage. They were not well developed, but they were the ancestral stock of the microfaunas living in the oceans today.

The east Texas excursion came to an end after three days. My argument with Doc was only an intellectual exercise for me. Unfamiliar with the subject matter, mindful that Doc was arbitrary and dogmatic in his administration and suspecting that he was equally so in his scientific judgment, I remained skeptical. Furthermore, I had other problems to worry about; for more than twenty years, I did not get involved again in a discussion of the boundary problem. Stenzel, however, did not put the subject aside. He persuaded his first graduate student at the University of Houston to research the Cretaceous-Tertiary boundary for his dissertation.

Bill Berggren worked as a laboratory technician at the Shell Lab during the day and attended evening classes at the university. After Berggren received his bachelor of science degree, Stenzel sent him to Scandinavia to study the foraminiferal faunas of the Maastrichtian and Danian.

* * *

FORAMINIFERS WERE FIRST DESCRIBED BY ALCIDE DES-
salines D'Orbigny, a French paleontologist, in 1826.
D'Orbingy thought they were miniature ammonites, because their shells bore a superficial resemblance to those
mollusks' coiled and chambered ones. Like people who
add on to a house when their older dwelling becomes too
cramped, foraminifers make a larger room, or chamber,
just outside the older one. The living creature occupies
only the outermost chamber. The name *foraminifer*
refers to the foramina, or holes, between successive
chambers, which are assembled in a coil or in a series.

Studies of living foraminifers soon revealed that these
animals are not dwarfed mollusks, but one-celled organisms. Many species dwell on the seafloor; they are called
benthic forms. Others inhabit the surface waters of the
oceans; they are called planktonic, or "floaters" (although that is a misnomer, because foraminifers swim or
dive rather than float).

Foraminifers are small, commonly less than 1 millimeter across, although unusually large ones have shells
more than 5 centimeters in diameter. The larger ones are
mostly benthic foraminifers, and because the shapes of
their shells are more distinctive as well as being easier to
see, they have been studied since D'Orbingy's time.
Fossil foraminifers have been found in rocks as old as
early Cambrian, but the larger benthic species called
Nummulites are known only from the Tertiary. By the
middle of the last century, it had become clear that
Nummulitic formations are as much the fossil signature
of the Cenozoic as the ammonites are a fossil signature
of the Mesozoic.

PLANKTONIC FORAMINIFERS ARE RARELY VISIBLE WITH-
out a microscope, and the forms that distinguish among
species are more subtle. Nevertheless, by the time Berggren was sent off in 1957 to Denmark to study Desor's
"Danian terrane" the technique of sieving out microscopic foraminifers had advanced, and the taxonomy of
various species had been largely established. Berggren

could, therefore, carry out systematic research on planktonic foraminifers in the Danish sediments. For comparison, he obtained samples of the same age from Japan,
West Africa, the Soviet Union, Sweden, Greenland,
Mexico, and the Gulf, Atlantic, and Pacific coasts of the
United States. By 1960 he was able to report to the International Geological Congress that "No species of Tertiary planktonic foraminifera occur in the Maastrichtian
strata in Denmark and Scania. Nor has the writer seen
any undoubted occurrences in the many faunal suites
studied in Maastrichtian sequences elsewhere." He also
noted what he called "one of the Gordian knots in the
science of geology": The shell shapes of species from the
Cretaceous were so different from the shell shapes of
the Tertiary species that there must have been considerable time for evolutionary development between the two
periods.

Yet the sediments from the two periods were separated only by the Fish Clay, in which no foraminifer fossils had been found. Berggren, influenced by the
Lyell-Darwin claim of a chasm between the Cretaceous
and Tertiary, saw a gap in the record of their evolutionary development. But he had no way of knowing how
long the missing period was. Radiometric dating of geologic formations had indicated only that the chasm was
not as great as Lyell had told us; it could not have been
more than a few million years. Could it be less?

FOR AN ANSWER TO THIS QUESTION, GEOLOGISTS WENT
to Gubbio in Italy. Gubbio is a small medieval town. Motorists emerging from the narrow streets of Assisi usually
ignore the sign *Città delle Arte* pointing to Gubbio. After
viewing all the Giottos in the monastary built for St.
Francis, few care to make a detour to inspect the few
altarpieces in Gubbio's provincial cathedral. The town
has become, however, a mecca for geologists. The sedimentary sequence called the *scaglia rosa* outside the city
provides one of the best records anywhere of the transition from the Mesozoic to the Cenozoic era at their
boundary between the Cretaceous and Tertiary periods.

The *scaglia* are sediments of the Tethys Sea, ancestor of today's Mediterranean and the Black, Caspian, and Aral seas to its east. Some 15 million years ago, a portion of the deep-sea floor was uplifted to form the Apennine Mountains of Italy. Through erosion the sediments of the Mesozoic and Cenozoic, including the *scaglia*, now lie exposed; samples of ancient marine life can be obtained from the roadside easily for paleontological investigation. Several years after Berggren's report on foraminifers, two other specialists in these microscopic fossils set out to see just what had happened in the evolution of foraminifers. Isabella Premoli-Silva, a red-haired countess from Tuscany who had studied micropaleontology at Milan, and her Swiss colleague, Hans Peter Luterbacher, felt excitement in the air: Something had happened at the end of the Cretaceous. Together they searched for a complete sedimentary section to study the remarkable discontinuity in evolutionary development, and they found it in the *scaglia* near Gubbio, not very far from Premoli-Silva's own hometown. Their joint report, published in 1969, confirmed Berggren's findings and added more detail. The last Cretaceous fauna included a diversified plankton population belonging to the foraminifer families *Globotruncanids, Ruboglobigerinids*, and *Heterohelicids*. Those "floaters" included dozens of species which had frolicked in the warm Cretaceous oceans for some 5 or 10 million years.

Clearly foraminifers had evolved rapidly since the middle of the Cretaceous and by the end of that period were at the zenith of their development. There was no sign of senility, no thinning of their ranks until suddenly, at a boundary so sharp you can mark it with a razor, all the Cretaceous forms became extinct. All three families, all the genera within them, and all the species within those genera disappeared, never to reappear among the faunas of the Cenozoic.

Foraminifers had been so abundant that their skeletons, together with the calcareous secretions of very small plants called nannoplankton, make up the bulk of the last Cretaceous sediments at Gubbio. The sediments are limestone, the typically white rock that forms from shelly debris. Directly on top of that limestone is a layer of clay. Like the Fish Clay in Denmark, the clay at Gubbio is almost devoid of any kind of fossil and thus seems to be the sediment of a practically sterile ocean. The clay, now known as the boundary clay because it is sandwiched between the last fossil layer of the Mesozoic and the first fossil layer of the Cenozoic, is only 1 centimeter thick at Gubbio. Above the clay is limestone again, and in this limestone Premoli-Silva and Luterbacher found fossils of extremely small foraminifers.

Whereas the Cretaceous forms were robust, about 0.5 or 1 millimeter in diameter, the first Tertiary species were dwarfs about one-tenth as large as their expired predecessors. They constitute the *Globigerina eugubina* zone, the very first faunal dynasty of floating foraminifers of the Cenozoic and the primitive ancestral stock from which the modern family of Globigerinidae evolved. Eugubinas had been overlooked by Berggren and other previous workers because they are so extremely small. The Cenozoic limestones at Gubbio show that their evolution proceeded rapidly. The more evolved species are progressively larger in size, and increasingly diverse. In limestones some 5 meters above the boundary clay, the puny, primitive species were entirely replaced by many species of robust floaters.

Luterbacher's and Premoli-Silva's discovery of the eugubinas, which had been made possible by use of an extraordinarily fine sieve, cast doubt on the notion of a gap in the fossil record. Although this episode in the evolution of foraminifers had been surprisingly rapid, the progression from small primitive species to a rich and robust fauna seemed quite complete.

Gaps in the geological record are common in shallow marine sequences on continents. The top of the continental crust stands thousands of meters higher than the ocean floor. Unceasing activity within the earth can lift a continent higher still and can also submerge its low-lying portions some hundreds of meters under seawater. An area of continental crust can thus be land at one time but become a shallow sea—like the North Sea or the Baltic —at another. Aside from the moderate ups and downs of the continents, worldwide sea level also changes slightly from time to time. The teaching of historical geology can thus be a tiresome recitation of seas coming in (transgressions) and seas going out (regressions). During transgressions, marine sediments are deposited on top of land sediments. So far, so good, because each new layer of sediment protects the one below it. During regressions, however, high ground is eroded, wiping out the record there, while over coastal plains marine sediments are buried under river deposits. When the sea comes back over the land again, new marine sediments are laid down on top of continental sediments or on an erosional surface where previous marine or continental layers have been wiped out. Gaps in the record of marine life are thus a rule of sedimentary sequences on land. The Paris Basin, the source of Cuvier's intriguing fossil collection, is an example. Because the Paris Basin repeatedly emerged from the sea during regressions, sediments there were exposed to erosion after each flooding, causing inevitable gaps in the record.

The light crust of a continent sits on a heavier substratum, earth's 2,900-kilometer-thick mantle, and it can never sink as deep as an ocean floor, where it would be permanently protected from rain and wind. The ocean bottom, however, remains protected under thousands of meters of seawater, to be lifted to the surface only during the rare event of a continental collision. The most complete record of marine life is, therefore, most likely to be found by sampling sediments on the ocean floor. Such sediments are called *pelagic* after the Greek word *pelagos* for open sea. These days, pelagic sediments are sampled aboard deep-sea drilling vessels, but the first deep-sea drilling voyage was still seven years in the future when the work at Gubbio was undertaken. Fortunately, the pelagic sediments heaved up by mountain-making processes in the Apennines and so clearly exposed at Gubbio were an excellent choice, revealing to Luterbacher and Premoli-Silva a continuous record of biological evolution across the Cretaceous-Tertiary boundary. The record is preserved because Gubbio had remained submerged until one final upheaval.

Continuity is, however, relative. Do we have at Gubbio a day-by-day record, a year-by-year record, or a millennium-by-millennium record? Or is continuity there measured in units of millions of years?

Daily sedimentation records are increasingly rare. Dutch scientists studying sandy deposits in channels on tidal flats have discovered daily sedimentation that reveals monthly rhythms. Thicker beds are laid down at spring tides, when the moon is new or full; thinner beds are deposited at neap tides. One can read rather well the twenty-eight-day-month cycles in these so-called tidal bundles; each "bundle" contains twenty-eight layers of diurnal tidal deposits. But geological diaries are practically never preserved; they are destroyed almost as fast as they are written.

Under unusual circumstances, we may obtain a year-by-year record. The most recent sediments of Lake Zurich, for example, are varves, or annual layers of calcium carbonate that reflect the summer blooms and winter deaths of algae in the lake waters. Minute white crystals of calcium carbonate precipitate during the summer, whereas the deposit each winter is a paper-thin layer of fine detritus. Undisturbed varves are therefore annals of sedimentation. Various types of varves are not uncommon in lakes, but they are rarely found in oceans.

Various other kinds of rhythmic bedding are present in deep-sea sediments. Unfortunately, their causes are not yet perfectly deciphered, and neither are the lengths of time represented by the rhythms.

The modern effort to even propose a scale of time appropriate to geological history began with seat-of-the-pants guess-work. Darwin ventured to pinpoint the middle of the Cretaceous at more than 300 million years before the present. He was chastised by Lord Kelvin, whose elaborate calculations indicated that earth itself could not be older than 24 million years. The credibility of any mathematical computation, whether done by hand or by high-speed computer, depends on its original premise. Kelvin's premise was wrong. We now know that the earth is at least 4.5 billion years old, or about two hundred times older than Kelvin thought, and that the middle of the Cretaceous was about 100 million years ago.

Darwin the geologist did err, but his guess was better than the superficially impressive calculations of the physicist Kelvin. Darwin got at least the order of magnitude right.

The clock that was finally used to measure geological history is radioactivity, and dating by this method is called radiometry, or radiometric dating. The technique was an outgrowth of the discovery of isotopes, atoms of an element that have the usual number of protons and electrons but vary in their number of neutrons.

Isotopes were not discovered until 1913, and then largely because the numbers involved in chemistry were pesky. William Prout proposed in 1815 that atomic weights of chemical elements should be whole numbers. This proposal seemed to make sense because the weight of an atom is in its nuclear particles, neutrons and protons, each of which is one unit of the atom's total mass (the mass of an electron is, for all practical purposes, nil). An element whose atom has two nuclear particles should have an atomic weight of 2, and the atom with three nuclear particles should have a mass of 3. It is all very simple. Yet when we were students working on exercises in chemistry, calculations involving the compound sodium chloride were a nuisance, because chlorine has an atomic weight of 35.45, nowhere near a whole number.

T. W. Richards of Harvard, one of the best chemical analysts of all time, proved in 1913 beyond any doubt that the atomic weights of elements are not whole numbers. But he was also upset to find that weights of one and the same element can be different. Radioactive elements, when they come apart, or decay, are transformed into other elements. Lead produced by the radioactive decay of uranium, Richards discovered, has a different weight from that of ordinary lead. The results puzzled Richards, but a young British chemist, Frederick Soddy, proposed a brilliant solution: A chemical element is not made up of one kind of atom, but is a mixture of two or more isotopes.

The word isotope is derived from Greek words that mean "same place." The "place" is the pigeonhole in the periodic table of chemical elements that decorates high school chemistry labs everywhere. Each pigeonhole used to be reserved for one chemical element, which has the same number of protons and of electrons. Now it is reserved for two or more isotopes of that element, which, although they all have the appropriate number of protons and electrons, possess different numbers of neutrons. All chlorine atoms, for example, have 17 protons in their nucleus, but one of that element's two isotopes has 18 neutrons, giving it an atomic weight of 35, while the other has 20 neutrons, giving it an atomic weight of 37.

The pigeonhole for chlorine is reserved for both of its two isotopes, chlorine 35, and chlorine 37. Chlorine is ordinarily a mixture of both isotopes. Chlorine 35 constitutes always 75.77 percent and chlorine 37, 24.23 percent of the mixture. The atomic weight of chlorine with this ratio of its two isotopes turns out to be 35.45, the inconvenient number we encountered in our exercises before computers were invented.

Chlorine 35 and chlorine 37 are stable isotopes; they remain the same kind of atoms through eternity. Uranium 238, uranium 235, and uranium 234 are three naturally occurring isotopes of uranium. They are not stable isotopes, but radioisotopes. Radioisotopes decay radioactively into other atoms, called their daughter product. Uranium 234 and uranium 238 decay into the daughter product lead 206 whereas lead 207 is parented by uranium 235. Common lead contains not only lead 206 and lead 207, but also lead 204 and lead 208. Its atomic weight is, therefore, quite different from that of lead produced by radioactivity alone. No wonder Richards was puzzled.

Minerals in a rock have not always been the solid substances we think of when we think of quartz or lead. They have at some point crystallized within cooling molten rock, or precipitated out of an aqueous solution. At the time a mineral crystallizes, a radioactive element, such as uranium, may become one of the constituents of its chemical composition. Over time, as the radioactive element decays, its daughter element accumulates in the mineral of which it was not originally a part. Therefore, in any particular mineral that contains a radioactive element the abundance of the radioisotope compared to its decay, or daughter, product depends upon the time that has been available for decay since the mineral first crystallized. As time passes, there is less and less uranium and more and more of the daughter lead into which it has decayed. The time during which half of the parent element is lost is called the half-life of that isotope. Uranium 238 has a half-life of about 4 billion years. Because that happens to be a little less than the age of the earth, almost half of the U-238 that was here when earth was first formed 4.5 billion years ago still exists; the other half has been converted into lead 206. In another 4.5 billion years, half of the remaining U-238 will be converted to lead 206. At that time, the ratio of U-238 to lead 206 will be one quarter uranium to three quarters lead, or $\frac{1}{3}$. The ratio of a uranium isotope to its daughter lead isotope in a mineral thus gives the mineral's radiometric age. Similarly, the radioisotope of potassium, potassium 40, produces argon 40 as one of its decay products; the potassium 40 to argon 40 ratio in a mineral can also give the mineral an age.

Which isotope is chosen for analysis might depend on which radioactive element is most abundant in that rock sample. The potassium/argon ratio is commonly used for dating sedimentary rocks which contain potassium-bearing glauconite, a not uncommon sedimentary mineral crystallized from seawater. The same method is also used for dating volcanic rocks interbedded in a sedimentary sequence because they contain potassium-bearing mica.

Quantitative analyses of isotopes are done with a mass spectrometer. A mass spectrometer, as the name suggests, separates out isotopes according to their mass, or weight. This it does by "bouncing" them against an electric or magnetic field. Although the analogy is crude, lighter isotopes are "bouncier" than heavy ones, and they are therefore deflected farther from the field. In this way isotopes of various masses are separated from one another and collected for counting. Since its invention in 1918 the mass spectrometer has had its design refined until now only a few micrograms of a sample is needed to perform an accurate isotope analysis for radiometric dating.

"Accurate," however, is another relative term. The accurate measurement that produces a perfect cake is nowhere near sufficient to produce a perfect chemical analysis. Arthur Holmes, a pioneer in the field, established the first numerical time scale for the geological eras and periods. Holmes's figures have been refined since the publication of his time scale in the 1940s, but not by a great deal. For example, Holmes dated the end of the Cretaceous at 70 million years ago. The now accepted figure is 65 million years ago. Nevertheless, uncertainties on absolute ages have been reduced only to the order of a few million years for rocks as old as the Cretaceous-Tertiary boundary in the pelagic sediments of Gubbio, so that the boundary date is most properly expressed as 65 million years ago, give or take 2 million.

The time interval represented by the top and bottom of a bed can be more accurately determined if we know its sedimentation rate. By the time Premoli-Silva and Luterbacher started their investigations, numerous sedimentary beds or interbedded volcanic deposits in the Cretaceous and Tertiary sequences had been dated by radiometric methods. The duration of a time interval between any two radiometrically dated beds is the difference in age between the upper and lower beds, and the average sedimentation rate of the interval is obtained when one divides the thickness of the sediment between the two dated beds by the duration of time that separates them. Using this method, geologists have found that pelagic limestones are commonly deposited at a rate of a few centimeters per thousand years, and pelagic clays at the rate of about 1 millimeter per thousand years. The record at Gubbio showed that the Cretaceous foraminifers had become extinct during the time interval represented by the 1-centimeter-thick boundary clay. If the clay was deposited in an open ocean at a normal rate, we might conclude that the Cretaceous faunas died out within a time interval of ten thousand years or so, although we are not sure whether the event took place 65 million years ago, or a couple of millions of years earlier or later.

Luterbacher and Premoli-Silva suspected that the dying-off of the old and the appearance of the new was as sudden as that, but they did not say so, because they were uncertain whether there were subtle gaps of record within the boundary clay at Gubbio. Movement of bottom water in the ocean can cause some erosion of seafloor sediment, as they had noted in faunal records across the Cretaceous-Tertiary boundary in northern Italy; at a number of localities not very far from Gubbio, some uppermost Cretaceous and/or lowermost Tertiary foraminiferal zones are absent. Erosion of even a meter of clay could mean 1 million years missing from the record. Nevertheless the radiometric dating of the various Cretaceous and Tertiary formations till 1960 had proved, at least, that there was no gap that could be called a "chasm" between the last Cretaceous and the first Tertiary: The Cretaceous period ended sometime less than 70 million years ago, and the Tertiary started more than 60 million years before present; a break in the record, if it existed at all, could not have been more than a few million years.

Because the term *Cretaceous* is defined on the basis of their extinction, both the dinosaurs and the Cretaceous plankton became extinct at the end of that period. But did they become extinct simultaneously? The question has not been easy to investigate, since dinosaurs and plankton did not share the same habitat. The radiometric ages for sediments bearing the very last of these faunas on land and in the oceans at various sites range from 63 to 67 million years. That range can be interpreted in two ways: Either there are real differences in age among the various sites where Cretaceous extinctions have been studied, or the discrepancy is an artifact of an imperfect dating technique.

Were the dinosaurs dying out at the same time as the plankton, during the same millennium, when sterile dust was settling onto the ocean floor to make the boundary clay at Gubbio?

4

C-29-R

THE EXPRESSION *C-29-R* IS NOT THE CODE NAME OF A secret agent or the signal for a football play. It is an abbreviation for Chron Cenozoic 29, reversed, the magnetostratigraphic epoch that has become crucial to the question of whether the dinosaurs and the old foraminifers became extinct at the same time.

Stratigraphy is the science of strata, or layers of sediment, and their sequential relationship. Magnetostratigraphy is a new branch of stratigraphy which determines the age of strata through an investigation of the "lie" of bits of magnetite "frozen" in rock as it was laid down or crystallized.

I first learned that we might be able to date rocks by investigating their magnetic properties from a talk by Keith Runcorn in 1953. That was back when I was a Chinese graduate student and Runcorn a British postdoc at UCLA. In fact, I did not attend the lecture because of a personal resentment. The reason was trivial: Runcorn and I both had to work with rock samples, and we had only one big rock saw in our laboratory. The intruder from England had studied physics and acquired little experience in rock cutting. We geology students were naturally experts. Runcorn was given the privilege of using the saw in the evenings. Alas, more than once we found a broken blade in the saw and had to start our day by replacing it. Besides, there was my arrogance; as a brash young graduate student, I thought my own research was the only endeavor of relevance. I presumed that a person who did not know how to handle a rock saw had nothing of importance to tell us. I erred. Runcorn's talk that day, as I was to find out from a classmate who did go to hear it, concerned the natural remnant magnetism of rocks, a subject of great relevance to geologists.

All rocks contain magnetic minerals, such as magnetite, the mineral the first compasses were made with. Those miniature magnets orient themselves along earth's magnetic field when they are free to move very much as iron filings align themselves with the magnetic field of a bar magnet. Bits of magnetite align themselves in a sediment while it is being laid down, or in igneous rock as it cools from the liquid state. Normally their north-seeking pole points toward the magnetic north pole somewhere in the Arctic, and, because the field is curved as it is around a bar magnet, their north end normally dips downward in the northern hemisphere and tips upward in the southern hemisphere. The angle of the tilt is called magnetic inclination.

Instruments constructed to measure the intensity and orientation of natural remnant magnetism were first used on volcanic rocks. A French geophysicist, Bernard Bruhnes, carried out a project in 1909 to investigate the natural remnant magnetism of basalt flows in central France, in the plateau country south of the Loire. Most of his samples showed the magnetic properties he had expected, but he discovered to his surprise strange magnetic "behavior" in some of his specimens. The north-seeking end of the miniature magnets in those rocks pointed to the south, not to the north, and pointed upward instead of downward. Their orientation was thus exactly the reverse of that of the present.

Some two decades later in 1928 Motonari Matuyama made similar measurements on volcanic rocks formed in Japan during the past 2 million years and found again the reversed polarity of natural remnant magnetism. Matuyama further noted that the anomalous polarity was consistently found among a group of older basalts, whereas the younger samples all had a direction of magnetization that accorded with earth's present field. He came to the very daring idea that the magnetic poles had flipped: At some time the magnetic north pole must have been located somewhere near the Antarctic, and the magnetic south pole was near the Arctic. Matuyama guessed that the flip had occurred somewhere during the Quarternary period, perhaps a few million years ago. If Matuyama was correct, Runcorn emphasized, geologists would have a new way to discriminate between rocks formed prior to the flip and those formed after. I would probably have scoffed at Runcorn's credulity if I had gone to listen to him; the notion that earth's magnetic field could ever have been upside down was incredible.

Not many scientists believed in Matuyama's explanation, not even his countrymen. Seiya Uyeda, then a young geophysicist fresh out of school, not only rejected this crazy idea but set out to discover a more believable explanation for the undoubted fact of reversed magnetism. Experimenting in his laboratory, Uyeda produced a self-reversal phenomenon. By 1958 he was able to demonstrate that rock could be artificially induced to acquire a reversed polarity under some special circumstances. That was fine, but the question remained whether the reversed polarity in Bruhne's and in Matuyama's volcanic samples had undergone such special treatment, or earth's magnetic poles had indeed flipped 180 degrees at some time in the past.

There was a way to check the two alternatives. If Matuyama was right, all the reversely magnetized rocks must have originated during an epoch in the past when earth's magnetic field was reversed and should therefore be of similar age. Their age could be confirmed by radiometric dating.

Volcanic rocks contain radioactive potassium. Certain refinements of radiometric dating had progressed far enough by 1960 that research teams in California and Australia were beginning to produce quite reliable numbers on the age of young basalts. Their data confirmed Matuyama's guess. All the basalt rocks that had reversed polarity had erupted during the late Pliocene and early Pleistocene epochs of the Cenozoic era between 2.4 and 0.7 million years ago, making it seem likely that the poles had indeed switched polarities for that interval. That period of time, known as a magnetostratigraphic epoch, was called Matuyama in his honor. Since the Matuyama epoch the earth's magnetic field has remained in its present familiar, or "normal," polarity. This present magnetostratigraphic epoch, 700,000 years long so far, was named after Bruhnes. Thus, in less than a decade after Runcorn's talk, geologists had themselves flipped. Matuyama's "crazy idea" had proved to be correct and had been formalized in the naming of the first two magnetostratigraphic epochs discovered.

As it turned out there were many other epochs still to be discovered. We now know that earth's magnetic field has been unstable. The north and south poles have alternated repeatedly between two states, normal and reversed, during the geologic past. Reversals have occurred at irregular time intervals, and each flip probably took thousands of years to complete. There are many layers of normally polarized rocks older than the Bruhnes epoch, as there are many layers of reversely polarized rocks older than the Matuyama epoch.

Intuitively one does not like the idea. In our naïvieté we tend to think that earth's magnetic field should be induced by a big solid magnet buried inside our planet. It would be physically impossible to turn such a magnet around. In fact, no solid magnet can be the source of earth's field, because all solids lose their magnetism at the high temperature that prevails within this planet's interior. Our magnetic field is electromagnetic; the field is induced by the flow of charged particles within earth's molten iron core, as magnetism is induced by the flow of an electric current through a coiled wire. Earth's core is thus a giant dynamo. Because the movement in the liquid core is influenced by the planet's rotation, the position of the magnetic poles has always coincided, more or less, to that of the geographic poles. Computations have shown, however, that random motions within the fluid core, turbulence resembling cyclones in the atmosphere, can result in a reversal of the earth's magnetic field whenever a certain critical configuration is reached. Polarity reversal of earth's magnetic field is a physical reality, not a supernatural wonder.

While the polarity of rock samples from land was being analyzed in the laboratory, geophysicists from Scripps Institution of Oceanography were surveying by ship remnant magnetism on the Pacific seafloor. When they plotted their data on a map, they found another strange anomaly: In the area surveyed by their ship-towed magnetometer, the intensity of the magnetic field varied in a peculiarly regular fashion. Narrow stripes of seafloor with high-intensity magnetism alternated with stripes of low-intensity magnetism. The stripes ranged from several kilometers to about 100 kilometers wide, and they were several thousand kilometers long. Eventually such magnetic stripes were found in all of the world's oceans.

Scripps Institution of Oceanography published its first magnetic field maps in the late 1950s, but the geophysicists working on the problem, Art Raff and Vic Vacquier, were at a loss to give an explanation. One might have thought that the stripes of high intensity were underlain by submarine ridges of magnetic basalt. But echo sounding had shown that there was no correlation between magnetism and topography. A submarine mountain may coincide with a zone of high intensity or with one of low intensity, and the same is true of submarine plains. The puzzlement did not last long. Fred Vine, a student from Cambridge who began his graduate work after the maps were published, soon came up with the answer.

I first heard of Fred Vine when we were both candidates for a keynote speech at the 1966 meeting of the

Geological Society of America at San Francisco. He was chosen and presented to the society his now famous theory of seafloor spreading. Again, this time burning with disappointment as a loser, I did not attend a crucial lecture. If I had gone, I might have joined Vine's Earth sciences revolution then and there, instead of tagging along three years later when my own work confirmed the same ideas.

I finally got to know Vine personally when, as the chairman of a search committee for a geophysics professor at our university, I invited him to Zurich for a visit. He told me then that two trains of thought had led him to the solution of the magnetic puzzle. The starting point was the theory of continental drift advocated by Alfred Wegener in the 1920s. Wegener had gathered a lot of odd facts which could not be explained except by a theory of displaced continents, yet how could continents drift, when all the earth is encased in solid crust?

Vine, following a suggestion by Harry Hess of Princeton, looked at the matter from a different angle: The continents had not drifted, but they could have moved if the seafloor had spread itself between them. Continued eruption of basalt lava along a central line, the axis of seafloor spreading, would form successive segments of newer seafloor in the middle, continually shoving apart the older segments on both sides, as well as the still more distant continents at the ocean's edges. The theory, since so well confirmed that seafloor spreading has been elevated to a fact, explains not only the apparent drift of one continent away from another, but also the collision of continents that we now know pushes up such mountain ranges as the Alps, the Apennines, and the Himalayas.

A second implication of Vine's theory was that if there was such a thing as a flip-flopping magnetic field, newly erupting basalt would acquire the magnetic polarity of the time. Each flip should, therefore, be recorded in sequence along the ocean floor to each side of the axis of seafloor spreading. Each segment of seafloor created along the length of the axis after a magnetic reversal should have a polarity opposite to that of the previous segment created before the reversal. With older seafloor on both sides constantly shoved aside by new seafloor in the middle, more and more segments, or stripes, would be added. Simple arithmetic, then, solved the puzzle of why segments should differ in magnetic intensity. Those created during epochs of normal magnetic polarity add their magnetism to that of earth's present, normal magnetic field, resulting in the stripes of high intensity Scripps Institution's magnetometers had recorded. Segments of seafloor created during an epoch of reversed polarity subtract their opposite magnetization from the Earth's present normal field, resulting in the stripes of low intensity. The alternating stripes of high and low intensities are thus comparable to a magnetic tape recording successive reversals of the earth's magnetic field.

The theory also implied that the width of a magnetic stripe was related to the duration of a polarity epoch. If earth's polarity remained the same for a considerable length of time, a rather broad segment of new seafloor, all magnetized in the same orientation, would be produced. We should then have a broad stripe, or even a segment so broad that it eventually came to be known as a "quiet zone." If the poles flipped back and forth frequently, the result would be a series of narrow stripes. Assuming that seafloor spreading has proceeded at the same rate, the width of a stripe should be proportional to the duration of the polarity epoch during which it formed.

By the time Vine published his ideas about seafloor spreading in a 1963 article, coauthored with his thesis adviser Drum Matthews, radiometric analysis had established durations for the four most recent polarity epochs covering a total span of 5 million years. Counting backward from the present 0.7 million-years-long Bruhne's epoch, the three others had timespans of 1.7, 0.9, and 1.7 million years, respectively. If Vine and Matthews' theory was correct, the ratio of the widths of the four magnetic stripes nearest to the axis of seafloor spreading should be 0.7:1.7:0.9:1.7. Those data were available from Scripps Institution's published maps, and Vine was able to show that the ratio was indeed what had been predicted. He found the same ratio for the width of the magnetic stripes of both the Pacific and the Atlantic seafloors. The record thus confirmed the assumption that both seafloors had spread at constant rates during the last 5 million years at least.

Going a step further, Vine reasoned that we should be able to determine the age of the seafloor at any particular spot if the rate of spreading had *always* been constant. To find the age at any spot one had only to measure the distance from there to the axis of seafloor spreading and divide that distance by the spreading rate. Where the rate of seafloor spreading is 1 centimeter per year, the seafloor at a distance 100 kilometers away from the axis should thus have an age of 100 kilometers per centimeter per year, or 10 million years. The prospect was exciting: The width of any magnetic stripe on the seafloor, not only the four most recent, could be used to calculate when that reversal epoch had begun, and how long it had lasted. Using regions of seafloor where surveys had been completed, Jim Heirtzler and his colleagues at the Lamont Doherty Geological Laboratory in 1968 constructed a magnetostratigraphic time scale extending back to 80 million years before the present.

I missed all the excitement of these discoveries at sea. My job in the early 1960s was to search for oil on land. Not familiar with the facts, and therefore blind to their implications, I remained aloof, still smug in my assumption that the new hypotheses of polarity reversal and seafloor spreading were nonsense.

As fate would have it, I changed my job in 1967, accepting employment in landlocked Switzerland, only to be invited one year later to an oceanographic expedition. The position was with a multinational research program known as the Joint Oceanographical Institutions' Deep Earth Studies, or, simply, JOIDES. This first venture of mine at sea was the third expedition of the newly started Deep Sea Drilling Project whose general mission was to explore the deep oceans. The particular purpose of this voyage was to test the Vine and Matthews theory.

Our plan called for drill sites in the South Atlantic located at 200, 420, 500, 700, 740, 1,000, and 1,300 kilometers from the axis of seafloor spreading, called in that ocean the Mid-Atlantic Ridge. The rate of spreading in that part of the Atlantic has been 2 centimeters per year during the last 5 million years. Using what seemed to me the simple minded formula of distance divided by rate, the predicted ages of the seafloor at the seven sites should be 10, 21, 25, 35, 37, 50, and 65 million years, respectively. After two months of drilling and rough onboard analyses, we had the results. The ages were 9, 24, 26, 33, 40, 49, and 67 million years. The agreement was amazing; my skepticism was shattered.

I hated to admit that I had erred in my scientific judgment, but I had no alternative. A scientific theory can predict and can be verified. Vine and Matthews had predicted, and their prediction had been stunningly verified.

Within a year, deep-sea drilling results confirmed the general validity of the magnetostratigraphic time scale. The next step was to see whether the polarity-reversal chronology as it had been deduced from horizontal seafloor spreading agreed with the chronology deduced from radiometrically dated fossil zones in vertically stacked layers of sedimentary rock. This second test demanded more effort. Only sediments and sedimentary rocks contain enough fossils for accurate dating by paleontologists, yet their magnetism gives far less clear signals than does the remnant magnetism in the volcanic rocks in which polarity reversals had first been discovered. High-sensitivity instruments had to be invented to investigate their more elusive remnant magnetism. The sampling technique had also to be improved. Deep-sea drill cores at that time were primitive, resulting in broken or incomplete samples of pelagic sediments. We could not proceed until a new technique was developed for obtaining complete and undisturbed samples from boreholes beneath the ocean floor. The technology for verifying Heirtzler's horizontal time scale by seeing whether it agreed with the chronology of vertically layered sediments had, in fact, to wait thirteen years. At last, in 1980, I led what was by then the seventy-third drilling expedition of the Deep Sea Drilling Project, again to the South Atlantic, to bore a chronology from the ocean floor. We found that the polarity epochs defined by natural remnant magnetism in sediments exactly correlated with the polarity epochs laid down in the magnetic stripes on the seafloor. The history of earth's flip-flopping magnetic field was coded in both sets of data.

C-29-R is a shorthand form of that code. Each magnetostratigraphic epoch is called a chron. Each chron is given a number corresponding to its position in the sequence of epochs. *C* indicates Cenozoic because this set of chrons is counted from the most recent Chron, Cenozoic-1, which corresponds to the Bruhnes and Matuyama magnetostratigraphic epochs. The letters N for normal and R for reversed are added, so Bruhnes becomes C-1-N and Matuyama C-1-R for short. Chron Cenozoic-2-N, or C-2-N, is the next oldest epoch of normal polarity, when the poles were as they are today. All chrons labeled N for normal correspond to the high-intensity stripes of magnetism on the seafloor, all of which formed during epochs of normal polarity. Between them lie the low-intensity stripes, formed during epochs of reversed polarity, and labeled R, for reversed.

Positively identifying a chron in a vertical sedimentary sequence is less easy than identifying a chron in the horizontal sequence of stripes on the seafloor. Nowhere do we find a continuous sequence from the present down to the days of the dinosaurs, so we cannot start from the top at any one locality to make a countdown to our destination. We make do with fragmentary information to find our place within an incomplete sequence. Fortunately polarity reversals took place at irregular intervals, so that the signals read like a Morse code. Reading outward from the center of seafloor spreading, and starting with Chron Cenozoic-25, for example, the width of magnetic stripe C-25-N on the seafloor is narrow, and C-25-R is broad. Continuing outward, C-26 stripes are narrow, broad; C-27 are narrow, narrow; C-28 are medium, narrow; C-29 are narrow, medium; and so on. The corresponding magnetostratigraphic chrons should have matching durations: Chron Cenozoic-25-normal should be short, and C-25-R should be long, and from there to C-29 should read short long, short long, short short, medium short, ending with short medium.

In fact the information is more precise than that expressed by the adjectives broad, narrow, long, and short because the width of magnetic stripes can be measured precisely and expressed numerically. If we use black and white bands to represent graphically the normal and reversed polarity intervals, the pattern will look very much like a standard product code on merchandise. Computers have no difficulty reading the information stored in the patterns of bands, and geologists similarly read the patterns of magnetostratigraphy. Already in 1969, during my first South Atlantic Expedition, we had indications that the last Mesozoic sediments were probably deposited during Chron Cenozoic-29-reversed. Using the abbreviated technical expression we could tentatively state that the Mesozoic era ended during C-29-R.

In the years since magnetostratigraphy became a handy dating tool to scientists, it has been applied to the question of when the foraminifers at Gubbio became extinct, when the last of the dinosaurs died, how long these minute or monstrous creatures took to expire, and whether they did so simultaneously. In 1979, fifteen years after paleontologists had pinpointed the horizon of the Cretaceous extinction at Gubbio, geophysicist Bill Lowrie and geologist Walter Alvarez, among others, joined paleontologist Premoli-Silva and her team at the site of her original foraminifera study to read the magnetostratigraphy of the Gubbio sequence. The group found the Cretaceous-Tertiary boundary, the place where the foraminifer-rich limestone gave way to the nearly sterile boundary clay, in Chron-Cenozoic-29-reversed. That confirmed the very tentative conclusion by the South Atlantic drilling team, which I had accompanied on my first deep-sea expedition, that C-29-R marked the end of the Mesozoic era. But how did the age of C-29-R, deduced on the basis of seafloor-spreading theory, correspond with the ages of sediments bearing paleontological evidence of mass extinction and dated by radiometry?

The low-intensity stripe of Chron-Cenozoic-29-reversed was located some 1,300 kilometers from the Mid-Atlantic Ridge. Assuming the constant rate of 2 centimeters per year for seafloor spreading in that part of the South Atlantic, the age of C-29-R should be 13 million centimeters divided by 2 centimeters per year, or 65 million years. Radiometric dating performed on layers of volcanic ash near the Cretaceous-Tertiary boundary had yielded ages ranging from 63 to 67 million years, plus or minus 2 million years in either direction. The magnetostratigraphic age of 65 million years for this boundary is a round number exactly in the middle of the radiometric dates. This age has therefore come to be the one commonly selected to mark the end of the Mesozoic era and the beginning of the Cenozoic.

Because of the margin of error in radiometric dating, it cannot be used to measure durations that are relatively brief, a few million years or so. Magnetostratigraphy has, however, given us a precise yardstick to measure duration. Denis Kent of Lamont Geological Laboratory found that C-29-R could not have lasted longer than half a million years. Based on the width of its low-intensity stripe, Kent's exact figure for this reversely polarized epoch was 470,000 years. Because the time span represented by a stripe corresponds to the time span represented by the layer of sediment laid down in the same polarity epoch, his figure set an outside limit on how long it could have taken for the mass extinction of the marine plankton recorded in the ocean sediment at Gubbio.

Another calculation was used to check whether the extinction had continued throughout the time period of C-29-R, or during only a part of it. The reversely magnetized sequence C-29-R at that site consists mainly of pelagic limestones and is about 5 meters thick. The sedimentation rate of such limestones is commonly on the order of 1 centimeter every one thousand years, so the entire span of time this layer represents is about half a million years. The extinction event, however, is recorded by the 1-centimeter-thick boundary clay. Clay is ordinarily deposited much more slowly than limestone, at a rate of only 1 millimeter every one thousand years. Therefore, the best estimate indicated that the marine microfaunas at Gubbio became extinct during a mere ten thousand years of Chron C-29-R. Furthermore, with the help of magnetostratigraphy, we are now sure that the record at Gubbio is complete; if a break exists at all, it cannot be a span of more than a few thousand years.

Was the extinction of the dinosaurs also confined to the same brief interval of time? Magnetostratigraphy has made it possible to focus more clearly on that question, although not to answer it with certainty.

We had radiometric dates on the terminal Cretaceous extinction from samples of sandstones and shales containing the last dinosaur remains that had been interbedded with layers of volcanic ash. Depending on the site from which they were collected, some samples suggested that the last dinosaurs at that place died out 67 million years ago, others that dinosaurs elsewhere survived until as recently as 63 million years before the present. Radiometric dating is uncertain enough that these figures could be interpreted to mean that dinosaurs expired very slowly over a period of at least 5 million years in various parts of the world, rather than that the range reflected analytical errors. The development of magnetostratigraphy allowed us at least to narrow the possible duration of their extinction. If all last remains of late Cretaceous dinosaurs occurred in sediments from C-29-R—and in no earlier or later sediments—then their extinction could have taken no longer than the half-million years of that polarity epoch.

This promising approach was unfortunately launched in confusion by a preliminary study in 1979 by E. H. Lindsay and others of an incomplete sedimentary sequence in the San Juan Basin, New Mexico. They claimed that the last dinosaurs lived during a normally magnetized epoch, probably Chron Cenozoic-29-normal, which followed C-29-R. Other investigators of the same area considered Lindsay's "last" dinosaurs to be next-to-last; they were convinced that the final sediments of the Mesozoic had been eroded away, and that Lindsay had found earlier, not final, fossils. The confusion was cleared up by James Fassett of the U.S. Geological Survey, who studied the eastern San Juan Basin where the sedimentation sequence had not been interrupted during the passage from the Mesozoic to the Cenozoic. Their results indicated clearly that erosion had indeed misled Lindsay. His "last" dinosaurs lived during C-32-N some 5 million years before the end of the Mesozoic. Lindsay's latest results have convinced him that the Cretaceous-Tertiary boundary event in San Juan Basin fell within C-29-R.

During the last several years additonal magnetostratigraphic studies have been carried out in various parts of western North America. The last dinosaur remains were always found in reversely magnetized sediments. J. F. Lerbekmo of Canada identified those sediments as C-29-R by reading through a substantial passage of the "standard product code" of remnant magnetism in a sedimentary sequence in Alberta. The dinosaurs' extinction during the half-million years of that epoch now seems very likely.

Did they die out as quickly as the foraminifers of Gubbio? The fossil finds of dinosaur bones are never abundant enough, and the technique of dating is not sufficiently perfected to permit a conclusion that the dinosaurs died out within thousands, tens of thousands, or hundred of thousands of years. The fact remains, however, that any time interval less than 1 million years is considered "short" and its passage "sudden" in geological terminology. Expressed in such terms, the interpretation that the dinosaurs on land ended their reign as abruptly or almost as abruptly as the plankton in the oceans would cause few paleontologists to disagree.

The question remains whether the great dying at the

end of the Mesozoic era took place everywhere, both on land and in the sea, and not only at Gubbio and in the American West, during the half-million-year epoch of C-29-R.

Magnetostratigraphic studies during the last few years have given an affirmative answer for marine organisms. Since I had the personal satisfaction of obtaining a confirmation during the South Atlantic drilling expedition in 1980, drill samples from several other Atlantic and Pacific deep-sea sites have all indicated that the Cretaceous-Tertiary boundary is at C-29-R. A number of studies of the boundary in ancient deep-sea sequences, now uplifted and exposed on land in Spain and in Germany, have also led to this conclusion. On land, paleobotanists have placed the last fossil pollen grains of an assemblage of plants that became extinct at the end of the Cretaceous at C-29-R, too. We have therefore become more and more confident that many forms of life, marine and terrestrial, plant and animal, did suffer mass extinction during the epoch Chron Cenozoic-29-reversed.

Magnetostratigraphic investigations in the last few years have certainly dealt the final blow to Lyell's and Darwin's postulate of a great chasm in time between the last record of the Mesozoic and the first record of the Cenozoic. The time of transition is laid out as a stripe on the seafloor, and as a layer in both oceanic and continental sediments. It has width, it has depth. C-29-R is real.

Therefore, we must believe our eyes. If many life forms make their last appearance in C-29-R, and never appear again, then they became extinct suddenly and simultaneously worldwide 65 million years ago.

5

The Enigma Of Extinction

THE FACT OF EXTINCTION, MUCH LESS THAN THE FACT of mass extinction, has been peculiarly difficult for people to accept. In the beginning, according to Linnaeus, God created a single pair, one male and one female, of every sexual species of living thing, and a single individual for each hermaphroditic species.

"There are as many species," Linnaeus wrote in 1751 in his *Philosophia Botanica*, "as the infinite being created diverse forms in the beginning, which, following the laws of generation, produced as many others but always similar to them. Therefore, there are as many species as we have different structures before us today."

In this belief the great classifier was in step with his time, for most eighteenth-century scholars believed that species were the basic entity created by God at the beginning of time. The essence of Linnaeus's division of organisms into "kinds" was his conviction concerning the immutability of species and of the fixity of their number.

Eventually Linnaeus was shaken in this conviction

when he considered that new species might have been originated by hybridization. He then drew a line of defense at the genus level, one step higher in his hierarchical system of nomenclature. Genera must be the essence, the "structures" created in the beginning. His followers, however, never wavered on the question of immutability and essentiality of species.

In 1753 Linnaeus had learned of about six thousand species; he thought the total number might be about ten thousand. New species described since Linnaeus's time are so numerous that we have lost count, but the latest estimates range from a conservative 2 million to as high as 30 million.

Number of species alone was no problem to Linnaeus, even if he had known how great that number is. The problem was immutability. When fossil species were described, many were found to be different from those living. Cavalier Lamarck faced that problem after he was appointed professor of insects, of worms and microscopic animals at the Paris Museum. He was too good an observer to overlook the distinction between fossil and recent shells in the museum's extensive mollusk collection, although he noted similarities too. To bring the possibility of extinction into line with biblical doctrine, his contemporaries suggested that the extinct were the evil ones, destroyed on purpose, or that they somehow missed *the* boat.

Young Charles Lyell, doctrinaire in his belief of uniform state, had difficulty in accepting the idea that a former world had been inhabited by other kinds of animals and plants. He was aware of Cuvier's discovery of four faunal dynasties whose fossil bones lay buried in the sediments of the Paris Basin. But large areas remained unexplored in Lyell's time; the descendants of apparently extinct fossils would be found, he felt sure, in faraway places. Even in modern times, such hopes are kept alive by newspaper accounts of a coelocanth, a fish previously known only from its fossil and thought to have been extinct for 300 million years, recovered from the waters off South Africa, or dawn redwood survivors from the Miocene, discovered in primeval forests of southwest China. That such finds are newsworthy serves, however, to emphasize that they are rare. Optimistic adventurers are still looking for proverbial dinosaurs in jungles along the Congo River or in the lochs of Scotland, but their chance of locating one is highly improbable, for none of the five thousand-odd dinosaur skeletons that have been found are of beasts that died in formations younger than the Cretaceous. Even if we should discover, against all odds, Nessie (and presumably her mate) we still face a problem in explaining the extinction of all those others.

Lamarck also could not, as a firm uniformitarian, agree with contemporary pleas for extinction through a diluvian disaster or by any other catastrophic means. Eventually, he gave up the hope that extinct species were still to be encountered by geographic exploration. While still not liberated from the bondage of his time— he clung to the notion that the number of species had stayed fixed since Creation—he ultimately took the revolutionary step of questioning the traditional view of immutability. He was particularly impressed by the fact that many fossil shells had a living counterpart, not identical, but nevertheless similar to a stony ancestor. He suggested, therefore, that species did not remain static. After many generations, changes crept in that gradually resulted in discrete differences between progenitors and their offspring. Not all species remained what they were; they had evolved since they were first created. With some groups of fossils evolutionary changes were so clear that he was able to arrange them into a chronological series terminating in an extant species.

Such chronological series are now called lineages, and the fact that so many lineages are now known is a mainstay of modern evolution theory. By invoking lineages, however, Lamarck sidestepped the issue of extinction. There was no extinction, he claimed, only "pseudoextinction." No older species had died out; all had been converted into new species by gradual, progressive evolution during the immensity of time since Creation. Although species change, lineages have never been broken and we have now as many species as God created in the beginning. It is ironic that uniformitarianism and evolution were the concepts invoked by a creationist to defend a theological creed. Gradualistic evolution had to be postulated so that the dogma of the fixity of number of species could be rescued.

Pseudoextinction is a useful concept. I remember an old-timer in the oil industry who once told me of the evolution of the famous "Seven Sisters." His theme was that oil companies never went broke: they just evolved, changing their structures gradually and their names abruptly. We no longer have on the stock exchange listings of Standard Oil of New Jersey, Secony Vacuum, Roxana, or Amerada. But we now have Exxon, Mobil, Shell, and AMOCO. Those were pseudoextinctions, of course.

But there have been real extinctions, too, as when, in the first years of this century, John Rockefeller demolished his competition. New "species," the old-timer went on, have also arisen, when the old Standard Oil was broken up by antitrust legislation into Standard Oil of New Jersey, California, Ohio, Indiana, and Texas. The paleontological record is likewise full of examples of lineages that can be thought of in terms of pseudoextinction, the wild forms that are now our domestic animals, for example, but the archive is even more impressively endowed with documents on extinction. The dinosaurs and other giant reptiles have become extinct. Hadrosaurs did not become kangaroos any more than ichthyosaurs became whales, or pterosaurs bats. The ecological niches vacated by the exterminated were subsequently occupied by new species of mammals that evolved along similar lines to fill similar jobs in similar work places, but who were by no means of the same lineages.

For all their mistaken efforts to rescue the doctrine of fixity in the number of species through such notions as pseudoextinction, uniformitarians were in a way right all along. From about 600 million years ago, when the fossil record is clear enough to count species, to the present, the number of species is surprisingly constant. The number of species extant at any one time corresponds to what paleontologists call *diversity*. By comparing the diversity of species in one period to that at another period, paleontologists have a fundamental quantitative and qualitative measure of change over geological time.

Measuring diversity is not, however, as simple as counting all known species from a geological period. Geological periods or epochs do not all have the same length. The Ordovician period was, for example, twice as long as the Silurian period, and so, not surprisingly, about twice as many species have been described from the former. The problem is similar to comparing the number of graves in a graveyard used for a century with one used for fifty years in the same village at another time. The long-used graveyard might have twice as many graves as the one used for only half as many years, yet the comparison does not warrant the conclusion that twice as many people lived then. To take care of the problem of different duration, David Raup of the University of Chicago proposed to use numbers of species per million years of an epoch to express diversity. According to the million-year yardstick the Ordovician and the Silurian faunas turn out to have about the same diversity.

Another problem is the volume of sedimentary rocks preserved in the geological record. The older sediments are, the more of them will have been eroded away or lost their integrity during episodes of mountain building. The Cenozoic era in which we live has had about the same duration as the Cretaceous period, or 65 million years for our era compared to about 70 million years for the previous period. But the volume of Cenozoic sediments is about twice as great as that of the Cretaceous, and presumably the number of fossils to be found in sediments is also doubled. In fact, twice as many Cenozoic fossils as Cretaceous fossils have been collected and described. Again, graveyards provide an analogy: The fewer graveyards exist intact from a certain time in the past, the fewer graves can be counted regardless of the actual population then. To arrive at the best estimate of species diversity, Raup had therefore to count the number of species per million years and also account for the sampling bias between sediments of various ages. Taking both sets of complicating factors into consideration, in 1976 Raup came to the surprising conclusion that species diversity for marine invertebrates, those best preserved in the fossil record at all times, has remained remarkably constant for 600 million years. Raup's conclusion was not accepted by all of his colleagues. There were numerous discussions and arguments in private. But four leading antagonists eventually came to a compromise and published a joint paper in 1981 to express their consensus that diversity increase, if there has been any, has been moderate during the last 600 million years.

A detailed breakdown shows that the apparent fixity in the number of species owes much to rapid recovery after mass extinctions. Geological eras—the Paleozoic, Mesozoic, and Cenozoic—were originally distinguished because scientists noted the drastic faunal turnovers at the transition from one era to the next. Species diversity was drastically reduced at the end of each geological era not only at the species level, but among genera and families too. For example, Dale Russell made a count of the number of genera before and after the end of the Cretaceous. He found that although organisms on land and in freshwater environments such as rivers or lakes suffered relatively little reduction in diversity in general, reptilian genera (including the dinosaurians) were reduced by more than half from fifty-four to twenty-three genera. The diversity of several groups of marine organisms was similarly drastically curtailed. Floating microorganisms suffered an average reduction in diversity of about 40 percent, from 298 to 173 genera. The great losses of the planktonic foraminifera and nannoplankton that build their skeletons of lime were partially offset by the lack of any damage at all to plankton that build their skeleton of silica, the major mineral in sand. Marine bottom dwellers had their diversity reduced by half, from 1,976 to 1,012 genera. Swimming marine organisms as a group suffered the greatest loss, from 332 to 99 genera, or a 70 percent reduction.

Russell's body count across the boundary between the Mesozoic and the Cenozoic eras included 2,862 genera described from the latest Cretaceous, and 1,502 genera described from the earliest Tertiary. At least half of the total genera perished during the last of the Cretaceous epochs. Actually, the figure is even higher. Russell included in his count of survivors not only genera that had been around before the extinction, but also new genera that arose after it. The actual proportion of genera that became extinct must therefore have been greater than 50 percent.

Paleontologists less skilled at biostatistics can be misled by naive body counts that fail to take into account the many factors affecting the diversity of a fossil assemblage.

Tove Birkelund, an otherwise excellent paleontologist who chairs the geology department at the University of Copenhagen, failed to notice that there had been any end at all to a marine community she studied in Denmark. On the basis of the species diversity of marine bottom communities that lived at the end of the Cretaceous she claimed that nothing unusual happened then. The news astonished Birkelund's audience, for she announced it in a paper presented to the Snowbird Conference at Snowbird, Utah, in 1981, where geologists had gathered to discuss the possible catastrophic end to the Cretaceous. Why should the invertebrates dwelling on the bottom of a shallow sea escape unscathed, while the floating plankton in the same shallow sea had been almost completely wiped out?

Birkelund was particularly impressed with the species diversity in a group of animals called cheilostome bryozoans. The bryozoans, also called moss animals, are small aquatic organisms that live in colonies. The group Birkelund studied produces calcareous skeletons decorated by complex ornamentation. Each species produces a unique ornamental pattern, so it is not hard to distinguish among them. Birkelund explained that there was an "immense diversity" of those bryozoans in the latest Cretaceous and also in the earliest Tertiary time, well over five hundred species living during the Maastrichtian and Danian in Denmark alone. She also noted that diversity "during the Danian is of the same order as the Maastrichtian diversity." She characterized this sameness across the infamous boundary as an "evolutionary standstill."

Birkelund's statistics, which appeared eventually in 1981 article for the Geological Society of America, spoke otherwise:

> A particularly detailed investigation of the cheilostome bryozoans in the boundary sequence Nye Klov in NW Jylland (by Hakansson and Thomsen, 1979) revealed a total of 115 species . . . : 60 species have a restricted Maastrichtian distribution . . . ; 11 species occur in both the Maastrichtian and the Danian; whereas 44 species are restricted to the Danian. . . . All Maastrichtian chalk populations are highly diverse. . . . In marked contrast to this, the basal Danian marly chalk contains an extremely poor fauna, increasing from only a single species at the very base to no more than four species within the first metre. It should be stressed that none of the species surviving the Maastrichtian-Danian boundary are present in this pioneer community. Following this extreme reduction, both diversity and density rise rapidly to a maximum of more than 40 species in the bryozoan limestone some 6 metres above the boundary.

Expressed in plain language, the good professor was telling us that all the cheilostome bryozoans disappeared from Nye Klov suddenly, to be replaced by a lone group of immigrants. More than 80 percent of the Cretaceous community never did return. During the first million years after the holocaust, the first pioneer in the Danian chalk was joined by a few more immigrants, several of which were survivors that had found refuge elsewhere.

But the "newly born" groups dominated. Newly evolved species constituted more than 80 percent of the Danian population; diversity, momentarily lost, was reestablished.

Birkelund's mistake, which others also have made, was to compare the "before" and "after," while ignoring the critical time of change. If we compared the economy of Germany a decade before and a decade after World War II we might conclude that the development of West German industry had been at a "standstill." The fact, of course, was a catastrophic total destruction in 1945, followed by an unexpectedly speedy recovery during the postwar years.

Abrupt extinction has been even harder to accept than extinction itself and has similarly been glossed over by unsophisticated analyses. For example, improper handling of statistical data has led some paleontologists to form the impression that ammonites, those swimming animals with a coiled shell shaped like a ram's horn, died out gradually over many millions of years and that whatever happened at the very end of the Cretaceous was only the straw that broke the camel's back. One paleontologist working in Spain counted in 1969 more than 150 genera in a middle Cretaceous stage called the *Albian* but found only three genera from the topmost Maastrichtian sediments, those deposited just before the end of the Mesozoic era. He interpreted that to mean the ammonites had suffered a prolonged decline before the last remnants of that once great group died out. Unfortunately, the taxonomy specialist was not a rigorous biostatistician. He did not consider the fact that the Albian epoch was much longer than the interval of time when the last Maastrichtian ammonites lived.

Tove Birkelund studied the last ammonites in Denmark. She was able to find seven other ammonite genera —in addition to the three genera found in Spain—just below the Fish Clay in the youngest Maastrichtian rock at Stevn's Klint, but she emphasized that each Maastrichtian genus of ammonites consisted of few species only. This lack of diversity suggested to her that the ammonites had been on the decline well before the end of the Cretaceous. She failed to take into account that not much Maastrichtian rock is found on land. Many more species of Maastrichtian ammonites might have turned up if the Maastrichtian marine sediments she studied were as widespread as those of the Albian.

Recent evidence from a fresh source points out how wary one should be of the potential for sampling bias. Toward the end of the Mesozoic Europe and North America were undergoing regression as shallow seas withdrew from previously submerged continental coasts. Not much marine sediment of that age is therefore exposed on land in the northern hemisphere, and few Maastrichtian ammonites are to be found. The situation in Antarctica was just the opposite: The continent was gradually being drowned by a transgressive sea, and the Maastrichtian marine deposits in that distant land are more widespread than those from the older Cretaceous. It was, therefore, not surprising when a young Argentinian scientist announced recently that ammonite diversity there, at least, was increasing, not decreasing, when the Mesozoic came to a sudden end.

Gradual decline, as opposed to abrupt extinction, is a uniformitarian prejudice, and one that paleontologists have often found appealing. Like Birkelund herself, they are commonly convinced of the truth of the time-hallowed senility theory—the assumption that ancient families, genera, or species of organisms lose their "evolutionary vigor." According to the theory, the ancient ammonites were destined for extinction as inevitable as the fate of old people waiting for their death.

The analogy is, however, far from perfect. Individuals have average life expectancies. Species, genera, and families do not. Few would claim that cockroaches have lost their vigor, yet they are descended from one of the oldest families of fossil insects and remain among the most primitive of winged insects. The direct ancestors of the American opossum were contemporaries of the last dinosaurs. The giant redwoods have come from a very ancient stock 200 million years old. Ginkgo trees preceded them by 50 million years at least. The most impressively ancient of all is a small lampshell genus, *Lingula*, which is found among the earliest fossils of the Cambrian period, more than one-half billion years of age. There seems to be no limitation to the longevity of a genus.

The particular ammonite genera Birkelund studied in fact belonged to ancient ammonite stocks and had lived for millions of years with little evolutionary change. So the obvious question is not "were they vigorous?" but "why, after living so long, did they meet their end abruptly?" A sudden death is a sudden death, no matter if the victim is youthful or aged.

DETAILED STUDIES OF DANISH SEDIMENTS HAVE INDI-
cated the same pattern of sudden extinction for creatures other than foraminifers and bryozoans. Finn Surlyk and Marianne Johansen investigated the Danish brachiopods or lampshells—sedentary clamlike animals that feed on shallow sea bottoms. The upper Maastrichtian chalk at Nye Klov contains twenty-seven species, and the Danian chalk contains thirty-five species. Of the twenty-seven Maastrichtian species five were found in the boundary Fish Clay that is the earliest Danian sediment, and only six others survived the crisis and ranged well up into the Danian. Meanwhile twenty-four new species appeared for the first time in the Danian. In other words, only six out of the twenty-seven species survived beyond the earliest Danian, a casualty rate of about 80 percent. But the almost equally sudden recovery led eventually to a net gain in diversity of 30 percent on the other side of the boundary.

Surlyk was a colleague of Birkelund at Copenhagen and was also trained in the best classical tradition. Some time before he had completed his study of lampshell fossils, he was asked by the editors of *Nature* to comment on an article of mine concerning the sudden extinction at the end of the Cretaceous. He was skeptical and preached caution. After the completion of his work at Nye Klov, his hesitation vanished. The change of brachiopod faunas at Nye Klov was not a matter of pseudoextinction. Surlyk and Johansen emphasized significant differences between the Maastrichtian and Danian genera. The Maastrichtian brachiopods were simply massacred; brand new species evolved from a handful of survivors. The pattern of extinction was exactly the same as that for the foraminifers at Gubbio.

Nor was there anything gradual about it—lampshells had not declined or lost "vigor." Surlyk and Johansen wrote in an article for *Science* that "there was no warning in the form of decreasing population density, diversity, or early extinction of specialized groups." Suddenly, in the less than half a million years trapped in that layer of clay, more than three-quarters of the brachiopod species became extinct. The Danian brachiopods, like the Danian bryozoans at the same site and the Danian *Globigerina eugubina* at Gubbio, started up as abruptly as the Maastrichtian fauna had disappeared, and their rapid diversification more than made up for the severe loss.

Body counts alone speak of the severity of extinction, but they do not clarify its rate. To measure the rapidity of extinction we must examine the percentage of species that have become extinct during a given interval of time. Extinction occurs all the time; judging from the well-studied extinction rate of Cenozoic mollusk species in the Pacific Ocean, about half the total number of mollusk species becomes extinct every 7 million years. This normal extinction rate is called background extinction, that which goes on quite steadily for many millions of years at a time. If the background extinction rate for mollusks is half the number of species per 7 million years, then reduction by half in 3.5 million years, or reduction by three-quarters in 7 million years, would be twice as rapid an extinction rate. The data by Surlyk and Johansen on Danish brachiopods indicate a reduction by about three-quarters in less than half a million years. That is at least twenty times faster than normal. The shorter the time span, the greater the disaster looks. Should the time interval represented by the Fish Clay turn out to be only fifty thousand years, those mollusks were becoming extinct at two hundred times the normal rate.

IN SPITE OF IMPRESSIVE EVIDENCE AS TO BOTH SEVERITY and rate of extinction at the close of the Mesozoic era, uniformitarian hopes die hard. Just as Linnaeus hoped to preserve the immutability of "kinds" by choosing to hold the line at the genus, rather than the species, level, today's paleontologists whitewash the matter of mass extinction by choosing units higher up in the taxonomic hierarchy in compiling casualty lists. If a general reports to his superior after a massive defeat that there are survivors from each of the regiments under his command, he is not saying much. Some of those regiments may have been almost completely wiped out, and others may have been left with a few stragglers only. He may cover up an even greater catastrophe by reporting that there are survivors from each of the divisions under his command when the majority of his regiments no longer exist. Some paleontologists use a similar approach to demonstrate that the Mesozoic era was not terminated by a mass extinction. I have seen records of extinction in which neither species nor genera, but families or whole orders were chosen as units for analysis. The higher in the hierarchy of classification one goes, the more misleading the results. If one were to choose classes as the unit of extinction, not even the end of the dinosaurs would appear because the class *Reptilia* survived. A graph based on these data would show that nothing at all happened at the end of the Cretaceous.

But at the family level, it is clear that numbers were rapidly and drastically reduced during a brief episode at the end of the Cretaceous. Dave Raup and his associates recently made a statistical analysis of the survival pattern for families of fossil marine organisms. They counted 289 families of marine organisms that lived at the beginning of the Cretaceous period 135 million years ago and calculated the rate at which they became extinct between then and the end of the period 70 million years later. Twenty-nine families had disappeared after some

28 million years, and sixty-five families had disappeared after 64 million years, making the background rate for that period about one family per million years. Then, during the final 5 million years of the Cretaceous, 10 percent of the original number of families, or almost thirty of them, perished. The extinction rate fell back to normal again after the beginning of the Cenozoic.

Raup did not specify the duration of the accelerated extinction toward the end of the Cretaceous. If the extinct families made their exit steadily during the 5 million years of the Maastrichtian, the extinction rate would be about six times normal; if they disappeared during the half-million-year epoch of C-29-R, the rate is about sixty times normal. If all those families died out during the brief time when the boundary clay was being deposited, the rate would be catastrophic: more than five hundred times the background rate for this marine fauna.

Properly treated and properly read, statistics say that the number of species is not immutable, that the rate at which they die out and are replaced is not steady. Not only that, measures of species diversity also show that mass extinction can come suddenly, without forewarning, for there was nothing about the healthy, numerous, vigorous, and diversified foraminfera, bryozoans, or brachiopods to indicate their end was near.

What body counts do not show is how these thriving marine communities met their end. Even more mysterious is the enormity of the catastrophe: Whatever killed plankton and lampshells in the sea probably also exterminated dinosaurs ashore, as well as the rest of the myriad organisms which failed to survive into the following era.

One cannot help but come to the conclusion that catastrophe of global proportion descended simultaneously on many different groups of organisms on land and in the ocean, bringing the Mesozoic era to a sudden end.

A NUMBER OF YEARS AGO, WHEN I WAS A YOUNG MAN working for Shell Research, I used to pack a brown paper bag and join my friend Alfred Traverse for lunch in his office. One day at noon, I found him at his desk deeply engrossed in the latest issue of a trade journal. I had sat down and started to munch on my sandwich when he handed me the copy and said: "Would you take a look at that article on dinosaurs? Do you think the guy is serious? Or do you think de Laubenfels is the pseudonym of someone who is pulling our leg?"

I scanned the pages as I ate. It was amusing reading. De Laubenfels wrote that the last dinosaurs were killed by hot air, after the fall of a large meteor. Since "hot air" is a slang expression for idle talk, Traverse thought the article was a satire. The author was telling us that we had talked the dinosaurs to death.

What kinds of hot-air stories did we have to explain their mass extinction?

My favorite tall tale was one concocted by Tony Swain, a chemical taxonomist, at Kew Gardens, London. The story, which Swain called "Cold-blooded Murder in the Cretaceous," was published in 1974. Swain's work concerned chemicals that are synthesized by plants to deter herbivores. Ferns and conifers employ condensed tannins, apparently not very harmful to dinosaurs because those plants were the basic diet of many herbivorous species. Toward the middle of the Cretaceous period, flowering plants underwent an explosive evolution, becoming the dominant vegetation everywhere, and the main fodder for vegetarian dinosaurs. Their deterrent chemicals are alkaloids that are unpleasantly bitter and cause illness when consumed in modest amounts, or are lethal in larger doses. Mammals apparently do not like the bitter alkaloids and cut down their intake to a safe level. Reptiles, such as tortoises in Swain's experiments, find the plants more palatable, overeat, and thus "suffer severe physiological disturbance, and even death."

Based on this difference in "taste" he had discovered between mammals and reptiles Swain made a rash leap. Identifying dinosaurs with tortoises, and impressed by the insatiable appetite of those beasts, Swain suggested that they had poisoned themselves to death and to extinction.

It was a good story, but not taken seriously by geologists. Even if Swain was correct in all his speculations, he only explained the demise of herbivorous dinosaurs. Who "murdered" the tyrannosaurs? How did he explain the delayed reaction, for the dinosaurs died out many millions of years after the rise of flowering plants? Swain had anyhow ignored the variety of reptiles, marine invertebrates, mammals, birds, and even quite a few flowering plants that also became extinct at that time. His idea would have been forgotten long ago if it had not been so amusing.

A scenario almost as implausible suggested that dinosaurs were not despatched with poison, but died of hunger. In this tale the food chain collapsed when phytoplankton, single-celled photosynthesizing plants that constitute the bulk of floaters at the ocean surface, became largely extinct at the end of Cretaceous, and the dinosaurs were the ultimate victims.

Phytoplankton are usually less than 0.01 millimeter across. They grow by taking in nutrients such as phosphorus and nitrogen during photosynthesis and thrive especially in coastal waters, where nutrients are abundant. Though tiny, there are billions and billions of these organisms in each liter of ocean water during their seasons of reproduction, when their rapid increase is called a bloom. Soft-bodied phytoplankton leave little trace of themselves after death, but the hard-bodied ones, calcareous nannoplankton, are among those that secrete skeletons of unique design, different for each species. These skeletons survive the death of their soft-bodied inhabitants and sink to the the seafloor. Therefore, the history of nannoplankton is preserved in the chalky sediments and limestone they become.

Nannoplankton get their name from the Latin word *nana*, or dwarf, a reference to their tiny size. Their fossils, called nannofossils, were first discovered in rocks by the German microscopist Christian Ehrenburg in 1836. Some two decades later, Thomas Huxley, Darwin's friend and defender, found in recent deep-sea sediments of the Atlantic a type called coccoliths whose shell is a ring of little plates surrounding a central hole, and his contemporary, Henry Sorby, discovered that coccoliths are the main constituent of English chalk. During the ensuing century many specialists joined in describing and classifying new fossil species, but nannofossils did not make headlines in science until 1964, when Bill Bramlette, who taught me sedimentology at UCLA, utilized nannofossil data to show that there was indeed a sudden mass extinction in the world of nannoplankton.

Nannoplankton were very diversified during the Cretaceous; Helen Tappan, a micropaleontologist at UCLA after Bramlette left, counted more than one hundred genera. Bramlette found a nearly complete extinction of the Mesozoic coccoliths at the end of the Maastrichtian. Only a few "inconspicuous" species survived. These few remnants, however, quickly gave rise to new species toward the end of the Danian stage, a few million years later. A diverse and flourishing nannoplankton community was reestablished.

The coincidence in timing of the nannoplankton extinction with that of many other groups of organisms suggested to Helen Tappan a cause-and-effect relationship. Phytoplankton are at the base of the food chain, Tappan noted. Biologist H. W. Harvey had estimated that an annual harvest of 100 tons of phytoplankton is required for the survival of 70 tons of zooplankton browsers such as foraminifers. The 70 tons of zooplankton in turn supplies nutrition for some 4 to 7 tons of fish, which fulfills the annual dietary requirement of a carnivore some 300 kilograms in weight. If the production of phytoplankton were drastically reduced, a chain reaction might be unleashed; the collapse of the food chain could lead to starvation of many other organisms. Giant dinosaurs, with their cavernous appetite, should be obvious victims of such a hunger catastrophe.

Tappan's story had two flaws. First, she merely side-stepped the main issue when she put the blame on a poor harvest. Why should that happen? Phytoplankton need nutrients and vitamins, Tappan reasoned. Perhaps the supply of nutrients was scarce, as Bramlette had proposed. Or was there a vitamin deficiency? The vitamins necessary to the coccoliths Bramlette had studied—cobalamin, thiamine, and biotin—are synthesized by soil bacteria, carried to the ocean by rivers, and distributed by currents. A snafu in the chain of supply could have led to the catastrophe. But that scenario is not convincing. Either rivers had to have dried up or been plugged up, or the ocean had to have stood still, or soil bacteria themselves would have to be added to the already troublesome list of extinctions.

The second flaw was even more serious. Large ocean-going reptiles that were contemporaries of dinosaurs fed on fish, and they might have died of hunger if phytoplankton production failed, but dinosaurs were terrestrial: Carnivorous dinosaurs ate herbivores who got their food from plants on land. Plankton's dying of malnutrition in the oceans should not prevent dinosaurs from gorging themselves on the luxuriant growth of terrestrial vegetation.

If neither poison nor hunger had done the trick, could dinosaurs have been killed by cold? Many paleontologists tended to think so. They started with a fact noted by paleobotanists, that the earth's climate has undergone a cooling trend during the last 100 million years, starting in the Mesozoic when warm global climate supported tropical and subtropical forests nearly pole to pole, and reaching a crisis with the Ice Age that began 2 million years ago. The dinosaurs originally evolved in a warm climate, and, it has been claimed, could adapt only so far as the weather gradually cooled. Inexorably, they came under stress. The straw that broke the dinosaurs' back finally came 65 million years ago; the limit was reached and they died of cold.

This idea was well accepted at a time when dinosaurs were assumed by everyone to have been cold-blooded animals like other reptiles. Large crocodiles, pythons, iguanas, and tortoises are found today in regions of warm climate. Those reptiles that do live in temperate zones, turtles as well as snakes, are small enough to burrow deep and hibernate. There was no hiding place for dinosaurs. A close examination of this hypothesis reveals, however, many questions, not least of which is whether all dinosaurs lived in the tropics and subtropics.

In fact, they did not. In the higher latitudes dinosaurs were adapted to a climate where, judging by the deciduous tree species such as elm and beech that forested their habitat, they experienced at least mild winters. Some small dinosaurs, crow to cat size, evolved the insulating feathers which were inherited by their descendants, the birds. (Pterosaurs, flying reptiles that were not dinosaurs, were furred.) And, according to a growing number of paleontologists, all dinosaurs were to some degree warm-blooded. Robert Bakker of Johns Hopkins University is the leading champion of this new view of dinosaurs as endothermic, energetic beasts that had no trouble staying warm.

Van Valen of the University of Chicago, another dinosaur expert, proposed that it was the shift from subtropical to temperate vegetation, rather than the cold itself, that did in the dinosaurs. His work was done mostly in Montana. He thought that as winters became more severe there at the end of the Mesozoic many subtropical plants disappeared from the scene to be replaced by temperate forests. The dinosaurs could not stomach this form of vegetation; furthermore, the increase of deciduous trees which shed their leaves made less food available in winter. Feed requirements could indeed be critical for survival if, like the pandas of China that subsist entirely on arrow bamboo, a species is adapted to a very limited diet. But although there may have been some dinosaur species that ate only one sort of sago palm or one brand of fern, the tribe as a whole ate everything in sight. They were everything from wood chewers to grasshopper catchers, conifer browsers to possum hunters. Furthermore, herds tend to move to where their fodder is, as predators follow their prey. If the zone of subtropical plants did shift southward, why didn't dinosaurs follow them? Such "movement"—a shift in population really—is measured in feet per year. Tropical dinosaurs would anyhow not have had the problems of those living in temperate climates, nor should a chill that killed Montana dinosaurs also have killed many hot little mammals, and birds, and every marine reptile except sea turtles.

If we have difficulty painting a gloomy picture of chilled dinosaurs, we have no reason at all to suppose that marine plankton would die off en masse by moderate decreases in ocean temperatures. We are on sure ground here because the record of fluctuating temperature in the 65 million years since the end of the Mesozoic is quite clear.

Geological studies of climate during the Cenozoic have indicated rapid temperature decline during the Eocene 50 million years ago, at the beginning of the Oligocene 35 million years ago, in the middle Miocene 14 million years ago, in the late Miocene 6 million years ago, and in the late Pliocene 2.5 million years ago. The final temperature drop led to the Great Ice Age, with its more drastic fluctuations of ocean temperatures during glacial and interglacial stages. None of the drops in temperature led to catastrophe in the oceans, nor did they cause changes on land on the radical scale of the dinosaur extinction.

Earle Kauffman, a specialist on Cretaceous marine invertebrates, had enough experience in paleontology not to subscribe to any simpleminded approach such as poisoning, starvation, or chilling. He gave me a lecture on paleontology when I visited him in 1982 at the Smithsonian Institution, in Washington, D.C. We continued our discussion during our lobster dinner and returned to the museum for some more arguments. Kauffman did not appreciate the record of sudden extinction at the end of the Cretaceous (although he has changed his mind since then). He preferred a gradualistic hypothesis and proposed a complicated scenario which invoked oxygen depletion in ocean waters related to climate changes that were in turn triggered by the comings and goings of the seas.

Early in the Maastrichtian the seas transgressed over the land, and the continental shelves were drowned. Transgressions of the sea over a continent tend to ameliorate climate because water holds heat well. But the ventilation of warm seas is inefficient. According to Kauffman, oxygen became depleted in seawater during this early Maastrichtian transgression, and that was harmful to many tropical faunas living on the shallow bottom. Mass extinction started at that point. Then the sea receded, the shelves were again exposed, and the climate became colder. For some reason not clearly explained, ventilation of the cold sea was also inefficient and oxygen became further depleted. That and the cold climate combined to deal the fatal blow to tropical faunas of the shallow seas. Mass extinction, already begun during the earlier transgression, reached its climax at the end of the Maastrichtian.

Kauffman's idea seemed sophisticated; many paleontologists liked the fuzziness of his impressionistic picture. But impartial laymen could easily spot loopholes. One question would suffice: Why should the Maastrichtian transgression and regression bring about a natural catastrophe of unprecedented degree when so many others did not seem to leave any imprint on the history of lives on earth? I can't resist one further remark. Dinosaurs living in the interior of continents would have had no idea that the sea was coming in or going out, or that the oxygen in seawater was depleted. And why should they care? It affected them not a whit.

Many experts who see no problem about dinosaurs' keeping warm have nevertheless questioned how well they could stand heat. Giant animals are just made for a cold climate; they have, compared to small, slender animals, less surface area through which to lose heat trapped in their bulky bodies and can thus hang on to body heat produced by their own metabolism. It is heat that is the "fat man's misery." Efficient heat retention would have been a disadvantage in a rapidly warming climate.

Dale Russell compared a 20-ton dinosaur to a ball

with a surface area of 9 square meters. Assuming that this large dinosaur was ectothermic like today's reptiles, its metabolic heat production would be 557 kilocalories per hour. Its surface area would radiate heat at just about the same rate for each degree that its body temperature exceeded the ambient temperature. Basking in the sun, it would heat up. If the ambient temperature were between 20 and 25 degrees Celsius—about room temperature—it would acquire 8,100 kilocalories of solar energy in addition to the metabolic increment. It would be able to keep its body to no more than 15 degrees above the ambient temperature, or in the range of a mammal's body. If the air temperature rose to 30 or 40 degrees—a summer heat wave—large dinosaurs would overheat unless they quickly found shade in which to cool off.

Edwin Colbert, curator of vertebrate paleontology at the Smithsonian, found that alligators die when ambient temperature is raised to only a few degrees above the optimum temperature, that at which they function best. The same is true of several species of desert lizards, as a study by his associate R. B. Cowles revealed. This low tolerance is understandable because cold-blooded, or ectothermic, animals do not have efficient means to dissipate body heat.

The question of whether large dinosaurs had difficulty with overheating is complicated somewhat by Robert Bakker's evidence that the dinosaurs were warm-blooded. If they had evolved endothermy, would they also have been more efficient than previously supposed in dissipating heat by such means as panting, sweating, or even blushing? Russell did not think so; he felt the problem of overheating would be worse for warm-blooded dinosaurs because of their much higher metabolic rates of heat production.

Dewey McLean, a micropaleontologist whose broad interest in biological science has tempted his imagination beyond the narrow confines of his field, published in 1978 an article on this subject in *Science*. He put forward an elegant argument that dinosaurs died in a "terminal Mesozoic greenhouse."

McLean reviewed the evidence that reptiles are notoriously incapable of tolerating heat and explored the unorthodox postulate that dinosaur extinction was induced not by falling temperature, but by rising temperature. Giant dinosaurs and other large reptiles, regardless of whether they were cold- or warm-blooded, would have died of heat stroke if the air temperature had risen 10 degrees Celsius above normal.

Even somewhat less elevated temperature could have affected reproduction. McLean cited, for example, research on male sterility as a result of overheated sperm, which become nonviable at only slightly elevated temperatures, and on heat stress in chickens, which causes hens to lay excessively fragile eggs. There is evidence of shell pathology in the most recent dinosaur eggs, and also of unfertilized, sterile eggs.

To explain so prolonged a heat wave, however, McLean had to resort to the failure of the plankton crop, as had so many others before him. This is not to say that the subtle scenario he proposed was implausible, for he suggested that with the mass death of phytoplankton in the oceans, the carbon dioxide these plants normally consume in photosynthesis would have been released to the atmosphere. It was already well known at that time that carbon dioxide acts as glass in a greenhouse, trapping heat that normally escapes out to space and raising temperature globally.

But all these explanations have the same flaw: They begin with the fact that is most in need of explanation: The death of oceansful of plankton. How that mass extinction could have happened was not to be guessed until a year after McLean's 1978 article. Meanwhile, one could begin to choose at least between chiller thriller and hot-air stories by investigating what the weather really was like 65 million years ago.

6

Witness from the Abyss

W HEN I WAS A STUDENT AT UCLA I STARTED MY dissertation research with the distinguished geophysicist David Griggs. His hero was William Thomson, better known to us as Lord Kelvin. On the door of Griggs's office was a quotation from Kelvin: "I often say that when you can measure what you are speaking about, and express it in numbers, you know something about it; but when you cannot express it in numbers, your knowledge is of a meagre and unsatisfactory kind; it may be the beginning of knowledge, but you have scarcely, in your thoughts, advanced to the state of Science, whatever the matter may be."

Another pearl of wisdom attributed to Kelvin was downright insulting. He was supposed to have declared that there were scientists—he meant physicists—who expressed their knowledge in numbers, and there were "stamp collectors." Stamp collectors were biologists, geologists, and other students of nature who, Kelvin was convinced, were interested only in specimens.

Putting aside his arrogance, Kelvin had a point: We

111

need quantification to verify ideas. Russell and others had estimated that dinosaurs could not have survived if the air temperature had suddenly risen 10 degrees Celsius. McLean had proposed that the temperature was that much warmer at the end of the Cretaceous, but he had no numbers to support him. De Laubenfels envisioned the demise of marine reptiles under scorching heat near boiling temperature, but he had not even a hint of a boiling ocean. The evidence for a cooling trend was likewise vague: A 100-million-year-long trend does not specify the temperature at any given time during that period.

WE USED TO DEPEND UPON PALEONTOLOGISTS FOR INformation on past climate. Plants are sensitive indicators of their environment. Some fossil plants have modern representatives, and we could presume a habitat of the past similar to that of the present. We found, for example, fossil palms of Mesozoic age in the Arizona desert, telling us that the climate was not much different there 250 million years ago. Other plants are, however, extinct, and we have to guess what the distribution of their fossils says on the basis of their relationship to modern plants or use plant morphology for our interpretation. For example, plants with broad leaves tend to grow in the tropics or subtropics; conifers or leguminous plants are more common in temperate or drier regions.

Animals have their preferences too. Coral reefs grow in the tropics, whereas seals and walruses inhabit polar waters. Diversity is another criterion: An abundance of species is found in optimal climates, but only a few hardy ones survive severe cold or other stressful conditions. Paleontologists have thus been able to recognize faunal provinces of bygone days and correlate them with climatic belts.

The distribution of one-celled organisms in the ocean is also related to climatic belts. One-celled organisms are these days called *protists* and are considered a kingdom of living beings separate from the animal and plant kingdoms. Protists include what used to be thought of as

one-celled animals, for instance the browsing foraminifers, and one-celled plants, for instance the browsed-on
nannoplankton. Foraminiferal and nannoplankton species that inhabit the tropics can be distinguished from
those that inhabit middle and high latitudes. Radiolarians
with lovely jewellike and glassy skeletons are abundant
in the equatorial Pacific, whereas diatoms, of whose
gritty skeletons polishing agents are made, are particularly common in polar oceans.

The study of climate-related fossil distribution is
called paleoecology. For more than a century, the
science of paleoecology developed ways to reveal the
changing climates of the past. Descriptive terms such as
warm and cold, tropic and temperate, were employed to
denote broad differences in temperatures of the environments in which various fossil organisms lived. We have
gained confidence in the work of paleoecologists because
results from different lines of evidence have tended to
converge to give the same conclusion. Diversified faunas
were found in seas that washed over the continental shelf
close to land where tropical floras grew, or adjacent to
open oceans where equatorial protists flourished. When
nonpaleontological methods were developed, many of
the conclusions were confirmed. The inclination of natural remnant magnetism, for example, can indicate latitude and therefore confirm that a seemingly equatorial
fossil assemblage was indeed at the equator and therefore "tropical."

One shortcoming of the paleoecological approach is,
however, that it offers no numbers. Most paleoecologists
use such expressions as "warm," "relatively warm,"
"warmer," "very warm." But one man's "warm" may be
another's "very warm." Also, paradoxical expressions
are often resorted to: "tropical faunas," for example,
may not be those living near the equator, but those of
high latitudes in existence at a time when the climate was
very warm globally. In fact, the precision required to
support any of the hot or cold theories of mass extinctions was such that the paleontological approach broke
down completely. On the question of the terminal Creta-

ceous climate, paleontologists engaged themselves in futile arguments over whether temperature rose or fell then; really, no one knew.

The technique that allowed us at last to measure the temperature of ancient climates—the paleothermometer, so to speak—had actually been in use for twenty years when McLean proposed his greenhouse theory to explain the dinosaurs' end. It sometimes takes that long, however, to debug a new tool and to find out exactly how to use it with the required accuracy, and results were for a long time confusing.

The method grew out of the work with isotopes that had made radiometric dating possible. It had originally been thought that the relative abundance of the various naturally occurring stable isotopes of a chemical element—those that cannot be used for radiometric dating because they do not decay—should be the same everywhere they are found, and under all circumstances. But back in the early 1930s, Harold Urey suspected that hydrogen, not yet known to have any isotope at all, may have more than one, and that there may be a way to enrich a sample of the element so that it contains an unusual abundance of a heavier isotope. Common hydrogen atoms have one proton and are that element's lightest isotope with an atomic weight of 1. Light atoms like that are agile. When liquid containing them is evaporated, such light atoms have the best opportunity to "jump" out of the liquid, to become vapor. When the vapor is condensed, atoms that weigh more, such as a heavier isotope of hydrogen carrying one or more neutrons, should have a better chance to get back into the liquid. Thus, by evaporating and recondensing a liquid repeatedly, the final, residual liquid should be enriched in the atoms of the heavier isotope, were it to exist. Urey evaporated some 6 liters of liquid hydrogen and found by mass spectrometry that the residual liquid was enriched with hydrogen atoms that had an atomic weight of 2. Thus a heavy hydrogen, called deuterium because of its doubled atomic weight, was discovered, and Urey received a Nobel Prize for his effort.

Deuterium has an atomic weight of 2 because its nucleus has a neutron in addition to the proton. Eventually, a third hydrogen isotope, tritium, was discovered; it has two neutrons. Deuterium is a stable isotope, but tritium is radioactive. Other very common elements also have isotopes. Carbon has carbon 12, carbon 13, and carbon 14. The last is radioactive and provides a means of radiometric dating of carbon-bearing materials. Oxygen has oxygen 16, oxygen 17, and oxygen 18; they are all stable isotopes that don't decay into daughter products and therefore cannot be used for radiometric dating.

All isotopes, however, can be fractionated as Urey fractionated hydrogen into its heavier and lighter isotopes. After his work for the Manhattan Project during World War II, Urey went back to basic science and started to think about the way in which fractionation of stable isotopes might happen in nature, and what the consequence might be.

The most common isotope of oxygen, oxygen 16, has eight protons and eight neutrons in the nucleus and constitutes 99.756 percent of oxygen atoms. Oxygen 17 has one additional neutron, and oxygen 18 has two additional neutrons; they constitute 0.039 percent and 0.205 percent of oxygen, respectively. When oxygen combines with another element or elements to make a chemical compound, the oxygen in the compound also contains a small proportion of the heavier isotopes oxygen 17 and oxygen 18. The percentage of the various isotopes of oxygen in that compound is referred to as its oxygen-isotope composition. Commonly oxygen 17 atoms are too few to be measured accurately; it suffices to express the isotope composition of oxygen in terms of the relative proportion of the heaviest and the lightest isotopes, oxygen 18 and 16.

Water, that familiar H_2O compound of hydrogen and oxygen, contains the ordinary proportion of light hydrogen and its heavier deuterium isotope, as well as all three oxygen isotopes. Water in the open ocean has been homogenized to such an extent that its ratio of oxygen 16 to oxygen 18 is practically the same everywhere and is, therefore, used as the standard: standard mean ocean water, or SMOW. Clouds, however, are like the hydrogen vapor that escaped from Urey's liquid hydrogen in his experiments to separate heavy from light isotopes by repeated evaporation and condensation. Clouds have less of the heavy oxygen 18 isotope than does the ocean water from which their vapor escapes. Oxygen compounds with less oxygen 18 than standard mean ocean water are said to have a negative oxygen 18 anomaly with respect to SMOW. Clouds, then, have a negative oxygen anomaly, and so do rain and snow that fall from those clouds, and so do the lakes and streams fed by rainwater and melted snow. Compounds that contain more oxygen 18 than does SMOW are said to have a positive oxygen anomaly.

UREY REPORTED THIS FINDING DURING A TALK IN 1946 AT the Swiss Federal Institute of Technology. Paul Niggli, professor of mineralogy then, immediately saw an application to geology. For many years geologists had had difficulty distinguishing between limestones deposited in a lake and those deposited in an ocean. Limestone (calcium carbonate, or $CaCO_3$) contains oxygen, which comes from the water in which the limestone formed. If fresh water has a negative oxygen anomaly compared to SMOW, limestones formed in a lake should also be low in oxygen 18 compared to marine limestones. A fossil shell in marine limestone from what is called the Pee Dee Formation of North Carolina was eventually chosen as a standard against which calcium carbonate deposits of undetermined origin could be compared.

Niggli's remark after the lecture may have altered the direction of Urey's life: He was to change from a profession in chemistry to Earth and planetary sciences, and his first contribution in his new career was a way of using the isotopic composition of calcium carbonates as a paleothermometer to measure the temperature of ancient oceans. A theoretical analysis showed that the temperature at which this mineral crystallized would influence the relative abundance of its oxygen isotopes even if all crystals were precipitated from the same SMOW. Higher water temperatures would lead to fractionation in favor of more agile atoms of the light isotope; heavier oxygen 18 should thus be relatively depleted in crystals precipitated in warmer seas. Calculations by Urey and his student J. M. McCrea resulted in a scale that told the temperature of ancient seas, and the differing values were great enough to be detected by the mass spectrometers of that day.

Since marine shells are made of calcium carbonate from ocean water, Urey reasoned that the isotopic composition of a fossil shell should indicate the temperature of the ancient ocean in which the shell was secreted.

Satisfied with his theoretical premise, helped by a young paleontologist named Heinz Lowenstam, and supported by a grant from the Geological Society of America, Urey went fossil hunting and found belemnites the most suitable paleothermometers.

Belemnites are called pen-rocks in Chinese because their cylindrical shells have a stubby and a pointed end like a Chinese writing pen. Urey chose pen-rocks because their original skeletons have been preserved, whereas many other fossils are made up of minerals that have replaced the original ones. The first measurement was made on a specimen from a Jurassic formation in England. Urey's Jurassic specimen had a diameter of 2.5 centimeters. It was brownish and translucent. When a section was cut, one could see well-defined growth rings. Samples from twenty-four rings were analyzed, and the oxygen anomaly ranged in values equivalent to temperatures of 14 to 20 degrees Celsius (57 to 68 degrees Fahrenheit). The temperature variation suggested that the Jurassic swimmer had lived through three summers and four winters after its youth and died in the spring, age four years.

The British Museum provided the Chicago team with belemnites, oysters, and brachiopods from the middle and upper Cretaceous chalk of England. The Copenhagen University Museum made a gift of three Maastrichtian belemnite specimens, the last of which was collected

17 meters below the top of the chalk; the creature had lived a million years or so before the end of the Cretaceous. Upper Cretaceous belemnites and oysters were also obtained from widely scattered outcrops of the United States in Mississippi, Tennessee, North Carolina, and from the Pee Dee Formation in South Carolina, whence the limestone standard had been selected. The English samples indicate a temperature decline from about 23 to 14 degrees Celsius at the end of the Cretaceous. The American samples at more southerly latitudes had similar ranges of paleotemperatures, but no clear-cut trend.

Although Urey's data were fragmentary and preliminary, he did not miss this first opportunity to jump into the controversy on dinosaur extinction. In an article with his colleagues published in the *Bulletin of the Geological Society of America*, Urey came out in favor of the hypothesis that the dinosaurs were chilled to death, perhaps on the hunch that although he had only single samples from each zone, more samples would show a clear trend toward lower temperature. The chilling school thus won the first round.

Urey's students Heinz Lowenstam and Sam Epstein continued in 1954 with a more systematic investigation, obtaining samples from Sweden, Denmark, England, Holland, Belgium, France, Algeria, India, Japan, Australia, and the United States. Their "average belemnite mean temperatures" reached a low of 15 degrees Celsius during the Cenomanian epoch 100 million years ago, roughly in the mid-Cretaceous, and attained a maximum of 20 degrees Celsius before dropping to another minimum during the Maastrichtian. Lowenstam and Epstein reiterated their earlier conclusions that there was "no evidence of a major rise in temperature" as the cause of dinosaur extinction. On the other hand, dinosaurs survived the chilly Cenomanian weather 100 million years ago, and Lowenstam and Epstein saw no reason to blame cooling for their extinction 65 million years ago, "unless it was in conjunction with other factors yet to be determined."

The numbers coming out of the Chicago campus did not receive universal acceptance. Old-school paleontologists used paleoecological arguments to question the validity of the paleothermometers. They noted the evidence of increased diversity of reef corals, tropical mollusks, and large foraminifers during both of the supposedly chilly epochs during the Cenomanian and at the end of the Maastrichtian. Ecologically speaking, ocean temperatures seemed to have been maximal at those times rather than minimal. They considered the possibility that marine organisms are choosy about which isotopes they pick up. If belemnites preferred the heavier to the lighter isotope for building their shells, they would show the higher proportion of oxygen 18 typical of a cold ocean even if they had lived in a warm one. This possible "vital effect" remained in doubt, and the "warming-up" school thus won the second round.

For a while the decision remained suspended; no further evidence turned up one way or the other to show whether climate warmed up or cooled down during the last 10 or 20 million years of the Cretaceous.

Data on the earliest Cenozoic were also not available because belemnites, whatever the weather was, did not survive beyond the end of the Mesozoic. Lowenstam and Epstein analyzed other fossils from Maastrichtian and Danian formations but found no significant differences in their oxygen isotope compositions. Furthermore, organisms that would be otherwise valuable because they are common and widely distributed, such as brachiopods, have been altered by mineralization and have acquired modified isotope signals. They are found in ocean limestones and chalks that later became land, where groundwater altered their chemical composition as they were converted from loose sediments into rocks. This problem in finding suitable fossils prevented the wide application of Urey's paleothermometer for many years.

Sediments in the open oceans have never been lifted onto a continent; samples retrieved by oceanographers contain the original skeletons of foraminifers and nannoplankton. Such deep-sea sediments thus held out the promise for finding out for sure whether the ocean was warming up or cooling down toward the end of Cretaceous. But sediments 65 million years old are rarely found on the ocean bottom: they are buried hundreds of meters lower, beneath the sediment that have been deposited in all the eons since.

IN THE SUMMER OF 1958 WHEN I WAS IN MIAMI ON A business trip, my friend Bob Ginsburg arranged a luncheon to introduce me to Cesare Emiliani, who was always full of ideas.

There was a fierce debate going on in the community of Earth scientists that year. A technological breakthrough, the dynamically positioned vessel, had finally enabled researchers to drill holes into the deep-sea floor.

Normally when one spuds an offshore hole, the drill platform is fixed by pilings driven into the sea bottom. Oil wells off the Gulf Coast or in the North Sea are drilled that way. But one can hardly drive pilings into a 5,000-meter-deep ocean floor; it would not be feasible even if it were possible. A dynamically positioned vessel is not moored in any way to the sea floor. Instead, it is kept in place by maneuvering four engines under the command of a position-monitoring computer that keeps it as steadily in place as any tether. Once the breakthrough was announced, the majority of the scientific establishment wanted to go for broke and drill a 5-kilometer hole, the so-called Mohole, deep into the ocean crust, rather as a child in America might dream of digging a hole to China. Many millions had already been spent for this venture, and many more were asked of the United States Congress.

Emiliani was incensed that money was being poured into what seemed to him an impractical project (as in fact it turned out to be). He felt that it would make better sense to drill a few shallow boreholes into ocean sediments in order to obtain samples for the study of climate fluctuations during the Great Ice Age.

Emiliani was trained as a paleontologist at the Univer-

sity of Bologna. He was very proud of his native land
and of his alma mater; he never lost an opportunity to
praise the beauty of Tuscany or to advance Bologna's
claim as the oldest university in the world. At Bologna,
Emiliani studied planktonic foraminifera, and after World
War II he received a fellowship to engage in postdoctoral
research at the University of Chicago, where Harold
Urey was trying to extend his still very limited paleothermometer principle to broader applications. The samples he was then studying were deep-sea sediments
(though by no means from as deep as the boundary lies).
Deep-sea sediments are lime muds made up of skeletons
of foraminifers and nannoplankton that are called *oozes*
because they ooze out of your hand when you try to
grasp them. Urey was discouraged; the fossil foraminifers in his samples included those which once had lived
on the cold ocean bottom as well as those which once
had swum in warm surface water. Random samples contained different mixtures of the two groups so Urey was
unable to get meaningful results. To perform a temperature analysis on the oozes, he would have to separate the
warm-water floaters from the cold-water bottom
dwellers. A chemist can't do that; without training and
experience with plankton those tiny creatures all look
alike. Therefore when Emiliani, the specialist, showed
up in Chicago, he was immediately grasped by Urey's
group. Emiliani knew how to tell one kind of foraminifer
from another, and he was the help they needed for a
study of the deep-sea record of past climatic history.

AT THAT TIME THE ONLY PAST CLIMATE THAT HAD BEEN
studied in detail was that of the Ice Age from about
2 million to about 10,000 years ago. Albrecht Penck, a
geographer and student of land forms who had spent
many youthful days in the mountains of Bavaria where
glaciers abound, was responsible for the first recognition
that there had been not one continual episode of cold for
all that time, but rather fluctuations in climate during
which glaciers had advanced over the continents and
then retreated again. Working in southern Germany dur-

ing the 1880s Penck noticed that modern streams meander weakly in valleys underlain by gravel deposits. He reasoned that modern streams did not have enough power to transport gravels, and that such coarse debris must have been brought down by much more powerful meltwater rivers coming out of glaciers during the Ice Age.

Penck further found that stream terraces on both sides of a valley are underlain by the same type of gravel deposits as those in the modern valley. Those gravels must, then, have been laid down at those higher levels during earlier stages of the Ice Age. Because he was able to recognize four levels of terraces, he postulated that there must have been four stages of glacial advance. Using the names of streams where he made his observations, Penck and his associate Brückner came up with the names of four glacial stages which are known to every school child of Europe today: Günz, Mindel, Riss, and Würm. In between were the interglacial stages, when the climate was as warm as, or even warmer than, that of the present.

Geologists in North America used a different approach. They pointed out that a glacier riding over the terraine pushes aside rock and mud debris as it advances, very much as a bulldozer shoves dirt from its path. Some of the debris gets trapped below the glacier. When the ice melts away, there is left a carpet of rough rock fragments in a muddy matrix, the deposit called a ground moraine. During the interglacial stage that ensues, the moraine material is weathered in part into soil, only to be covered when the glacier returns and deposits the next moraine on top of the first. One can, therefore, count the number of moraines and the intervening soil layers to determine how many times ice has come and gone. Like Penck, North American geologists also found four glacial stages. They named them after the states where they are best exposed: Nebraskan (the oldest), Kansan, Illinoisian and Wisconsin. When I learned geology as a student, it was generally assumed that the four American stages corresponded to the four European stages.

Neither the American nor the European classic approach promised a complete record of glacial history. Debris deposited during one glaciation may have been scraped away by the next. In Switzerland, for example, the Riss glaciers seemed to have been the most powerful, and they removed much of the record of earlier glacial stages. Also, counting river terraces that have been partially obliterated with time and correlating them from one stream valley to another presented problems and controversies. Penck, in fact, at first thought that there were only three terraces corresponding to three glacial stages before he adopted his fourfold division. Later on other scientists found more than four river terraces, suggesting that there had perhaps been more than four episodes of continental glaciation. Nevertheless, theories tend to become incontrovertible truth once they are written in schoolchildren's textbooks. We have to preserve our Günz, Mindel, Riss, and Würm, even if we have to invent "substages" Riss I, Riss II, and Würm I, II, and III, so as to retain our magic nomenclature.

THE OCEAN, THAT GREAT RECEPTACLE OF SEDIMENTS, can provide a continuous record of various aspects of Earth history, but in Penck's day only grab samples scooped from the surface of the seafloor were obtainable. They revealed recent history, but nothing as old as the Ice Age whose sediments lie buried below. To sample from below the surface sediments requires removing a core of the seafloor.

The first cores that reached into Ice Age sediments were taken during the German *Meteor* Expedition to the Atlantic in 1925–27. Those earliest types are called gravity cores. A hollow steel tube was hooked to the end of a steel cable, which was lowered into the sea. The momentum of the descent drove the tube into the seafloor, and, when the tube was raised on board the vessel, a sediment core was extracted. Gravity cores are about a meter long. Scientists studied the foraminifera fossils in the *Meteor* cores from the equatorial Atlantic and made an interesting discovery. In the topmost portion of the

cores, among many foraminiferal species, was one called
Globorotalia menardii that lives in tropical waters today.
But this typical warm-water species was present in none
of the sediments from the middle part of the core. Apparently the ocean was too cold during the period represented by that portion, which, the researchers reasoned,
was deposited during the last, or Würm, glacial stage
when the equatorial Atlantic was much cooler than it is
now. Farther down, in the sediments near the bottom of
the cores, specimens of *Globorotalia menardii* were
found again; this deeper sediment seemed to represent
the climatic record of an interglacial stage before the last
glaciation.

The results of the *Meteor* Expedition showed promise
and raised expectations, but sampling was limited by the
technology of the time. Because ocean sediments commonly accumulate at a rate of a few centimeters per
thousand years, a meter-long core can clarify the history
of only hundreds of thousands of years. The gravitational force of descent simply cannot force a corer much
deeper than a meter or so into the seafloor. A more complete history of the Ice Age climate had to await the
technology to retrieve longer cores.

THE FIRST MAJOR BREAKTHROUGH WAS THE KULLEN-
berg corer, a piston device named after its inventor
Börge Kullenberg, a Swedish oceanographer who led the
Swedish Deep Sea Expedition of 1947–48. The principle
of the Kullenberg corer is similar to that of a hypodermic
needle. A piston is pulled out of a coring tube as the tube
is pushed down into the seabed. This displacement of the
piston makes room for and sucks up the incoming sediment. Since the late 1940s when the new device was first
put to use, Earth scientists had been able to obtain much
longer cores and thus extend their knowledge of climate
deeper into the past.

Using long Kullenberg cores obtained from the Atlan-
tic Ocean and Caribbean Sea by the Lamont Geological
Observatory in Palisades, New York, Dave Ericson and
Goesta Wollin found in 1950 that the warmth-loving *Glo-*

borotalia menardii registered by their conspicuous absence four episodes of cooler climate during the last 2 million years, corresponding, one hoped, to the four beloved glacial stages on the continents of Europe and North America.

At about the same time, Gustaf Arrhenius, a young Swedish geochemist who had recently joined the staff at Scripps Institution of Oceanography, perceived another way in which data from fossil plankton in ocean sediments could reveal past climate. In the oceans today, the equatorial zone produces a rich crop of plankton because the nutrients they require are delivered by bottom currents that flow from the Antarctic to the equator, where they ascend with upwelling water to feed the surface pastures. On the basis of what is known about the behavior of bottom currents, Arrhenius reasoned that during the Ice Age when the Antarctic glacier advanced, the ocean bottom current would have been stronger, and thus more nutrients would have been delivered to the equator, and more plankton would have been produced. The relative size of the plankton population could be measured: When plankton die, those which have skeletons of calcium carbonate sink, enriching bottom sediments with their calcareous fossils. The more nannoplankton that existed, the more calcium carbonate should have been deposited. Glacial and interglacial deposits of the equatorial oceans could thus be distinguished by their calcium carbonate content, for ocean sediment laid down during glacial stages should have a higher calcium carbonate content than that deposited during interglacial periods. Using this principle to study the cores from the Pacific Ocean, Arrhenius's colleagues at Scripps did not find the classic pattern of four glacial stages. Instead there seemed to have been at least nine repetitions of intensely cold climate.

A discrepancy in conclusions from two different lines of approach necessitates critical appraisal by a third method. Emiliani, at work in Urey's isotope lab at the University of Chicago, wanted to use Urey's newly developed technique to determine ocean temperatures directly. The core he used for his analysis was from the Caribbean and, as it happens, was one of the cores used by Ericson and Wollin for a population count of *Globorotalia menardii*.

The results of the two different methods of assessing temperature agreed fairly well for the top part of the core. However, the two methods suggested drastically different conclusions about the bottom part. *Globorotalia menardii* was absent in the whole bottom segment, implying one cold episode. Emiliani's isotope data, on the other hand, indicated that the same period of time had been characterized by two warm stages and an intervening cold stage. Emiliani got into an even more heated dispute with the Lamont scientists when he made a correlation of the climatic record at sea with that on land as indicated by Penck's studies of river terraces. Emiliani thought that all four of Penck's glacial stages were represented by the Caribbean core, whereas Ericson and Wollin thought that the record only reached the top of the Mindel, or second-oldest, glacial stage. Both groups suspected the methods used by the other: Emiliani thought that factors other than climate influenced the presence or absence of *Globorotalia menardii*; Ericson and Wollin did not trust the reliability of the isotope technique.

That was where matters stood when I was introduced to Emiliani over lunch in Miami in 1958. No wonder he felt so urgently the need for Ice Age cores instead of a Mohole!

EMILIANI HAD JUST COME DOWN FROM CHICAGO TO AC-cept a post with the University of Miami, where he intended to continue the work on isotopes. His first need was for a mass spectrometer. Emiliani himself was not an experienced instrument maker, so he persuaded his Swiss friend Hans Geiss to come and help. They borrowed and tinkered until they scraped up a mass spectrometer, and they proudly showed me their laboratory during my Miami visit. Emiliani talked excitedly about his new findings. He had tried to correlate the cold stages recorded by his first Caribbean cores to Günz,

Mindel, Riss, and Würm but had been sufficiently uncertain of the correlation that he assigned numbers instead of names to the epochs of climatic variation. Now, at Miami and working with long cores, Emiliani had found seven cyclic changes. The climatic pattern found by the Scripps scientists seemed to be the rule, and no correlation with Penck's chronology was possible any longer. Evidently, we were on the threshold of a revolutionary change in our thinking about the Ice Age. To carry out the revolution, we needed more sample materials, particularly long cores.

With immigrant optimism that America is a land of opportunities Emiliani applied to the National Science Foundation in the early 1960s for support to obtain long deep-sea sediment cores to investigate the history and cause of past climatic changes. Scientists at the U.S. National Academy of Sciences had been discussing establishing a program to explore the sediment and upper crustal layers of ocean basins and hoped for the initiative from some leading institutions. Emiliani's proposal came at the right time, but Miami was not yet sufficiently staffed and equipped to do it alone. In fact, more than a little initiative from a lot of universities would be needed before Emiliani got his long-sought cores.

In 1963 Maurice Ewing, then director at Lamont Geological Laboratory of Columbia University, jumped on the bandwagon and campaigned actively for an ocean sediment coring program. Eventually, senior representatives from Miami and Lamont joined with their counterparts at Scripps Institution of Oceanography, Princeton University, and the Woods Hole Institution of Oceanography to form the LOCO (for LongCores) Committee to explore the possibility of acquiring funds to charter a dynamically positioned drill ship. Maneuvering for position is the rule in science politics as in that of other fields, and partnership in the new venture became a game of musical chairs. Miami and Princeton were at first dropped when LOCO became the Consortium for Ocean Research and Exploration (CORE). Later, Miami rejoined Lamont, Scripps, and Woods Hole to become the founding members of the Joint Oceanographical Institutions Deep Earth Sampling (JOIDES). Still later, the University of Washington also joined JOIDES when congressional politics convinced the National Science Foundation of a need to increase regional representation from the Pacific Northwest.

Finally, in 1965, JOIDES received the loan of the dynamic-positioning vessel *Caldrill I* and drilled fourteen holes in the Atlantic during that April and May. The impressive results from these cores convinced more and more people that an oceanwide program of sediment sampling was bound to be a success. A contract for a Deep-Sea Drilling Project (DSDP) to carry out scientific programs formulated by an advisory panel from JOIDES was awarded to Scripps Institution of Oceanography in 1967. A new drilling vessel was built specially for the project by Global Marine, Inc., and christened *D/V Glomar Challenger* after its illustrious predecessor of ocean exploration HMS *Challenger*. The ship was launched in March 1968, only four years after Emiliani's optimistic request to the National Science Foundation.

Glomar Challenger departed from Orange, Texas, on July 20, 1968, for DSDP's first phase of seabed drilling in the Gulf of Mexico. The honor of leading the inaugural cruise was given to Maurice Ewing, the chief proponent of JOIDES. I joined the activities of JOIDES-DSDP later that year for the Leg 3 cruise that tested the seafloor-spreading theory in the South Atlantic. Compared to those results, which revolutionalized the Earth sciences, Emiliani's wishes were modest. They were soon fulfilled with 100-meter-long cores of Ice Age sediments.

THE CORES RETRIEVED DURING THAT VOYAGE ALSO opened up a whole new round in the battle over climate at the end of the Cretaceous. Holes were drilled more than a kilometer deep to sample materials laid down during the 150 million years since the middle of the Mesozoic era, and we took back with us samples for isotopic analysis. DSDP Hole 21, drilled into a submarine hill called Rio Grande Rise in the Southwest Atlantic, penetrated the Cretaceous-Tertiary boundary. Tsuni Saito, who served as paleontologist on board the *Glomar Challenger*, separated floating foraminifers from bottom dwellers. His colleagues at Lamont analyzed the two groups of fossils separately and obtained figures for the bottom and surface temperatures. The results of the analyses, completed in 1974, indicated that both the surface and bottom temperatures at DSDP Site 21 dropped by about 5 degrees Celsius during the last few million years of the Mesozoic; the ocean during early Cenozoic times was even colder. Thus the Lamont team concurred with Urey and his colleagues at Chicago that the climate had turned colder toward the end of the Mesozoic. Furthermore, the cooling trend continued across the Cretaceous-Tertiary boundary into the Cenozoic. The third round in this seasaw battle over terminal Cretaceous climate was won by the chilling school.

The work by the Lamont scientists, however, proved only to be an opening salvo. Their conclusions were immediately questioned because their cooling trend was defined by three samples spanning a time interval of 3 or 5 million years. Short-term climatic fluctuations take place over 0.1 million years or less. More sampling could yield completely different results.

The *Glomar Challenger* drilled more than two hundred holes during its first five years and obtained many thousands of meters of cores. Very few of those samples were analyzed for paleotemperatures, not because of a lack of interest, but because few samples were adequate. We had, for example, also penetrated the Cretaceous-Tertiary boundary at Site 20, but bottom-dwelling foraminifers were too rare in those sediments to provide any results from isotope analysis.

THE SAME PROBLEM PLAGUED MY OWN RESEARCH WHEN I joined my second deep-sea drilling expedition aboard the *Glomar Challenger* to the Mediterranean. There, in 1972, we found paleontological evidence that the Mediterranean bottom water was colder 5 million years ago than it is now, but I wanted to have some real numbers. I talked to my old shipmate Saito at Lamont about the isotope technique. He explained to me the difficulties. Ocean oozes contain so few specimens of bottom-dwelling foraminifers that not enough material can be gleaned for routine analysis. However, Saito had heard that a young physicist at Cambridge University was working on a gadget that could measure isotopic composition in very small samples; perhaps he could help us. After processing 2 meters of under-populated deepsea core, Saito picked out three tiny Mediterranean bottom dwellers, sealed them in a vial, and had them hand-carried to Nick Shackleton at Cambridge.

Shackleton is the son of a well-known geologist. He decided to study physics to escape the shadow of a famous father. Physics brought him to Cambridge's botany department, where a subdepartment devoted to paleobotany, including its implications for past climate, needed physicists able to perform isotopic analysis. Shackleton thus successfully eluded a department of geology, but he did not escape geology. With his knack for sophisticated instrumentation he soon established himself as a leading expert on the geology of the Pleistocene and Holocene epochs.

The importance of Shackleton's technique to determine the isotopic composition of samples weighing only dozens of micrograms was not easily appreciated. I wanted to bring Shackleton to Zurich in 1979 to help improve our isotope laboratory (and he did eventually come), but when I extolled his virtues in an academic senate meeting, my colleagues questioned the merit of his invention. Professors of materials testing would have liked to see bigger and bigger samples tested; they saw no need to work with micron-sized specimens. I had to explain that small is beautiful when one needs precision. Isotopic analysis of foraminifers picked out from 2 meters of cores could give us the average temperature for a quarter or a half million years, but foraminifers from a centimeter-sized sample could give us the average ocean temperature over a mere few hundred years.

Shackleton's technique thus gave us the possibility of seeing even a very short-term change.

Shackleton's gadget had been at work since the early 1970s, and my sample from the Mediterranean bottom had been among the first he analyzed with it. His work in the next few years rapidly began to fill in temperature fluctuations that preceded those of the Ice Age. The major objective of the second phase of the Deep Sea Drilling Project was to study ancient climates, and for that purpose *Glomar Challenger* was sent to the Antarctic in 1973. After a successful venture to the Ross Sea, the vessel sailed to the waters south of New Zealand and drilled three holes there; one penetrated 472 meters to Paleocene sediments, the oldest of the Cenozoic era. Jim Kennett, a New Zealander then teaching at Florida University and co-chief scientist of the expedition, was also a specialist on foraminifers. Kennett took more than eighty centimeter-sized samples at intervals that represented about a million years each and separated the planktonic from the benthic foraminifers. Shackleton made the isotope analyses. Their cooperation produced, for the first time, a numerical record of changing temperature per million years in the Southern Ocean during the Cenozoic era. The record indicated that the decline in temperature did not proceed at a linear rate. Instead, seven major steps during the Cenozoic were detected. The last step was 2.5 million years ago and was the one that led to the advance of continental glaciers during the Great Ice Age.

This epoch-making contribution by Shackleton and Kennett became one of the most cited articles in geology, even though it was published in an expedition report of limited distribution. We in Switzerland certainly did not overlook this important work, and Shackleton was invited to Zurich in 1978 to present his data from the Southern Oceans.

Shackleton surprised us with new data. One hole, DSDP 384, drilled into the Western Atlantic bottom, penetrated not only the early Tertiary but also the upper Cretaceous. Shackleton could thus extend his temperature record across the Cretaceous-Tertiary boundary. His technique had advanced so far that he now could analyze samples consisting of only a few fossil foraminifers, all belonging to the same species. Mixed assemblages gave mixed signals, he explained, but signals from a single species were loud and clear. He flashed a graph on the screen and showed his latest results from DSDP 384. His data showed a sudden rise of ocean-bottom temperature at that site after the end of the Cretaceous. There had been an increase, not a decrease, of 5 degrees Celsius. The "warming-up" school won the final round.

Shackleton habitually spoke in a monotone. He produced wonderful numbers, but he had no intention of entering the great debate on the demise of the dinosaurs. After the talk doubts were raised because his results seemed to be at odds with the conclusion of the Lamont scientists. There was no problem. "Previous workers," Shackleton explained, "did not have samples representing the million-year time interval immediately across the boundary. They missed the signal!" Was he certain of his measurements? Yes, he was. What was the cause of this sudden rise? He did not know, but to warm up the oceans 5 degrees so very suddenly seemed inconceivable by any known cause of climatic fluctuation.

THE WORKING OF THE MIND IS STRANGE INDEED. IT HAD been more than two decades since that lunchtime when I had flipped through the pages of de Laubenfels's outrageous article, I could no longer remember exactly in which journal and in what year the article had been published, nor could I recall the name of the author.

But the "hot-air" story had been stashed away in the computer that is the human brain and was retrieved immediately when Shackleton flashed his graph on the screen.

With the help of our librarian I tracked down the article and checked the author's credentials. The article, modestly titled "Dinosauria Extinction: One More Hypothesis," had been published in the *Journal of Paleontology* in 1956. De Laubenfels had been a professor of palentology at Oregon State University, Corvallis, Oregon. He was a specialist on fossil sponges, but he had not published much. His article on dinosaur extinction was a swan song; he died two years after its publication.

De Laubenfels contended that heat, not long continued but very brief, was the doom of the dinosaurs. He envisioned air temperatures near boiling in the tropics and up to 50 degrees Celsius (122 degrees Fahrenheit) at high latitudes: "Fierce gales of heated air swirled here and there, missing only scattered small areas." Under such circumstances all the dinosaurs perished. Giant reptiles could not hide; they also perished. Turtles "have an ability to hold their breath for hours at a time under water." They survived. Crocodiles also survived. As de Laubenfels put it, "one batch of eggs, well buried in mud...lived through (the) catastrophe." Lizards survived because they crawled into cracks or hid in their burrows to keep cool. Snakes survived because they, too, could hide amazingly. The birds and mammals survived best of all, because they lived in the "snow-covered high latitudes. ... Even boiling hot air, blowing over miles of snow, would cool down to a breathable degree." Brief heating would let enough vegetation escape to reseed the world. Many plants were burnt, but their roots could sprout again.

De Laubenfels did not say what happened to the ammonites or the marine plankton. Perhaps he assumed that no swimming organisms could survive in surface waters when air temperature was near boiling and thought it not worth discussing.

As to the cause of this brief, hot doomsday, de Laubenfels believed that a large meteorite had hit the earth. He figured that an iron meteorite 100 meters in diameter and weighing 30 million tons would do the trick: Its impact would release an explosive power of about 3,000 megatons of TNT dynamite, or the equivalent of 200,000 Hiroshima bombs.

When I had first read de Laubenfels's story in 1956 it could not have attained the stature of a scientific theory even if it had seemed plausible then, because no possible verification of the postulate was suggested. Like many other premature ideas, de Laubenfels's meteorite-impact hypothesis had to remain dormant until there was a way to look for evidence of its reality. Now, with Nick Shackleton's numbers, it seemed possible that that obscure paleontologist had been a prophet. Could hot air from a meteorite impact have heated up the oceans?

7

Death from
the Sky

I GO DOWN TO THE LIBRARY ONCE A WEEK TO SCAN THE current journals. It has become a habit, like reading the newspaper at the breakfast table, and the exercise serves the purpose of providing relief from more pressing duties in the office. *Nature* and *Science* are my favorite journals; they are weeklies and always bring something new. It may be a report of a new drug for birth control, or a new theory on Stonehenge, or the discovery of lizards that reproduce without benefit of males. One day in the early 1970s, in the aftermath of the publicity over comet Kohoutek, I came across a reference to an old article written by Fred Whipple in 1950 on those strange visitors from outer space.

The Chinese named four kinds of stars. The sun is a constant star, fixed in position in our solar system. The earth is a walking star, rotating around the sun. Meteors are dying stars; they fall to the earth. Comets are wise stars. Why wise? I don't know.

Whipple wrote that the word comet comes from the Greek *aster kometes*, meaning "long-haired stars." The long hair refers to the tail; the comet's head is the *coma*, which includes the nucleus of the comet surrounded by an atmosphere of ice crystals, dust, and ionized particles, atoms that have lost electrons, that are actually the beginning of the comet's tail, which can stream for tens of millions of kilometers to the rear. We do not see the nucleus of a comet through its veil of icy dust, but computations have shown that its diameter rarely exceeds 10 kilometers.

Comets strew debris behind them in interplanetary space, and pieces may be as large as a grape. For many years, therefore, the generally accepted notion was that the cometary nucleus was some kind of "gravel bank" hurtling through space. The solid bits, which have been compared to the pea gravel sometimes used for driveways, were thought not to be cemented together, but to be only loosely bound by their mutual gravitational attraction.

A loose aggregate of pea gravel in space will, like a fluid body, break up if it comes too close to the more powerful gravity of a large star. According to the calculations of a nineteenth-century French astronomer, E. Roche, such a body will be torn apart by the pull of a star if it approaches within a distance 2.5 times the star's diameter. This critical distance has been called the Roche limit.

Fred Whipple proposed in 1950 the new idea that a comet is more like a dirty snowball than a gravel bank. He suggested that the debris in the nucleus of a comet is not loose stones, but solid particles embedded in ice. Whipple was inspired by the idiosyncrasy of cometary motions. According to Newton's law of gravity, the periodicity of comets should be as regular as clockwork. Yet comet Encke has always come two and a half hours too early on its triennial visits. Halley's comet, on the other hand, seems to have been a procrastinator; it has always been late by an average of 4.1 days during its last eleven apparitions. Such odd behavior, Whipple surmised, can only be explained by an assumption that comets lose a little of their mass when they approach the sun. He suggested that solar radiation causes the ice in the dirty snowball to sublime—to evaporate without melting first—and that the jet action of the vaporized molecules streaming out from the comet could push it either toward or away from the sun, thus accelerating or delaying its reappearance.

A critical test of Whipple's idea that comets are held together by ice came in 1965 when comet Ikeya-Seki passed the sun at a distance only one-third the sun's diameter, and thus well within the Roche limit. If the comet were a gravel bank, it should break up. If it were cemented together by ice, its nucleus should be strong enough to hold together. The comet was not pulled apart by the tidal forces induced by the gravity of the sun and went away practically unscathed. Whipple had been right.

WHAT IS THE SNOW OR ICE MADE OF? FROZEN WATER, OF course. Whipple's article explained, however, that many substances other than water are also frozen in the extreme cold of outer space. Ice on Mars, for example, is "dry ice," or frozen carbon dioxide. Dry ice is also present in the nucleus of comets. In addition to carbon dioxide, ammonia, methane, and carbon monoxide are also frozen together with dust made up of various rock materials and metals.

The article had been informative and interesting so far, but I began to sit up in my chair when I learned that frozen cyanides are also found in comets. There had always been indications that comets contain cyanides, but the latest investigations of comet Kohoutek left little doubt that these deadly chemicals are not only really there, but in quantities that constitute some 10 or 20 percent of a comet's mass.

When I read about the cyanides, I was disturbed. Halley's comet has a mass of a trillion tons. If cyanides make up 10 percent of the comet, what kind of catastrophe would it be if 100 billion tons of poison were dumped into the ocean?

The thought came and went in a flash. There was not

a chance in a billion years that a comet as large as Halley's would hit the earth. I read on and forgot about the horrifying prospect.

But that was fifteen years ago, when I had little appreciation of the significance of geological time for catastrophe. I did not realize then in what way time is related to probability, nor did I consider the adage that anything that can happen does happen—given the time. My intuition was right—there is not a chance in a billion years for a big hit—but there have been more than 4 billion years of earth history. Smaller collisions have happened frequently, as evidenced by many ancient impact craters. Even during the brief period of human history, there was the very real event at Tunguska.

Tunguska was a quiet little hamlet in central Siberia. At seven o'clock on the morning of June 30, 1908, a fireball appeared above the horizon to the southeast. More luminous than the rising sun, the bright blue light streaked across the cloudless sky and exploded somewhere to the northwest. The scale of the explosion was unprecedented in recorded history. When seismographers consulted their instruments and calculated the energy that had been released, they were stunned. Translated into today's terms, computations indicated that the explosion had the force of a 10-megaton nuclear detonation, or about that of seven hundred Hiroshima bombs.

The brilliant object had been seen for hundreds of kilometers around, and the explosion was heard from as far away as 1,000 kilometers. A pillar of fire and smoke, followed by a mushroom cloud that rose to a height of about 20 kilometers, was also reported by distant observers. A farmer 60 kilometers from the target site was seared by the heat, thrown off the steps of his house by a blast of hot air, and crashed to the ground several meters away. The shock wave of wind circled the globe twice, and the ejecta from the explosion glowed over northern Europe through the next two nights. Vast amounts of fire debris arrived at California some two weeks later, noticeably depressing the transparency of the atmosphere over the Golden State.

Fortunately the object had exploded at a height of 8.5 kilometers above the ground, and the fall region was very sparsely populated. Native hunters who were the first to enter the disaster area reported that the whole forest had been flattened and gave accounts of wild forest fires. Systematic investigations did not begin until two decades later. The first team of experts, Soviet scientists under the direction of Leonid Kulik, visited the target area in 1927. Kulik's team endured great hardship to penetrate the devastated forest with horse-drawn wagons to investigate the aftereffect of the blast. Their mapping showed that trees within a radius of 30 to 40 kilometers had been uprooted and blown radially outward from the center of the blast. Within the blast zone, a 2,000-square-kilometer area had been ravaged by fire, and there was evidence of scorching over an area 18 kilometers in diameter.

The target site itself was a large swamp marked by numerous pits and shallow depressions. Kulik thought he had found craters made by small meteorite fragments. A trench was dug to drain water from one of the larger pits, but no meteorite was found. Later investigators sent out on three additional expeditions, before work was interrupted by World War II, believed that the pits had been there before the fireball struck, and that no sizable fragments from the incoming object survived to strike the ground.

Study of the Tunguska site resumed after the war and is still continuing. Although no meteorites have ever been found, soil samples from Tunguska contain small spherical objects similar to tektites, black glassy objects found in soil or sedimentary rocks and commonly believed to result from the impact of a meteorite. The chemical composition of impact tektites is similar to that of terrestrial rocks; they are apparently fragments blasted from the impact crater, melted in the extreme heat of the explosion, then reconsolidated in a typically droplike form during descent. The material of which they are made is only slightly contaminated by extraterrestrial substances from the meteorite itself. The spherules found at Tunguska have been compared to small tektites, or microtektites, which are commonly a fraction of a millimeter in diameter, but the chemical composition of the Tunguska spherules resembles cosmic dust. Apparently they were not ejecta thrown out of an impact crater, but were derived directly from the explosion many kilometers above the earth, and descended as extraterrestrial fallout.

What was it that exploded on that sunny morning over Siberia?

Astronomers have conjured everything from black holes to balls of antimatter, but dramatic as the Tunguska event was, it does not seem to require an exotic explanation. The more likely interpretation is conventional: The object was a large meteor.

Meteors, familiar to sky gazers as "shooting stars," are pieces of matter heated to incandescence by passing into or through the earth's atmosphere. The name came from the Greeks because they mistakenly considered them a meteorological, or atmospheric, phenomenon. We now know that such pieces of matter are either fragments of asteroids, themselves the result of an ancient planetary collision, or cometary fragments that originate in the far reaches of the solar system. Those that survive their plunge to earth without being vaporized to nothing are called meteorites. Meteorites are commonly stony, or composed largely of iron. The larger the meteor and the denser the material of which it is composed, the more of it will survive as meteorites.

An iron meteorite that entered the atmosphere over the east coast of Siberia in 1947 and broke up at an altitude of about 6 kilometers left some 380 fragments totaling more than 23 tons. This was a far smaller event that that of Tunguska; the explosion had an energy of about 2 kilotons, or less than 0.1 percent that of the 10-megaton Tunguska blast. On March 31, 1965, another fireball flashed over the sky of British Columbia. Instrument readings suggest an impact energy of 20 kilotons, and many fragments of stony meteorite were found. If a meteor exploded over Tunguska, where are the pieces? The size of the event in Tunguska argues against an iron or stony meteor so small that it would disintegrate to nothing larger than microtektites. Yet the much larger Tunguska explosion left those small spherules of cosmic composition but neither macroscopic meteorite fragments nor craters. This fact gives credence to an explanation first proposed by Whipple and several Soviet scientists in the 1930s: The object was composed of very weak material; it was a comet or a cometary fragment on a collision course with earth.

The 1908 comet was probably traveling in a direction opposite to that of earth. A head-on collision with our planet would give a speed of 60 kilometers per second. The cometary nucleus, or a part of it, exploded and disintegrated. The explosive energy, resulting mainly from the release of kinetic energy (the energy of motion) upon collision with the atmosphere, has been estimated to have been the equivalent of 10 million tons of TNT. Based upon that estimate, the mass of the comet was about 30 million kilograms.

That would have been a very small comet: Its nucleus would have measured only about 40 meters in diameter. A Czech astronomer suggested in 1978, therefore, that the Tunguska object was only a cometary fragment. He noted that comet Encke changed its orbit in 1908 and that the change could have been induced by the loss of a fragment of the size of the Tunguska object.

WAS THE TUNGUSKA EVENT UNIQUE? AN IMPACT THAT leaves no crater also leaves little in the geological record for scientists to study. Three-quarters of earth's surface is ocean, where craters are hard to find. On the continents erosion quickly obliterates small craters, and eventually even the largest are wiped clean from the record. Because of this paucity of evidence, meteorite impacts had not been considered an important geological process, and the frequency of meteorite impact over the history of our planet was not studied seriously until the dawning of the space age. Then, much to the astonishment of geologists, photographs transmitted to earth from spacecraft showed that the surface of the moon is covered with craters, large and small. They have been produced by bombardment of meteorites during the last 4.5 billion years. There, where there is no atmosphere or ocean, even a fragile comet core leaves the scar of its impact, which is preserved because there are neither winds nor waves to erode the evidence. The surface of Mars also preserves a record of billions of years of meteorite cratering, although some erosion seems to have taken place there. The kind of debris that collided with our neighboring planet and our own moon could hardly have missed us. Space research forced us to realize that bombardment by meteorites has been the rule rather than the exception in our solar system.

One of the best known impact craters on earth is the Meteor Crater in Arizona. I visited the impact site many years ago on the way back from a geological excursion to the Grand Canyon. The circular depression has a diameter of 1.2 kilometers. No meteorite fragment had then been found, and in those pre–space age days we were skeptical that it was indeed a crater produced by impact with an extraterrestrial object. Eventually a mineral called *coesite* was found in the crater. The mineral has the same composition as a normal glass sand but is much denser and can be formed only at pressures of hundreds of thousands of atmospheres. Such high pressure cannot be naturally produced at the Earth's surface except by collision with an impacting object.

Gene Shoemaker, who did his dissertation on Meteor Crater when he was at Cal Tech when I was a graduate student at UCLA, found evidence that the impact occurred between twenty thousand and thirty thousand years ago, and that the object was an iron meteorite. The Arizona event was relatively rare. Events producing small craters a few tens of meters in diameter, such as the 14-meter Haviland Crater in Kansas or the 51-meter Sobolev Crater in Siberia, are much more common. Ones as large as Meteor Crater are sufficiently unusual to become a tourist attraction. Only a few craters on earth exceed 100 kilometers in diameter, although such large impact scars are numerous on the moon and on Mars.

Robert Grieve of Canada made an inventory of all the meteor craters known on earth. He found that the size of the crater is inversely proportional to the frequency of its occurrence. That is, the most disastrous impacts are the least common, and the smallest impacts are the most common. This is the same relationship between the magnitude and the frequency of an event found by seismologists for earthquakes, by engineers for landslides, and by geologists for natural phenomena of all kinds such as storm floods, tidal waves, and volcanic eruptions. Events are not rare because of their nature, but rare because of their size, their magnitude. Small shooting stars are seen every summer night. Small meteorites are found every decade or so. Very large impacting bodies are rare, but they have hit during the long course of Earth history.

Grieve's equation gave the probability of impact; astronomer David Hughes, in a 1979 commentary published by *Nature*, translated the mathematical formula into plain words: 1-kilometer craters should be produced every 1,400 years, 10-kilometer craters every 140,000 years, and 100-kilometer craters every 14 million years. Were the record preserved here as it is on the moon, we would find not a few, but hundreds, of scars of devastating impacts each as large as the whole of Los Angeles County.

Grieve's equation and Hughes's translation gave me a way to think about the probability of catastrophic impacts, but it was another article that brought meteorites almost too close for comfort. I was looking through a copy of *Scientific American*, which I had subscribed to for my teenage son, Andreas. Georg Wetherill's article on Apollo objects caught my attention.

Apollo objects are stony bodies whose orbits cross the orbit of earth. They come so close to us so frequently that Wetherill thought that they could have been the principal cause of cratering here and on the moon during the last 3 billion years. More than twenty Apollo objects had by then, in 1979, been discovered. The total number lurking near the Earth must be much greater. The largest known ones are more than 3 kilometers in diameter; probably as many as six hundred as yet unseen Apollo objects are larger than 0.5 kilometers across. The average life span of an Apollo object before it is eliminated by planetary collision on its swing through earth's orbit or ejected from the solar system on its swing back out toward its distant edge is about 20 million years. But steady replacement from a long-lived source seems to have kept the total number of Apollo objects more or less the same.

WHAT WAS THE SOURCE THEN? WETHERILL THOUGHT Apollo objects are the condensed nuclei of comets, which are continually supplied from an area known as the Oort Cloud in the far reaches of the solar system. The conversion of a comet's icy coma to a stony object is, as Whipple explained, advanced each time its orbit takes it close to the sun. Comet Encke, for example, whose earth-crossing orbit is like that of an Apollo object, loses a little of its ice on each of its triennial visits. After one thousand visits, or three thousand years, comet Encke can be expected to lose all of its volatiles and become an Apollo object. In another 20 million years or so, the stony nucleus of the former comet should collide with the earth.

Wetherill's article got me thinking. If a comet in such an orbit is destined to fall after having lost all of its volatiles, is it possible that a comet could also hit the earth when it was still a "dirty snowball"? If it could, wouldn't the impact be greater before it had lost the mass of its ice? And just how great an impact would it make?

George Wetherill, one of the foremost planetary scientists today, chairs the International Commission on Planetary Geology. He was elected professor at UCLA shortly after I left. I had heard stories about his "treasure hunt" for meteorites from friends of my student days at the university, but our orbits did not cross until one winter day in Moscow a few years back. We had both been called to the Soviet capital to help organize an International Geological Congress. Five days of consultations were scheduled. The Soviets listened to our suggestions politely, but it became clear that our role was only to approve the plans they had already made and intended to follow anyway. So Wetherill and I had plenty of time for sipping vodka in the small bar at the Academy Hotel's restaurant. I found an occasion to ask him whether a comet could hit the Earth.

Yes, Wetherill answered me; the soft-spoken man had to raise his voice to overcome the band music that is ubiquitous in Russian restaurants. Comets have collided with the moon and probably also with the earth. In fact comets, with their massive icy coma and their very high speed, meeting the earth on a head-on collision course, may have produced the largest craters of all. What was the energy of a cometary impact?

As to the impact energy of a comet the size of Halley's, Wetherill performed some on-the-spot calculations. The impact energy is equal to the mass of the object times the square of its velocity. If Halley's comet should hit earth at 40 kilometers per second, the impact energy would be comparable to that of the explosion of 400 billion kilotons of TNT, or more than 20 billion times more powerful than the bomb dropped at Hiroshima. The surface of the earth has an area of about 500 million square kilometers. A collision with a Halley-sized comet would thus release the equivalent of 500 Hiroshima bombs per square kilometer of the earth's surface, or enough to wipe out all living things. Fortunately the energy of collision would be concentrated near the impact site so that a doomsday scenario is not applicable. Nevertheless the consequence of such a hit is truly frightful.

Naturally I became suddenly concerned about the rate of cometary bombardment. "There are two ways to look at that," Wetherill told me. Paul Weissmann of the Jet Propulsion Lab at Cal Tech had calculated that the odds of a comet's actually colliding with earth are about one or two in a billion. "Those odds can be translated into rate or chance," Wetherill explained. "Let's say the odds of your hitting a jackpot in a slot machine are one in one thousand. If you play the one-armed bandit day and night, and you pull the arm every two minutes one thousand times, you should hit the jackpot, in two thousand minutes, or thirty-three hours. You may not win any money, but the probability is that you are sure to hit the jackpot at an average rate of once every one and one-half days."

It is the same with cometary collisions. The odds may be one in a billion that any particular comet will hit, but crossing earth's orbit every year are some nine hundred comets big enough to produce on impact a crater with a diameter of 10 kilometers or more. The odds might be one in a billion for each comet, but the chance of having a collision with one of the nine hundred is much greater. The probable rate is, in fact, one collision every 5 or 10 million years. However, only a small fraction of the comets lurking around are very large, so that the chance of collision with one capable of producing craters of a few hundred kilometers across is only one or two in a billion years.

A second way of calculating the rate of cometary collisions is to figure out the size of the crater that would be produced by a comet of a particular size—Halley's was on my mind more than ever—then apply to the crater size Grieve's formula, which relates size to frequency. Wetherill referred me to a book called *Impact and Explosion Cratering*, edited by scientists at the Jet Propulsion Lab at Cal Tech.

I looked up the answer in the book. A systematic relation between impact energy and crater size has been deduced on the basis of laboratory experiments and of atomic bomb testing. Meteor Crater in Arizona, with a diameter of 1.2 kilometers, was produced by an impact energy equivalent of 15 megatons of TNT. An iron meteorite about 42 meters in diameter could have done the trick. According to Grieve's formula, such a small event may happen every two thousand years.

Gene Shoemaker made a more conservative estimate

of once every five thousand years for impacts of the magnitude of Meteor Crater. He also computed probable frequency in terms of energy. A 6-kiloton explosion could be an annual event, a 200-kiloton event could be expected every twenty-five years, a megaton event once a century, and a 10-megaton Tunguska-type event every millennium or so.

If there have been several impacts comparable to the Tunguska event during the last few thousand years of human history, do we have any historical records of such happenings? It is unlikely, because most of those events, if they did take place, can be expected to have disappeared in the ocean or vented their destruction in uninhabited areas. I am nevertheless intrigued by the story of Sodom and Gomorrah in the Bible. We are told that God sent a rain of fire and sulfur down and the cities of sin were burnt instantly. Could that be taken as a garbled account of the twin cities' destruction by death from the sky?

Thousand-year impact events do not produce a big enough splash to be detected in the geological record. Geological history is, however, almost a million times longer than human history; evidence of rare but more powerful events is preserved in the geological record in the form of impact craters, tektites, and other relics. The impact energy of a Halley-sized comet, for example, is millions of times greater than that of the largest nuclear bombs ever tested. To extrapolate on the basis of atomic explosion data to extremely high-energy impacts introduces some uncertainties. Nevertheless the best educated guess is that the 400-million-megaton hit of an object as large as Halley's comet would produce a crater 250 kilometers in diameter. Substituting this relation to Grieve's formula on cratering rate, one finds that the chance of a collison between a trillion-ton extraterrestrial object and the earth is about once in 100 million years. A hundred million years seems an eternity to us ephemerals, but the earth is 4.5 billion years old. Advanced forms of life have existed since the Paleozoic era some 600 million years ago. Several such catastrophes should have hit our planet since that time. One crater at least, 100 kilometers across in Ontario, Canada, records an event almost as powerful as that.

THIS MENTAL EXCURSION OF MINE INTO THE PROBABILity of catastrophe had, of course, little support in hard evidence. I had not stumbled into any 250-kilometer craters, and I had more pressing duties than to indulge for long in scientific fantasies. In the spring of 1979, the Chinese government invited me as a consultant to help modernize their geological research and teaching programs. My wife, Christine, our four children, and I spent six months in the land devastated by the "Great Proletarian Cultural Revolution." I traveled and gave lectures until I lost my voice, and I sat through endless sessions of consultation and discussion. I was totally immersed in the practical problems of the country of my birth, so real, so urgent that I did not think again about comets nor about mass extinctions. However, I was immediately made restless by the new excitement in the air when I came back to Europe in September. The controversy surrounding the Cretaceous-Tertiary boundary had intensified. Two new hypotheses for the terminal Cretaceous extinctions had been proposed earlier that year. One was advocated by my former student, Hans Thierstein, and his colleague at Scripps, Wolf Berger. Another had been proposed by Walter Alvarez; his father, Luis Alvarez; and their coworkers at Berkeley.

Thierstein and Berger thought that the world's oceans may have received at the end of Cretaceous a big dose, or what they referred to as an "injection," of fresh water from the Arctic. This was not an altogether new idea. The same rather outlandish notion had been proposed earlier by paleontologist Steve Gardner of Texas A & M, who thought he had found Cretaceous diatoms native to the Arctic province in earliest Tertiary sediments from middle latitudes. The finding has since been discredited by knowledgeable experts.

Thierstein and Berger picked up the freshwater injection idea, however, because it could explain two anomalous facts. First there was the curious occurrence of the nannoplankton *Braarudosphaera* in earliest Tertiary sediments. Various species of this genus are now found in waters of unusual salinity, for example in the Black Sea, where water is less salty than normal seawater, and also in the Red Sea, where water is more salty. The presence of such nannoplankton species in earliest Tertiary marine sediments, deposited where salinity should have been normal, suggested to Thierstein and Berger a dilution of surface seawater by an injection of fresh water from somewhere. The second piece of evidence for the Thierstein-Berger hypothesis was the oxygen-isotope anomaly across the Cretaceous-Tertiary boundary that Nick Shackleton had discovered, and that since then had been confirmed by a group at the Scripps Institution analyzing a different set of samples. The fact that oxygen 18 was depleted in the earliest Cenozoic nannofossils indicated, according to Harold Urey's paleotemperature scales, an incredible 5 degrees Celsius rise in ocean temperature. Because fresh water is deficient in the heavier oxygen isotopes, the signal could, however, also mean that a large dose of fresh water had spilled into the ocean. Because a sudden 5-degree increase in ocean temperature seemed impossible, Thierstein and Berger preferred the idea of freshwater injection.

According to their hypothesis, the Arctic Basin during the Cretaceous had been a great freshwater lake, separated by a land barrier from the world's oceans. At the end of the Cretaceous, a large earthquake broke the barrier and the lake water flooded the oceans, lessening the salinity of surface waters. Few marine creatures can adapt to lowered salinity. The dose of fresh water caused the extinction of mollusks such as ammonites, and of zooplankton and phytoplankton. Only the *Braarudosphaera* species of nannoplankton and some of their tough relatives survived.

I was enchanted when I read this ingenious idea in an offprint of an article in *Nature* by Thierstein and Berger that I found among the pile of letters on my desk upon my return from China. On second thought, I had to dismiss the brilliant postulate. The world's oceans have such enormous volume that their saltiness is not easily changed. All the fresh water from a lake the size of the Arctic Basin might dilute its upper-most layer somewhat; it could hardly have affected the salinity of the whole ocean. Yet Shackleton's data had indicated the same oxygen isotope anomaly at the bottom of the ocean as at its surface. We have to conclude, therefore, that the bloom of *Braarudosphaera* does not necessarily mean abnormal salinity.

I saw Thierstein and Berger in late September when we met at Barbados to select drill sites for the JOIDES Deep-Sea Drilling Project. We were guests of the Marine Biology Station of the McGill University at St. James on the west side of the island. After a long day of business sessions most of us were too tired to go downtown to enjoy the turmoil of calypso music. We went instead to a quiet restaurant next door on the waterfront. Over gin and tonics, I told Berger and Thierstein my reservations about their clever postulate. Berger shrugged his shoulders; he is a man of many ideas and does not mind if one does not pan out. He used to tell me a parable by the scientist-writer C. P. Snow: Ideas to scientists are like mistresses to philanderers. If one has many, one does not mind losing a few. Nevertheless the isotope data demanded an explanation.

Perhaps the signal was indeed what it seemed to be—an extraordinary and catastrophic rise in temperature. I told them of the article by de Laubenfels. Berger smiled and mentioned that I was not the only one entertaining an "E.T." hypothesis. A Berkeley geologist, Walter Alvarez, had reported in the 1979 spring meeting of the American Geophysical Union the discovery of extraterrestrial trace metals in the boundary clay at Gubbio, where the lack of any chasm in time across the boundary had first been demonstrated years before. Alvarez and his team believed they had found evidence to support an earlier speculation by Otto Schindelwolf, a Tübingen paleontologist, that the terminal Cretaceous catastrophe had been caused by an exploding star.

Encouraged by this exotic theory and the gin and tonic, I put forward my own pet notion: "No, not a supernova," I disagreed. "It must have been a comet, a comet big enough to dump sufficient cyanides to kill off practically all the marine plankton at the end of the Cretaceous."

My friends did not think I was serious. Just the same, they suggested that I join a certain "party" at Copenhagen. Tove Birkelund of the University of Copenhagen had organized a symposium, "Cretaceous-Tertiary Boundary Events," for the following month, October 1979. It was fitting that she should have done so—the remarkably complete sedimentary sequences at Stevn's Klint and other outcrops near Copenhagen had been central to our understanding of the Cretaceous-Tertiary boundary, and Birkelund had contributed her share of interpretation. The plural form *Events* reflected the outlook of the organizer, who clung to her belief that a series of happenings, rather than a single catastrophe, was responsible for extinctions toward the end of the Cretaceous.

Thierstein was to present his and Berger's idea at the symposium. Walter Alvarez was on the program too, and they hoped I would further enliven the sessions with a cyanide-poisoning plot. But I had had a few drinks by then, and I was not sober enough to seriously consider registering.

I was not the only one who took the excitement of that fall in a spirit of levity. As the meeting approached the explosive proliferation of outrageous hypotheses induced two humorists, Peter Vogt and John Holden, to contribute a short satire to the Copenhagen symposium, entitled

THE END-CRETACEOUS EXTINCTIONS: A STUDY OF MULTIPLE WORKING HYPOTHESES GONE MAD

Concerning the end-Cretaceous kill-off, we conclude that the data can be dangerous. New data, regardless of reliable sources of high quality, have scarcely ruled out any past theory, but have fueled the promulgation of newer and even more outlandish proposals. We illustrate this phenomenon (modestly termed the "Vogt-Holden Effect") by adding several possibilities to the list—including a late Cretaceous Noahcean fleet of which only one ark survived, the tampering with Cretaceous faunas by extraterrestrial beings, and the existence of an "extinction machine." Somehow there are fields of science where the data become progressively harder as the theories put forth to explain these data become progressively softer.

The results of the symposium that October were reported to me by Anna Katharina Perch-Nielsen von Salis. A Swiss married to a Dane, she had taught at the University of Copenhagen before she came to join our staff at Zurich. As a specialist on nannoplankton, an expert on the transition from Mesozoic to Cenozoic, and chairman of the International Working Group on the Cretaceous/Tertiary Boundary, she naturally attended the Birkelund symposium. I went to see her after her return from the meeting.

Vogt and Holden did not show up; no research funding agencies would grant travel stipends to them to air their satire. Thierstein and Walter Alvarez did, and they both presented their interesting ideas. But nobody, Perch-Nielsen reported, was convinced. So it was just as well that I did not make a trip to Copenhagen to present my thoughts on poisonous comets.

HERE THE MATTER RESTED AS FAR AS I WAS CONCERNED until one morning in November when, during one of my weekly interludes at the library, I read an article on cometary collision by astronomers Vic Clube and Bill Napier in *Nature*.

The Oort Cloud, which Whipple had identified as the renewable source of comets and Apollo objects, lies on the outermost fringe of the solar system, several thousand times farther out from the sun than Pluto. Comets are "shaken loose" from the Oort Cloud when a star passes sufficiently close and are launched on their long journeys to the inner part of the solar system. Comet Kohoutek received such a send-off and came to visit us in 1972, when it was first discovered.

The Oort Cloud was itself assumed to be leftovers, the far-out remnant of the primordial cloud that collapsed and gave rise to the solar system. Clube and Napier proposed in their article, however, that comets originate in interstellar space within the spiral arms of our galaxy, the Milky Way. They have been sporadically captured from the spiral arms as our sun moves through them. Each capture event replenishes the population of comets in the Oort Cloud, periodically enhancing the chance that escaped comets will end up on a collision course with earth.

Recent computations by a Japanese astronomer had suggested that long-period comets, those that are infrequent visitors, could have been captured from interstellar space by the solar system 10 million years ago. Clube and Napier had set out to discover whether the solar system actually had passed through a spiral arm at that time. They found that it had: the solar system entered a large conspicuous spiral arm feature known as Gould's Belt some 20 million years ago and emerged from it 10 million years ago. The two astronomers boldly suggested that that and previous captures have been the cause of periodic terrestrial catastrophes in Earth history.

That hypothesis by Clube and Napier has since been criticized because comets do not seem to come from interstellar space; their chemical composition is typical of the solar system. Nevertheless their boldness emboldened me to action. I chose for my debut in the arena of the terminal Cretaceous extinction the same journal, *Nature*, in which their article had been published. A former editor of *Nature* had told me of the liberal publication policy of this prestigious science weekly: "We publish all original ideas that are not pornographic." Of course, there have been some lemons, but these can be forgiven compared to Watson and Crick's revelation of the structure of DNA, or of Vine and Matthews's seafloor-spreading theory, both of which were first published in *Nature*. I thus rather imprudently decided to throw my hat into the ring with a manuscript on "Terrestrial Catastrophe Caused by Cometary Impact at the End of the Cretaceous."

I reviewed de Laubenfels's article on Dinosauria extinction. I also reread Whipple's paper on comets and Hughes's report on impact cratering. While tracing down these articles with the help of our librarian, Esther Chappuis, I came across a reference to an article by Harold Urey, called "Cometary Collision and Geologic Periods." The article had been stimulated by the controversy surrounding Velikovsky's *Worlds in Collision*, a best-seller that had popularized the idea of catastrophic cometary impacts.

Immanuel Velikovsky, born in Czarist Russia and a distinguished scholar of classics, took an unorthodox approach to natural science: He began with the premise that all reports by ancient chroniclers were factually correct. If Herodotus said that the world had changed its direction of spin, then it had; if the Bible said that the sun had once stood still, then it did. Unlike geologists, Velikovsky was not concerned that those phenomena are physically impossible. Earthly catastrophes, according to Velikovsky, had their origin in a succession of planetary and cometary collisions. The chief villain was Venus, which, the classic scholar claimed, was really a comet in disguise. Naphtha from its tail fell on the earth and caused the rain of fire reported by the Bible; Venus —alias comet—also caused the draining of the Red Sea that enabled Moses to escape from Egypt. It did not bother the author that Venus had no tail, or that it is as solidly placed in its orbit as our own planet.

Velikovsky's books were good science fiction; they might even be considered interesting literature on comparative mythology. The trouble was that they were listed by the publisher in its catalog under "Science." In the resulting confusion the news and literary media went after noted scientists to get their opinions. Albert Einstein himself had to make a comment: He thought the book not "really bad. . . . The only trouble with it is, it is crazy." Nobel laureate Harold Urey pondered over the matter and came up with a new version of *Worlds in Collision*, the article I had stumbled across in our library.

Urey's scientific method was impeccable. He started with a premise not physically impossible that a comet the size of Halley's could collide with earth and explored the logical consequences of his assumption. He concluded that environmental destruction from such a catastrophic event would be tremendous. Cometary collisions might thus indeed have caused widespread damage: not catastrophes in historical times as proposed by Velikovsky, but mass mortality and extinction of animals and plants on earth for which there is evidence in the geological record. He offered the terminal Cretaceous extinction as an example. The great dying of the dinosaurs some 65 million years ago could have been the consequence of a cometary hit. But he did not insist that comet catastrophes must actually have happened.

Urey's thoughts were first published in *The Saturday Review* and later in a short note for *Nature*. Both articles were ignored in the scientific community, because scientific ideas, good or bad, are doomed to oblivion unless tests can be devised and performed to support or negate them.

With that lesson in mind, and having gathered all my references, I started writing. The first section of the article demonstrated the catastrophic nature of what happened at the end of the Cretaceous. Too many species had become extinct over too short a time in environments too suddenly and too drastically perturbed to be accounted for by terrestrial processes. In the second section I reviewed the statistics on frequency of cometary collisions and discussed the consequences of an impact by a Halley-sized object. In the third section I explored the consequences of chemical pollution, including possible cyanide poisoning of swimming organisms, and changes in seawater chemistry that might inhibit plankton reproduction, with the resulting collapse of the food chain. Chemical pollutants must have been carried over the ocean by surface currents, I reasoned. The most devastated marine life—ammonites, belemnites, surface-water foraminifers, and nannoplankton—were all swimmers carried along by the equatorial currents of the oceans; the dwellers of deep ocean bottom had been largely spared.

Ocean pollution could not have been an effective killer of terrestrial animals. Following the suggestions of de Laubenfels, McLean, and others, I suggested that the large vertebrates perished under a brief thermal stress. Small or aquatic animals on continents survived because they could tolerate the heat better or get away from it.

Hoping not to fade immediately into oblivion, I proposed a number of tests of my ideas and called for a search for the impact crater. I sent the manuscript away before Christmas to the editor of *Nature*. I also gave a copy to Perch-Nielsen, who, subjected already to so many outrageous ideas at the congress in Copenhagen, steered me away from a few ridiculous pitfalls. She made copies of the manuscript and sent one to each member of her working group on the Cretaceous-Tertiary boundary. I also sent a few copies to colleagues then actively engaged in the problem.

The repercussions came back in rapid succession. A Dutch colleague, Jan Smit, wondered how I had come to almost the same conclusions as he had. His manuscript, coauthored with colleague J. Hertogen, was submitted to *Nature* the following month, January 1980, and I was soon contacted by the editor, who requested a delay of the publication of my manuscript so that the two contributions could be published back to back in the same issue.

Just after the beginning of the new year, I came across a newspaper clipping about a report given by the Alvarez team in the December meeting of the American Association for the Advancement of Science. After further trace-element analyses, they had abandoned the idea of a supernova or star explosion, postulating instead the fall of a 100-billion-ton asteroid, 10 kilometers in diameter, to account for the catastrophic extinction at the end of the Cretaceous period. Soon I received a preprint of their article and a long letter from Walter Alvarez. They had completed their manuscript in November 1979, at about the same time I had started writing mine.

That same November, 1979, Cesare Emiliani, inspired by Shackleton's isotope data indicating the warming of the oceans after the end of the Cretaceous, announced in a talk he gave at UCLA that the mass extinction of dinosaurs and plankton had been caused by a catastrophic rise in temperature.

Eventually four articles—by Smit and Hertogen, Alvarez, Emiliani, and me—advocating an extraterrestrial cause of mass extinction at the end of the Mesozoic era were published in three journals within one month in the spring of 1980. That may seem pure chance or arouse suspicion that we knew of one another's latest ideas through the scientific grapevine. In fact, when I composed my own article, Jan Smit had not yet betrayed his thoughts on meteorite impact. Alvarez and his group were, as far as I knew, still talking about supernovas; I had no inkling that Emiliani was chewing over the same data and thinking about the same problem. Simultaneous publication of nearly identical theories is neither coincidence nor the result of communication. When the data point to the obvious, all those quick on the draw will come up with the same answer at the same time.

8

Neutron as Detective

IN 1958 THE MURDERED BODY OF A TEENAGE GIRL WAS found in an abandoned quarry near a small town in New Brunswick, Canada. The suspect was a young man named John Vollmer. Witnesses had seen him pick up the girl at a drugstore counter on the evening of her disappearance, others had seen her in his car driving out of the downtown area, and a farmer, coming home late that night, had noticed the suspect's car parked in the quarry where the girl's body was later found. Vollmer admitted all that but claimed he didn't kill her. Who could prove that the victim had not returned to the quarry later with another man, the actual killer? The jury had to have more concrete evidence.

The only material evidence the police had found was a strand of dark hair caught in the victim's fingernail, apparently as the result of a struggle. It could not be her own hair; she was blonde. Vollmer had dark hair, but so do many others. How could one prove that the hair belonged to the suspect?

Fortunately for justice, a forensic scientist at the

crime laboratory in Ottawa had developed a technique for classifying human hair on the basis of trace amounts of certain metals that, excreted by the body, accumulate in hair. His investigations had shown that an individual's hair can be as distinctive as a finger print. The 6-centimeter strand was sent to the capital together with a sample from the suspect. The answer came back in a week: The hair in the victim's fingernail and the sample from the suspect definitely belonged to the same person. Vollmer was convicted.

IF THE DINOSAURS WERE DONE AWAY WITH BY A COMET, did such a "long-hair star" not leave a strand of its hair behind? I thought of that possibility while I was writing my manuscript for *Nature*.

The major constituents of a comet are oxygen, hydrogen, nitrogen, and carbon, which are also the major constituents of earth. Such common stuff could hardly betray a comet's identity after it had been mixed with the much larger volume of common terrestrial stuff. Are there any trace metals so characteristic of a cometary tail that they could identify a comet the way the trace metals in human hair can identify an individual? Yes, there are, and that was what Walter Alvarez and his coauthors had discovered. Looking back, I have the uneasy feeling that I had missed my chance of making an important discovery, because I was not modest enough in my younger days to pay attention to what my elders had to say.

I came to Zurich for the first time in 1957 fresh out of graduate school and with my doctoral work completed. I did not feel compelled to register as a student again, but I went to the Geological Institute every day to read in the library and attend a few courses. I was especially interested in geochemistry then. Geochemistry was developed in the last century to investigate the chemical composition of the earth. V. M. Goldschmidt, a pioneer in the field, extended the study from terrestrial to extraterrestrial composition. It is to him that we owe much of our knowledge of cosmic abundance of chemical elements, which allows us, for example, to distinguish between tektites of earthly origin and those like the Tunguska microtektites whose composition betrays an origin elsewhere in the solar system. Goldschmidt's kind of geochemistry was, however, no longer taught in the United States when I became a student. We no longer cared about the tedious data on elemental composition that Goldschmidt had worked out for various heavenly bodies. We were interested only in processes, the chemical reactions that have changed the earth. But as it happened, the geochemistry course at Zurich University was taught by Fritz Laves, to whom Goldschmidt, his former teacher, was a hero. Laves liked to tell anecdotes of his youthful days at Göttingen, where he, as an Aryan, had to protect his mentor from the rowdies of the Nazi party. Eventually Goldschmidt had fled to Britain and had died in Norway shortly after the war ended.

Laves remained faithful to his memory. Goldschmidt's *Geochemistry* was the textbook of his choice. At the beginning of the first lecture, we were handed mimeographed copies of a table, *Abundance of Elements*, Goldschmidt's masterpiece, which compares the abundance of each element in the lithosphere, earth's rocky crust, with its abundance in meteorites. Laves then started lecturing, or, more precisely, reading. His voice droned on, punctuated only by initials, *n.b.* for *nicht bestimmt*, or "not determined," and *p.p.m.* for, in English, parts per million. "Wasserstoff [hydrogen], n.b.", he began. "Helium, n.b.; Lithium 65 p.p.m. in der Lithosphäre, 4 p.p.m. in Meteoriten; Beryllium, 6 p.p.m. in der Lithosphäre, 1 p.p.m. in Meteoriten; Kohlenstoff [carbon] 320 p.p.m. in der Lithosphäre, 300 p.p.m. in Meteoriten; Stickstoff [nitrogen], n.b.; Sauerstoff [oxygen] 466,000 p.p.m. in der Lithosphäre, 323,000 p.p.m. in Meteoriten. . . ."

After half an hour Laves had progressed to lanthanium, cerium, and proactinium. Never having been noted for my patience, I did not even worry about courtesy; I walked out of the room before he finished proactinium. If I had sat through the hour, I might have learned something. Unquestionably Laves would have gotten to the tail of the list, when he would tell us: "Osmium, n.b. in der Lithosphäre, 1.92 in Meteoriten; Iridium 0.001 p.p.m. in der Lithosphäre, 0.65 p.p.m. in Meteoriten; Platin, 0.005 p.p.m. in der Lithosphäre, 3.25 p.p.m. in Meteoriten; Gold, 0.001 p.p.m. in der Lithosphäre, 0.7 p.p.m. in Meteoriten. . . ."

If I had gone to his second lecture, I was almost certain to have learned that osmium, iridium, platinum, and gold all belong to a class of elements called platinum metals or siderophiles (iron lovers). They are very rare in the outermost shell of rocks, the lithosphere, on earth, but they are much more abundant in meteorites.

Goldschmidt spent his last years working on the cosmic abundance of the platinum metals. The natural concentrations of those trace metals are very minute, and the analytical methods of the first postwar years were barely adequate to detect them. Platinum metals are, however, on the average about a thousand times more abundant in stony meteorites. The siderophiles are even more enriched in iron meteorites, reaching concentrations greater by another order of magnitude.

Stony meteorites are generally considered to have a composition like that of the primitive earth before it had settled into its present layers. The current theory of the origin of earth is that our planet accreted from a multitude of small chunks and dust that balled together through their mutual gravitational attraction. Radioactive elements in the infalling material generated heat at too fast a rate to be dissipated in the rapidly growing planet, so the stony materials of primitive earth melted. Molten iron and nickel, both among the heaviest elements, sank and became concentrated in the center of the planet to form its iron-nickel core. The siderophiles, "iron lovers," have a chemical affinity to iron and accompanied it to the core. The lighter stony silicates, now depleted of their iron, nickel, and siderophiles, formed a mantle that is some 2,900 kilometers thick around the core, and that remains hot enough to have a somewhat plastic consistency. The cold brittle rocks of its surface, the earth's crust, derive their materials from the mantle, and they are thus correspondingly impoverished in nickel, iron, and siderophiles.

Stony meteorites are the same material of which the earth was made, but because they never underwent chemical segregation, they retain their original cosmic proportions of siderophiles. The same is true of cosmic dust, minute particles that have never become consolidated within larger bodies, or have since been blasted from them by collision. Cosmic dust continually rains down on the earth, but the amount of perennial cosmic fallout is too trivial compared to the bulk of sediment in most places for its peculiar chemical signature to be detected. Sedimentary rocks are therefore about as impoverished in siderophiles as igneous rocks derived from the mantle. Those metals should be enriched in deep-sea deposits, however. Little detritus from land reaches as far out as the central North Pacific, for example, and clay is deposited there at the very slow rate of less than a millimeter per year. Cosmic fallout becomes a significant component of oceanic sediments.

Goldschmidt predicted these results but was not able to confirm them. The primitive instruments of the first postwar years were simply not capable of the precision needed to measure such small quantities. Goldschmidt was a remarkable scientist, but his career, interrupted by political persecution and war, was cut short by an untimely death. If he had lived a decade longer, he might have had the satisfaction of obtaining figures that thoroughly confirmed his predictions, for the necessary precision was achieved through neutron-activation analyis, the technique used to obtain an exact profile of the trace metals in the suspect's hair in the Vollmer trial.

Neutron-activation analysis can detect trace metals in concentrations as little as ten-trillionths the weight of the sample. The Vollmer trial was the first successful application, and the method has since become routine practice.

Neutrons are the nuclear particles that add extra weight to isotopes. Unlike protons, which are positively charged and therefore repel one another electrically, neutral neutrons wandering about by themselves have some chance to meet up with and join the nucleus of an atom, thereby transforming it into an isotope. When there is a concentrated flow of neutrons the chance of their joining with atoms to make isotopes is even better.

Neutron bombardment is a natural process that has gone on throughout earth history, for free neutrons are a component of cosmic rays, the stream of energy and particles that continually radiate from the sun. The natural product of neutron bombardment is radioactive isotopes. Carbon 14, for example, is produced as atmospheric nitrogen is bombarded by neutrons from cosmic rays. Each radioactive atom spontaneously disintegrates into daughter products, such as the nitrogen 14 into which carbon 14 decays.

The traditional method of chemical analysis was to separate out from a sample the chemical element one was interested in, and to weigh the purified substance. This required much work in chemical separation, as well as much sample material. Neutron-activation analysis bypasses the difficult process of chemical separation. The sample, which can be quite small, is bombarded by neutrons. Numerous nuclear reactions take place between the neutrons and parent elements, such as platinum or iridium, within the sample. The various radioactive isotopes that result then decay. As each does so, it emits particles and energy in a pattern characteristic of the decay of that isotope. This decay pattern, detected and recorded by instruments, serves as a signature that identifies the isotope, and therefore the parent element from which it was formed by neutron bombardment. The number of decay "events" for each isotope betrays the relative amounts of each parent element in the sample. Thus the analysis tells the researcher both what the sample contains, and how much.

The first application of neutron-activation analysis to geology, published in 1968, realized the dreams of Goldschmidt. Two scientists from Scripps Institute determined the concentration of osmium and iridium in Pacific Ocean sediments in order to evaluate their cosmic content.

When I came back from my first drilling expedition to the South Atlantic in 1969, less than a year after this first application of neutron-activation analysis, I was asked by nuclear chemists from Texas A & M University whether we needed trace-element analysis of our cores. I was then fighting a losing battle against quantization in geology. The trend in research emphasizing instrumental analysis had already produced data, data, and more data, but little had been digested. I was irritated. Only in later years did I realize my mistake in not seeing that new data lead sooner or later to new levels of understanding. Perhaps I might have reacted positively to the offer from Texas if I had listened attentively to Fritz Laves that day when he recited the list of the cosmic abundances of elements. But for all my pondering on long-haired stars, and even though we had penetrated the Cretaceous-Tertiary boundary at two drill sites, it did not occur to me at all that trace-element analysis might reveal extraterrestrial debris in our precious boundary sediments.

Space scientists and astronomers had not forgotten Goldschmidt's prophecy. When the new analytical method became available, the search for siderophiles began. The Scripps scientists found that cosmic debris must have been accumulating at a rate 1.2 times 10^{-8} grams per square centimeter per year to account for the concentrations of iridium and osmium in North Pacific sediments. That is not very much, only about 120 grams per square kilometer, or not quite 2 ounces per square mile per year. The next step was to isolate and identify cosmic debris in other samples of ocean sediments.

The samples used were small spherical objects, or spherules, a fraction of a millimeter in diameter, obtained from sediments more than a hundred years earlier during the cruise of HMS *Challenger*. Some are rich in iron; others are stony. The major elements iron, nickel, and cobalt are present in those spherules at proportions similar to those in iron meteorites. An emigrant from India, R. Ganapathy, who was working for a chemical company in New Jersey, decided to check their trace-metal content by using neutron-activation analysis. Fifteen elements were analyzed, including the platinum metals iridium, osmium, ruthenium, and gold. Ganapathy found that stony spherules in ocean sediments have an elemental composition identical to that of a stony meteorite; the data convinced him that the tiny, stony spheres must have come from outer space. The spherules look, in fact, similar to the ones found at Tunguska, but they are mostly cosmic dust, originated from less spectacular meteor falls.

IT WAS AT THIS POINT THAT THE ALVAREZES STUMBLED upon the iridium anomaly. Walter Alvarez is the son of a famous physicist; his father, Luis, won a Nobel Prize in 1968 for his contributions in nuclear physics. Like Nick Shackleton, the young Alvarez chose a different profession to avoid his father's shadow. Like Shackleton, he did not escape. But Walter Alvarez did not enter a career in physics; he made a geologist of his father.

Walter Alvarez's first job after his studies at Princeton and postdoctoral research in Italy was at the Lamont-Doherty Geological Observatory, just outside New York City.

Lamont had grown under its first director, Maurice Ewing, from a two-man team into an institution housing, by the early 1970s, several hundred scientists. Neil Opdyke had established a first-rate laboratory there to study the remnant magnetism in ocean sediments, and the Lamont scientists contributed much to the establishment of magnetostratigraphy. Working in Opdyke's laboratory at that time was a young physicist, Bill Lowrie, who, liberating himself from the confines of the oceans, had turned his attention to ancient ocean sediments that had been lifted high in mountain building. The Mesozoic and Cenozoic oceanic sediments exposed at Gubbio in the Apennines were logical rock sequences to examine. Alvarez had become familiar with those rocks during his postdoctoral work in Italy, and he helped Lowrie get started on the project near Gubbio that demonstrated that the boundary clay in which Luterbacher and Premoli-Silva had found evidence for the mass extinction of foraminifers fell within the brief epoch of Chron C-29-R.

Alvarez, no paleontologist, was in those days not at all involved with the question of the terminal Cretaceous extinction. He was, however, concerned about the reliability of the magnetostratigraphic time scale.

The conclusion that C-29-R spanned less than half a million years was based on interpretation of the width of magnetic stripes on the seafloor. Although few now argued against the seafloor-spreading theory, the validity of assuming a steady rate of spread was still debatable. If there were another way, Alvarez thought, to check the duration of C-29-R, the soundness of the assumption might be vindicated.

While mulling over the problem, Alvarez came across the article by the Scripps scientists estimating by trace-element analysis the rate at which cosmic debris accumulates in deep-sea sediments. One should, he realized, be able to estimate how long it had taken for the boundary clay at Gubbio to accumulate by determining the content of cosmic debris in the clay.

Bill Lowrie had meanwhile joined the Geophysics Institute at our university in Zurich, and Alvarez had left Lamont to work at Berkeley, where his father was. He brought up the matter in a discussion among the family. The senior Alvarez had retired from the Berkeley Lawrence Laboratory, but he was professionally still active. Father and son decided to join forces. To detect very minute amounts of platinum metals by neutron-activation analysis requires sophisticated instruments, know-how, and personnel. The Berkeley Laboratory had them all. Frank Asaro and Helen Michel, well respected in the profession because of their analytical skills and perfectionism, joined the Alvarez team.

Of all the siderophiles, iridium was singled out for investigation by the Berkeley team in their initial study because it is most easily analyzed by the neutron-activation technique. Iridium captures slow neutrons well, and its decay pattern is easy to recognize. Samples were obtained from Gubbio of the various sediments accumulated during C-29-R, both the nearly fossilless clay and the fossil-rich sediments above and below it. Samples of all three were prepared by dissolving away calcareous skeletons with acid, leaving behind only insoluble clay. This was done to make them comparable to the ocean clay samples on which the Scripps scientists had performed their analysis.

The prepared Gubbio samples were put into a Berkeley reactor for neutron-activation, and the identification was made: The iridium concentration of the insoluble clay sediments below and above the boundary clay at Gubbio turned out to be 0.3 parts per billion: exactly what the Scripps scientists had predicted for the accumulation of cosmic iridium in deep-sea sediments.

The reasonable conclusion about the iridium sedimentation rate was a confirmation that magnetostratigraphy did provide reliable estimates of the duration of geological epochs; Chron C-29-R must have lasted about half a million years, as Denis Kent had suggested on the basis of the width of that stripe on the seafloor.

But what of the boundary clay itself, that single centimeter so peculiarly devoid of life? Alvarez was startled to find an anomalous concentration of iridium in the boundary clay. The maximum was nearly 10 parts per billion, detected at a horizon a few millimeters above the base of the clay. The anomaly is about thirty times the norm. The iridium concentration then falls off, back to the background level in a sediment 1 meter above the boundary, or at a time about fifteen thousand years after the end of the Mesozoic era.

Their curiosity aroused by discovering this strange anomaly at one site, the Alvarez team analyzed samples collected at the famous Stevn's Klint site in Denmark where the boundary sediment is known as the Fish Clay. There was an even more remarkable iridium anomaly at that locality. The background concentration was found to be about 0.3 parts per billion, the same as in Italy. The maximum found in the Fish Clay reaches 65 parts per billion, more than two hundred times the normal concentration. The iridium content then falls off to 0.4 parts per billion at a horizon 0.7 meter above the boundary, and to the background norm another half-meter higher.

The least far-fetched explanation for such a high concentration of iridium is that the boundary sediment at both sites was deposited at an unusually slow rate. If the 1-centimeter-thick boundary clay was not deposited during 5,000 years, but during 1 million years, enough cosmic dust could have accumulated to account for two hundred times the normal concentration of iridium. If this had been the case, other trace metals should also have been concentrated by a factor of 200 or so.

The Alvarez team, therefore, analyzed in Gubbio samples of twenty-seven elements in addition to iridium, including sodium, aluminium, rare earth elements, and trace metals other than siderophiles. Whereas the iridium increases by a factor of 30 in the boundary clay at Gubbio, none of the other elements shows as much as a doubling of their normal concentration. The rare-earth elements are in fact depleted in the boundary clay compared to the sediments above and below. This makes the "behavior" of iridium all the more extraordinary. Magnetostratigraphy had been accurate: An exceedingly slow sedimentation rate of the boundary clay could not have been the explanation for the anomaly. There must have been an extraordinary input of detritus rich in iridium.

The only known source of debris much enriched in platinum metals is extraterrestrial, and so it was that Luis Alvarez, Walter Alvarez, Frank Asaro and Helen Michel presented in that exciting year of 1979 the first hard evidence for an end-Cretaceous extraterrestrial event.

To check that hypothesis Frank Asaro carried out another test. If the iridium had been of extraterrestrial origin, other siderophiles should be proportionally enriched in the boundary sediments. He and Helen Michel analyzed the concentrations of osmium, platinum, gold, nickel, and cobalt from the Danish Fish Clay. The relative abundance of these elements compared to iridium in stony meteorites had been analyzed by Urs Krähenbühl in Bern. Asaro found an extraordinarily close match in his Fish Clay samples.

Ganapathy, who had identified the deep-sea spherules as cosmic debris, learned from local newspapers of the discovery of an iridium anomaly by the Berkeley team. He carried out a series of analyses of nine noble metals, including palladium, ruthenium, and rhenium, in addition to those analyzed by Asaro in the boundary clay of Denmark. All those metals are relatively abundant in meteorites and very rare on the surface of the earth. Ganapathy confirmed the presence of an iridium anomaly in the boundary clay. He found further that all other noble metals are also enriched, and that all except rhenium have an abundance ratio similar to that in meteorites.

Rhenium was proportionally more enriched. Ganapathy noted that because this element is very soluble, its extraordinary enrichment may have resulted from chemical processes in the oceans. But if rhenium abundance could be influenced by ocean chemistry, how could we exclude the possibility that the other metals had not been similarly enriched in the boundary clay? The clay in Denmark contains little calcium carbonate, which is the main constituent of the chalks, and it is black. Such differences suggested that an unusual chemical environment existed in the oceans when the boundary clay was being deposited. If ocean chemistry could explain the rich concentration of iridium and other rare metals, the same anomaly would not exist in sediments laid down on land. On the other hand, if the platinum metals were indeed cosmic debris, an iridium anomaly should be found ubiquitously in all sediments at the Cretaceous-Tertiary boundary, no matter whether the sediments had been deposited on the bottom of the ocean or on top of a continent.

The Alvarezes obtained from their colleagues in the paleontology department at Berkeley samples of sediments deposited on ancient flood plains in Montana. The Cretaceous-Tertiary boundary had been determined for the samples by the extinction of the dinosaurs—that is, the last of their fossils were below the samples—and by fossil pollen counts. Unlike dinosaur bones, which became fossils only if the creature laid down its life under very particular circumstances conducive to preservation, fossil pollen is nearly ubiquitous. Plants produce astonishing amounts of pollen every year. Each grain is jacketed in a nearly impervious coat that resists decay. Some pollen grains are commonly trapped in the sediments that accumulate in the beds of lakes, on flood plains, or in swamps, there to become microfossils in rock.

A group of parasitic plants and their relatives, known collectively to paleobotanists as the Cretaceous *Aquilapollenites* flora, died out at apparently the same time as the dinosaurs, and the extinction horizon of this flora as determined by fossil pollen counts can be designated as the Cretaceous-Tertiary boundary at places where fossil dinosaur remains are rare or altogether lacking.

In the spring of 1980 we heard through the grapevine that an iridium anomaly had been detected in the boundary sequence of the ancient Montana flood plain. The exciting news should have shut up all skeptics who had fantasies of unusual seawater chemistry. I waited in vain, however, for publication of the results. In June, at a workshop in Ottawa called by Dale Russell to discuss the question of the boundary, I blurted out the question to Asaro: "Where does the iridium anomaly occur in the Montana section?"

"On the platinum engagement ring of the person who prepared our samples," Asaro replied.

It so happened that the newly employed technician who had wrapped the samples in aluminium foil had recently been married. A touch of her hand with its brand-new platinum wedding and engagement rings was sufficient to spike all the samples with the three siderophiles they contained—platinum, gold, and iridium. The Berkeley scientists had to toss their original samples and start collecting again.

The team was eventually to find an iridium spike at the Cretaceous-Tertiary boundary in Montana, but the delay caused by the ring episode enabled a Los Alamos team to make the first discovery of an iridium anomaly in continental sediments, at Raton Basin.

Raton Basin is a small sedimentary basin east of the Sangre de Cristo Mountains in Colorado and New Mexico. The climate is dry now, and motorists hurry their way through the discomfort of a semidesert landscape to and from Denver, but the same region between 60 and 70 million years ago was warm, humid, swampy, and overgrown by dense forest like that Amazon today. Occasionally silts and muds carried by river floods overwhelmed the lush growth. Trees died, and over the ages were converted to coal.

Modern interest in coal had done much to reveal the area's past history. In an effort to locate economic deposits, sedimentary strata at roadcuts had been studied, boreholes had been drilled in the basin, and fossils had been studied for paleontological dating of the strata. Dinosaur fossils were abundant in the San Juan region to the west, where numerous fossil bones had been collected, but they seemed to have failed to penetrate the Cretaceous forests of Raton. The Cretaceous-Tertiary boundary of the Raton sequence was therefore determined by the extinction of the *Aquilapollenites* flora. Samples were collected from the cores of a borehole and from roadcuts. They were analyzed by Carl Orth and his colleagues at the Los Alamos Laboratory, using the most refined neutron-activation analysis that allows detection of parts per trillion. Orth found the anomaly exactly at the predicted horizon, in a white boundary clay near the top of a muddy sediment below a coal bed. The maximum iridium concentration of 5 parts per billion was 250 times the normal concentration. Doubters could no longer suppose that the extra iridium in the boundary clay of ocean sediments had arrived there by exotic chemical processes.

The discovery of an iridium anomaly at the paleobotanically determined Cretaceous-Tertiary boundary also gave much support to the supposition that the *Aquilapollenites* flora became extinct on land at about the same time that swimming organisms became extinct in the oceans; the iridium anomaly was proving to be a very accurate event marker.

But again, cross-checking with magnetostratigraphy was needed. If the iridium on land and at sea came from the same cosmic fallout, the layer containing that anomalous concentration should have been deposited during the magnetostratigraphic Chron C-29-R. If the iridium anomaly were to be found within a positively magnetized sediment, the theory that impact with an extraterrestrial object had dumped iridium everywhere simultaneously would be in jeopardy—and for a while that seemed to be the case.

An oil company scientist from Houston, Texas, studied a suite of cores of the Raton Basin in 1982. He found that the iridium-rich horizon lay within a zone of normally polarized sediments, not within an epoch of reversal. However, he overlooked the fact that, under certain circumstances, a rock acquires additional magnetization long after the time its sediments were laid down. A process called magnetic cleaning is then necessary to wipe out the later imprints, and to reveal the original magnetic signature. When Gene Shoemaker and his colleagues from the U.S. Geological Survey studied the same Raton Basin sequence, their cleaned-up signals came loud and clear: All the sediments near the boundary have remnant magnetism with reversed polarity.

Meanwhile the Berkeley team, discouraged but not deterred by the platinum ring fiasco, continued their search for the iridium anomaly in Montana sediments. Magnetostratigraphic measurements and neutron-activation analysis were carried out on a new suite of samples. The results were in full agreement with those of Orth's and Shoemaker's teams. An iridium spike was found in a boundary clay below a coal bed; the 4 parts per billion maximum iridium enrichment was similar to that found in the Raton Basin and lay within an epoch of reversed polarity. Three meters below the iridium-rich coal were the remains of the last dinosaur of the area, a thigh bone from a *Tyrannosaurus rex* that could not have lived more than thirty thousand years before the iridium fallout.

The segment examined by Shoemaker was not a long one; there was too little of the "standard product code" for him to ascertain that the reversely polarized boundary sediments in the Raton Basin belonged to C-29-R, or to another reversely polarized epoch. The same was true of the samples studied by the Berkeley team and samples from three more localities in Montana, although all were reversely polarized. Farther north in Alberta, Canadian scientists finally established beyond any reasonable doubt that the dinosaur extinction lay within C-29-R. The boundary there lay within a layer of volcanic ash which could be dated by the potassium/argon method. The ash was reversely polarized, and the radiometric dating placed its deposition at about 65 million years ago, the time of C-29-R.

Still, when a theory as earth-shaking as an extraterrestrial collision is put forward to explain an event as controversial as the Cretaceous extinction, there are bound to be doubters. Over the next few years, during the early 1980s, every test that researchers could devise was put to work to prove or disprove the cosmic origin of the iridium anomaly. The relentless progress of scientific techniques had, by 1980, opened up the possibility of counting single atoms by using an ultrasensitive detector called an accelerator mass spectrometer. That method easily found the enriched iridium in the Danish boundary clay. However, it was so sensitive that it found enriched platinum in sediments well above the boundary clay, suggesting that cosmic fallout, after it had settled down, may indeed have reacted with seawater. Dissolved platinum appears to have stayed in the seawater for some time before its final precipitation thousands of years after an extraterrestrial event, although the extra iridium was confined to the boundary clay.

The fact that platinum, at least, may have been chemically precipitated raised again in the minds of skeptics the possibility that anomalous concentrations could be explained by ordinary chemistry.

Karl Turekian of Yale University, a specialist on marine geochemistry, suggested to us one day over lunch during the conference at Snowbird, Utah, that analysis of the isotopic composition of osmium in the boundary clay could settle once and for all the question of a cosmic or terrestrial origin.

Osmium has two stable isotopes, osmium 186 and osmium 187. Osmium 187 is a decay product of rhenium 187. Because radioactive rhenium decays to produce osmium 187, materials rich in rhenium have a correspondingly large amount of osmium 187 compared to osmium 186. There is more rhenium in the lithosphere than in meteorites, so the ratio of the two isotopes of osmium should be greater in terrestrial sediments than in cosmic fallout. Turekian estimated that the ratio should be about 10 in continental rocks, but only about 1 in meteorites.

Turekian is a doer, and he also knew the instrument necessary for the job—the MIT-Brown-Harvard Consortium Cameca IMS-3f ion probe. The ion probe is a special kind of mass spectrometer, whose advantage, like that of the accelerator mass spectrometer, is its ability to determine the isotope ratio of elements present at very, very small concentrations—another marvel of modern analytical techniques. Together with an enthusiastic young associate, Turekian analyzed the osmium isotopes in the boundary clays from Denmark and from Raton Basin and compared their isotopic composition with that of normal samples dredged up from the oceans.

The osmium isotope ratio for normal ocean sediments, as it turned out, ranged between 6 and 8.5. The value is not exactly 10 as Turekian predicted for purely terrestrial detritus because all abyssal sediments contain significant cosmic contamination. The osmium isotope analysis of the boundary clays yielded dramatically different values. The samples from Raton Basin contain osmium with an isotope ratio of 1.29, and that from Denmark about 1.65. Again, the deviation from the predicted value of 1 for meteorites is due to contamination, for the cosmic material is mixed with earthly sediments.

Turekian had entered his research as a skeptic. He emerged convinced by his own data, and since then still more analyses—of isotopes, of the enrichment or deple-

tion of numerous elements besides the siderophiles—
have convinced most doubters that the peculiarities of
sediments at the Cretaceous-Tertiary boundary do indeed reveal an abnormal input of extraterrestrial debris
at the end of the Cretaceous. The next question was the
nature of the extraterrestrial source: Did the excess of
siderophiles come from an asteroid or from a comet, or
was the cosmic fallout debris from a nearby supernova
explosion?

THE IDEA OF A SUPERNOVA CATASTROPHE WAS FIRST PRO-
posed in 1954 by paleontologist Otto Schindelwolf of
Tübingen.

A supernova, an exploding star, can radiate as much
energy as about 10 billion suns, or 10^{52} ergs, or a billion
trillion (10^{21}) times more energy than that of a Halley-
sized cometary impact. Only a very small fraction of this
energy would be emitted as a radiation flash, and only a
much smaller fraction of that would reach the earth.
Still, terrestrial environments might be affected somewhat even if the explosion were at a distance of 100 light
years. If the earth were twice as close to the supernova,
the radiation from the explosion would cause severe
damage to life.

It has been estimated that a supernova explodes
within 50 light years of the earth every 70 million years
or so. When the Alvarezes got their first indication of
cosmic enrichment of iridium, they thought they had detected the debris of the postulated explosion. The idea of
mass extinction by supernova explosion became immediately popular.

The Alvarez's initial conviction was based on a critical test suggested by a chemist friend at Scripps. Iridium
has two isotopes, 191 and 193. Different supernovas produce iridium with different isotope ratios. Our solar system, astronomers maintain, was formed from debris that
had accumulated over time from the explosions of many
supernovas. Because our sun and planets condensed
from this assorted debris, the isotopic ratio of iridium
anywhere in the solar system, whether on earth or in a

meteor, should represent an average of many different supernovas. That ratio was well known. If fresh debris from a single supernova fell to earth's surface at some later time, the layer containing such cosmic debris should have a signature in the form of an isotope ratio different from the average in our solar system. Frank Asaro and Helen Michel of the Berkeley team undertook to compare the isotopic ratio of iridium from the boundary clay to that of ordinary iridium in other layers by neutron-activation analysis.

Their first measurement was the one that lead them to believe the iridium had originated in a supernova, for it indicated an iridium isotope ratio in the boundary samples differing by 5 percent from the value of the solar system. Their second measurement yielded, however, a 5 percent discrepancy in the opposite direction. They began to suspect that there had been analytical errors. Probability also suggested to Luis Alvarez that a supernova explosion was an unlikely explanation. The iridium concentration in the Gubbio samples was so high that the distance of an exploding star would have to have been a mere tenth of a light year away—hardly more than a month's distance at the speed of light. The chance of a supernova explosion so close to the solar system is 1 in 1 billion during the last 100 million years, or once in 100 million billion years. The 4.5 billion years of Earth's history shrinks by comparison. By the end of 1979 the Berkeley group was convinced they had indeed been misled by experimental errors. Upon further testing, the iridium isotope ratio in the boundary clays had proved to be about the same as that elsewhere in the solar system.

Just to be sure, the neutron detective was once more called to the scene of the crime. Astrophysical theory predicted that of the heavier elements produced by neutron capture during supernova explosions, there should be one plutonium 244 atom for each thousand iridium atoms. Plutonium 244 is radioactive, but, with a half-life of 80.5 million years, it does not disintegrate very fast. If cosmic debris had come from a supernova explosion 65 million years ago, more than half of the plutonium

244 should still be there, and neutron-activation analysis should easily detect it. The analysis found no plutonium 244.

With the exploding star no longer a contender, the remaining choice of villain was between an asteroid and a comet.

The Alvarezes opted for an asteroid, by which they meant an Apollo object. Although Wetherill had theorized that these objects whose orbits overlap earth's orbit are degassed comets, others considered them more likely to be asteroids ejected from their normal orbits by gravitational perturbation of a passing star. Whatever their origin, Apollo objects are solid rock, whereas comets are icy.

There was a chance, particularly if Clube and Napier had been right in their idea that comets are captured from beyond the solar system, that something in the chemistry of asteroids and comets could distinguish between them. Could neutrons be used to single out from the two suspects which had struck earth 65 million years ago? D. E. Brownlee and others collected from the stratosphere dust particles from 5 to 50 micrometers in diameter from disintegrated comets. They had a composition identical to that of any stony meteorites (and like an asteroid), and spectral analysis of cometary fragments performed by Ian Halliday arrived at the same result. Neutrons had done all the detective work they were capable of performing.

If our most powerful forensic tools could not discriminate between a comet and an asteroid, perhaps we could return to primitive detection. After all, there should be a humungous crater and, buried in it, the remains of the villain itself. A number of us are intrigued by the fact that some four or five craters in southern Russia and in northern Siberia have an age of about 65 million years. None of them is very big: One at Kamensk in the Ukraine is only 25 kilometers across, and the largest, a 60-kilometer crater at Kara in Siberia, is of a less certain age. A trillion-ton meteorite should blast a hole 200 or 300 kilometers wide. One might nevertheless assume that the Russian craters were produced by the terminal Cretaceous hit and seek explanations why there are several small ones instead of one giant. On the other hand, the object may well have plunged into the ocean. Chris Hartnady of South Africa wrote to me in 1985 that he had identified a 300-kilometer-wide crater of the right age in the Indian Ocean southwest of the Seychelles Islands. Preliminary studies of the oceanographical data gave credence to his idea, and a deep-sea drilling cruise is being considered in an effort to determine whether this is the watery grave of the fallen meteorite.

9

Darkness at Noon

A POPULAR SCIENCE WRITER USED THE TECHNIQUE OF a murder trial to report the mass extinction at the end of the Cretaceous. Following the practice of an inquest he asked why, who, and how.

Why pertains to the motive or lack of it. Contrary to Darwin's supposition, we have little evidence that dinosaurs died off because they lost a struggle for existence; they had no competitors capable of killing them off in order to take their place in the sun. If there was a killer involved, his crime was not willful, premeditated murder, but manslaughter, or, more accurately, saurslaughter. The killing was accidental, without malice, and apparently without purpose.

Who did it, then?

The detective called neutron found circumstantial evidence incriminating a meteorite. The suspect, described as weighing up to a trillion tons, when "last seen" was heading toward earth at a speed of tens of kilometers per second. It was a suicidal hit: "Strands of hair" from the killer were found, but not the killer's body. The smoking pistol in the form of an impact crater was also not positively identified. So far the coroner remained uncertain whether the meteorite was an asteroid or a comet.

How did it kill?

This is the most difficult question, but its solution may ultimately distinguish the innocent from the guilty, because asteroids and comets may use a different modus operandi to accomplish their destructive deeds.

The first of four conferences that were to be held during the academic year 1981/1982 to explore such questions about the terminal Cretaceous extinction was called by Dale Russell, the dinosaur expert, in May 1981. About two dozen of us met at the National Museum of Natural Sciences in Ottawa, Canada. Many of us were there to present our own scenarios: the Alvarezes, Vic Clube and Bill Napier, Jan Smit, Dewey McLean, Hans Thierstein, and I. Also invited was a graduate student from UCLA, Frank Kyte; he and his professor, John Wasson, had analyzed Cretaceous-Tertiary boundary clay samples from the North Pacific and found in them the same very high concentration of iridium and other siderophiles that the Alvarezes had found in their samples from Stevn's Klint. We were joined by a number of specialists on astronomy, impact mechanics, toxic chemistry, paleobotany, and paleobiology of dinosaurs. They kept us honest.

Yet such a conference is intended to be freewheeling. However offtrack early scenarios may prove to be, their presentation within a knowledgeable group hones off rough edges and sharpens the best of the ideas. Most of us came away convinced that an impacting body triggered the Cretaceous catastrophe, but we could not agree on any one scenario. The publication that followed the conference was therefore in the form of minutes of our round-table discussions.

A compelling scenario of how the culprit killed was offered by the Alvarezes' Berkeley group. It was playfully referred to as "darkness at noon." If, they suggested, a meteorite 10 kilometers in diameter were to have hit the earth 65 million years ago, pulverized rock debris from the explosion and impact crater would have been injected as dust into the stratosphere and rapidly distributed over the whole globe, cutting out most of the light normally reaching the surface. In the ensuing darkness photosynthesis would come to a halt, and disruption of the food chain at its very base would produce very nearly the pattern of extinction that is observed in the paleontological record. The layer of clay in which they had found the iridium anomaly in Italy and Denmark must be, they surmised, the dust that over the next few years after the impact gradually settled over the earth.

"Darkness at noon" seemed reasonable at first glance, but we were particularly ignorant of the consequences of an unusual impacting event, and many questions were soon raised:

Pulverized rock debris would be injected into the stratosphere for sure, but would the ejecta be rapidly distributed over the whole globe? Would the quantity of dust be sufficient to block out the sunlight? Would the darkness last long enough to suppress photosynthesis of plants effectively and to cause extinction of many organisms? And, finally, was the Danish boundary clay a layer of ejecta debris deposited during the few years after an impact event?

Answering those questions required help from many kinds of specialists, and they jumped into the act soon after the publication of the Alvarez manifesto. John O'Keefe and Tom Ahrens of Cal Tech; Bill Melosh of State University of New York, Stonybrook; Don Orphal of Livermore; Peter Schultz and Steve Croft of Houston Lunar and Planetary Institute; Eric Jones and John Kodis of Los Alamos; Brian Toon of NASA Ames Research Center, California; Don Gault of the Murphy Center for Planetology; and numerous other experts carried out investigations of impact mechanics and studied the effect of a direct hit by an extraterrestrial body 10 kilometers across. Some used computers; others performed laboratory experiments. They were all invited to the second conference about the Cretaceous extinction that year held at Snowbird, Utah, in October 1981 and sponsored by the Lunar and Planetary Institute of Houston, Texas.

The Snowbird conference, entitled "Large Body Impacts and Terrestrial Evolution: Geological, Climatological, and Biological Implications," was organized by Lee Silver of Cal Tech. I had known him very well during my student days in southern California when we both investigated the metamorphic rocks of the San Gabriel Mountains. While my professional wanderings led me finally to the realm of marine geology, Silver had become a specialist in planetary science. He was among those who had instructed the astronauts on lunar geology before they landed on the moon. Our paths had long since diverged, and I had not heard from him for ages, except for a letter in which he, as the president of the Geological Society of America, informed me of my election as an honorary fellow of that august body. I was, therefore, surprised when I was told one day in August 1981, during a three-month lecture tour to New Zealand and Australia, that Lee Silver from Pasadena had called. It was urgent, and I was to call him back immediately.

On the phone, Silver asked me to go to Snowbird. I did not want to go. I thought I had said all I had to say at Ottawa already. Also, I had traveled far too much that year. But Silver would not take no for an answer. After having tied up a trans–Pacific line for half an hour, my telephone phobia got the best of me. I consented reluctantly, mostly to escape that discomfiting machine. In October, I had hardly unpacked my bags before I had to repack them and catch a plane for Salt Lake City.

My performance at Snowbird was disappointing. In my hurry I forgot to take the illustrative materials for my talk. I was embarrassed and told a lie, blaming the airline for having lost my baggage, but my friends knew well that I was too experienced a traveler to trust important documents to check-in baggage. Aside from that I was very happy that I did go to Snowbird, because I learned a great deal. With my ignorance of the consequences of huge impacts somewhat diminished, I was able to steer myself away from mistaken notions and begin to try new, viable alternatives.

The impact mechanics of a large body differ radically from that of a small one. Small meteors burn up or disintegrate in the air because their trip through the atmosphere is a distance many times greater than their own diameter. The atmosphere is about 7.1 kilometers deep; the ocean's mean depth is about 3.6 kilometers. A trillion-ton meteorite with a diameter of about 10 kilometers is as thick in the middle as atmosphere and ocean put together. O'Keefe and Ahrens pointed out that the impact would simply punch a large hole in the atmosphere. The hole would remain when the object hit the earth and suck up the ejecta to make a fireball. Even a 5-kilometer-deep ocean could not stop a large meteor traveling at 20 kilometers per second, although sufficiently great shock pressure would build up to slow its descent, perhaps reducing its speed to 6 kilometers per second. At any rate, the maximum amount of energy taken up directly during the passage of a massive meteor through the atmosphere and ocean cannot be very great—certainly less than a 5 percent loss through the air, and 15 percent through water. The lion's share of energy would be released on impact. A large crater would be produced, and melted rock would floor the crater. Meanwhile, the debris ejected from the crater together with air, water, vapor, and vaporized meteorite would rise as a giant column of smoke, tens of kilometers in cross section, and spread out laterally as a mushroom cloud in the stratosphere.

The amount of debris thrown out of the crater would be enormous and made up of particles of all sizes. Coarser debris would be dumped around the crater as ballistic fallout or as avalanches spreading out from the target area. Finer particles would be melted, vaporized, and lofted up at supersonic speed in a column of fire and, if the impact object should hit an ocean, a tremendous volume of water vapor. Jones and Kodis gave a dramatic description of the first few minutes after an impact: The fireball would start as a thin disk of hot gas. The disk would expand explosively, become nearly spherical after one second, and then change into a rising column of hot gases reaching 30 kilometers in height within the first half minute. Finally, the ejecta would spread out as a mushroom cloud one minute after the impact. Fine ejecta debris could be carried to an altitude of 100 kilometers or more.

O'Keefe and Ahrens suggested that only the finest particles, less than 1 micrometer in diameter, could stay in the stratosphere long enough to be distributed globally. Millimeter- to centimeter-sized initially molten particles would be projected upward and lofted backward along the initial meteorite trajectory. As they cooled, they would reenter the earth's atmosphere as glassy tektites and glassy, stony, or iron microtektites.

Among the differences between various scenarios presented the previous fall in Ottawa had been the identity of the meteorite. I preferred at first to put the blame on a comet because of the poison it could bring, but the Alvarezes stuck to their opinion that it was an asteroid. One point in their favor was the large amount of iridium the object had delivered.

A comet, a "dirty snowball," contains far less stony material and thus less iridium than a solid-rock asteroid of the same dimension. The amount of iridium found in the boundary clay is stupendous. To have deposited that much, an asteroid would have had to weigh 100 billion tons; a comet would have had to weigh ten times that, or a trillion tons. The Alvarezes thought the postulate of a smaller body more credible, as Luis indicated in a talk he gave to the U.S. National Academy in 1982. Credibility is of itself, however, not a convincing argument.

Robert Grieve, basing the calculation on all the many craters he had studied, figured that in round numbers an ordinary stony or iron meteorite can excavate a volume of terrestrial ejecta one hundred times its own size. A 100-billion-ton asteroid could thus throw up as much as 10 trillion tons of ejecta debris. Although only a small fraction of that would be distributed as fallout via the stratosphere, the dusting of particles that eventually drifted down from the sky should be much more terrestrial than cosmic.

The iridium concentration of the boundary clay at several European localities, however, is so high that there cannot be one hundred times more terrestrial debris than cosmic debris. There cannot be more than ten times the amount of material in the impacting object. Even if all the particles in the clay are fallout from the impact, those blasted from the crater cannot account for any more than ten times the amount of material in the impacting object.

Tackling the problem of "excess" iridium Frank Kyte and John Wasson of UCLA came to the conclusion that the impacting object must have had a low density of 0.1 gram per cubic centimeter—not much different from that of a snowball—in order to account for the very high extraterrestrial component in the ejecta fallout of the boundary clay. Such an object could only have been an icy comet, not a rock-solid asteroid. The estimated fallout volume convinced the two scientists that the impacting comet must have weighed a little more than a trillion tons and must have measured more than 10 kilometers across. It must have been a Halley-sized comet.

But nothing is ever that easy in science. Attention focused on the nature of the ejecta. Jan Smit had discovered two kinds of microtektites in Cretaceous-Tertiary boundary clay at Caravaca, Spain. The smaller of the two kinds of microtektites resemble in size and chemical composition the spherules found in the Tunguska area, which have an iridium concentration as high as 56,900 parts per billion, similar to the content of an iron meteorite. The high concentration suggests that the material was derived directly from the meteorite as it exploded in the atmosphere and is uncontaminated by terrestrial materials. The larger microtektites have an iridium content of only 10.4 parts per billion. Smit and his coworkers concluded, therefore, that these round, disk-, or dumbbell-shaped objects had originally been droplets of molten ejecta material, excavated largely from an impact crater, but substantially contaminated by extraterrestrial material. Further study revealed a trace-element chemistry similar to that of oceanic rocks. It seems, therefore, that the ejecta were derived from a crater at the ocean bottom. Both kinds of dust—the larger microtektites with a composition similar to oceanic crust, and the tiny particles with a much more cosmic composition—had, in fact, previously been found in the boundary clay at Gubbio. Such fallout debris from the impact has since been identified at many other localities.

This finding, after a good deal more analysis, cast doubt on the theory that the smallish amount of terrestrial debris that had been mixed with cosmic debris in the boundary clearly indicated a comet rather than an asteroid impact. Working on just how ejecta might have been distributed after the impact, O'Keefe and Ahrens, with the help of the big computer at Berkeley, found that the destinies of the two types of dust are not the same. The initial ejecta have an extraordinarily high extraterrestrial component and an extremely high velocity. Those initial ejecta particles could have a concentration of cosmic material as high as the tiny particles found at Gubbio, Caravaca, and Stevn's Klint. It was their high velocity, the Berkeley team claimed, that enabled an ascent of 10 kilometers or more into the stratosphere for global distribution. Later, less speedy, and more terrestrial debris derived largely from the crater itself would mostly fall before reaching such heights and thus would not be generously distributed. The least contaminated fallouts should be found near the crater, but not in the boundary clay. That would make the cosmic-spherule-enriched boundary clay a poor measure of the total ratio of terrestrial to cosmic debris, and therefore no help at all in figuring out whether a stony asteroid or an icy comet had made the excavation. We were thus back to square one: The iridium concentration of the boundary clay cannot tell us whether the impacting meteorite was an asteroid or a comet.

Nevertheless the evidence had become impeccable that a meteorite did strike, and that the hit did throw up a lot of dust. The nature of the microtektites proved that the extraterrestrial body did not simply disintegrate completely in the atmosphere like the Tunguska object. Any lingering doubt was nullified a few years later when Bruce Bohor, a clay mineralogist from the U.S. Geological Survey at Denver, studied the boundary clay of the Raton Basin and discovered among hundreds of normal sand and silt grains, a number of quartz grains whose structure was similar to that of the ceosite found at Meteor Crater in Arizona and at other large impact sites. The pressure required to make such grains is so high that they can only be produced on the surface of the earth by a high-speed meteorite impact. But the question remained whether the ejecta of this impact had once caused a blackout everywhere on Earth.

O'Keefe and Ahrens believed that the ejecta would have had to stay in the atmosphere for several weeks at least before a worldwide distribution could be achieved, and that that was unlikely for any but the finest dust. Particles larger than 1 micrometer would fall out rapidly from the stratosphere. Smaller particles that collided and fused together would also be large enough to settle rapidly. Brian Toon and his associates made computations and found that particles coarser than 4 micrometers should settle in a couple of weeks, those coarser than 2 micrometers in a few months. Particles 0.5 micrometer in diameter would fall within three years even if they did not stick together to form larger, faster-falling aggregates. The results suggested, therefore, that larger particles like microtektites would have come down very quickly and have had a limited distribution.

The spherules of the boundary clay were first found in Spain, Italy, Denmark, and at DSDP Site 465 in the North Pacific, all of which are situated at middle to high northern latitudes. I had, therefore, thought that an east-west strewn tektite field had been discovered. Such fields made up of fast-falling particles mark the trajectory of many well-known meteorite hits, and, if the giant hit at the end of the Cretaceous had behaved according to Toon's calculations, its tektite field would provide an indication of where the object had actually hit. But Jan

Smit wrote to me recently that terminal Cretaceous microtektites had been identified at many localities in both the northern and southern hemispheres. The iridium anomaly is also worldwide. Luis Alvarez reported in 1982 that wherever the boundary sediment is in place, it is invariably enriched in iridium. The concentration ranges from a few to several tens of parts per billion. Thirty-six localities from Italy, Denmark, Spain, the Caucasus, New Mexico, Texas, Montana, the North Pacific, the South Atlantic, and New Zealand were plotted on Alvarez's map. From his experience tracing the radioactive fallout of Soviet hydrogen-bomb tests in the 1950s, Alvarez estimated that it would take not weeks, but a year or more for ejecta debris to be transported by stratospheric winds from the northern to the southern hemisphere. All but the very finest particles should have settled long before they could be transported to the other hemisphere. The presence of ejecta debris in both northern and southern hemispheres of the earth requires, therefore, that mechanisms other than stratospheric winds must have been at work. Alvarez, citing work by Jones and Kodis of Los Alamos, suggested that the impacting object may have hit the earth at a shallow angle. If there had been such a glancing blow, the bombarding and the ejected fragments could have ricocheted off the surface into a ballistic orbit, so that tektites and spherules could spread worldwide in a matter of hours. Whether or not a bouncing meteorite is the right explanation, the fact is that debris did spread worldwide and, judging from the degree of the iridium anomaly, there was a lot of it.

WAS THERE ENOUGH TO FORM AN ENVELOPE OF DUST that blocked out the sunlight and prevented photosynthesis? Siegfried Gerstl and Andrew Zardecki of Los Alamos investigated the reduction of photosynthesis under an extreme cover of dusty aerosol up in the stratosphere. The figures were based on what we know actually happens after volcanic eruptions that emit large quantities of ash. Sunlight necessary for photosynthesis was reduced by 10 to 25 percent after the 1883 Krakatoa eruption which released about 100 million tons of stratospheric aerosols, and by about 20 percent after the 1912 Katmai eruption which released about half as much ash. Gerstl and Zardecki's model calculations indicated that to reduce solar radiation to a thousandth of normal sunlight—or pitch-black darkness—would require 40 billion tons of dust in the stratosphere.

A large comet need not even hit the earth to produce that much dust; a near miss would leave enough debris in earth's atmosphere to produce a complete blackout.

Using a somewhat higher figure of 50 billion tons of stratospheric dust and assuming the envelope to have been evenly distributed at about 10 milligrams per square centimeter, Toon's computations agreed with Gerstl and Zardecki's model: The day would indeed be as dark as the darkest night, bringing photosynthesis to a complete halt. Because, however, plants can survive on stored energy for some time and resume photosynthesis as soon as the skies brighten, the settling rate is critical to the question of whether plants actually died, as in the darkness at noon scenario. Toon figured that the dust would settle quickly and photosynthesis could resume by about three months after the initial blackout.

Even when computations are made for much larger volumes of dust—trillions or tens of trillions of tons—the sky would be as bright as a moonlit night three months after the impact, and bright enough for photosynthesis to resume in four months' time. Toon's calculations assumed that small particles would form aggregates and therefore fall rapidly. If they should remain separate, and therefore settle more slowly, darkness might last longer than a year, but this possibility was considered highly improbable. Most likely darkness could not have lasted more than a few months no matter how massive a comet or asteroid had hit.

If the meteorite fell into an ocean, the "fireball of ejecta" would be enveloped in a giant "steam bubble." Steven Croft modeled oceanic impacts: A stony object 10 kilometers across hitting an ocean at 15 to 30 kilometers per second would vaporize a volume of ocean water twenty to one hundred times that of the object, or 1,000 to 5,000 cubic kilometers, weighing 1 to 5 trillion tons. The pillar of vaporized water would measure 20 or 30 kilometers across and rise tens of kilometers high one minute after the impact. The ocean would indeed have boiled above the target site!

The amount of water vapor thrown into the air would supersaturate the stratosphere above an area several thousand kilometers across. The vapor would rapidly recondense, and rain or snow out of the atmosphere. Croft estimated that most of the vapor would return to the earth's surface in a few months. Total precipitation would amount to a thousand meters or so, coming down at an average rate of 5 to 10 meters, or 200 to 400 inches, per day. I cannot help but remember the biblical story of Noah's Flood again. It rained for forty days, we were told. It is not physically impossible, if a large meteorite hit the ocean then. Thick cloud cover after an oceanic impact should, of course, further darken the sky. On the other hand, rain and snow would have cleansed the air of dust and accelerated the return of sunlight. No one had yet computed these two opposite effects, but the scenario of a temporary blackout seemed applicable no matter whether the meteorite hit the land or the ocean.

WHAT WAS THE CONSEQUENCE, THEN, OF SEVERAL months of darkness to the world of living organisms? Although none of the Alvarez team claimed to be a biologist or a paleontologist, they did venture some biological consequences of the darkness scenario. Their conclusions were neither new nor very well thought out. Wedding the blackout theory to the old hunger hypothesis, they proposed a collapse of the food chain caused by the temporary cessation of photosynthesis in all plants, and the permanent mass extinction of phytoplankton in the ocean. Phytoplankton extinction, in their view, explained the extinction by starvation of marine animals at successively higher levels in the food chain, with nearly total extinction of the foraminifera and complete disappearance of the belemnites, ammonites, and marine reptiles.

As for the second food chain based on land plants, they proposed that during the interval of darkness existing vegetation would die, or at least stop producing new growth. Even though new plants would sprout from seeds or resprout from still-living root systems after light returned, large herbivorous and carnivorous animals that were directly or indirectly dependent on vegetation would become extinct. The smaller terrestrial vertebrates that did survive, including ancestral mammals, may have done so by feeding on nuts, seeds, insects, and decaying vegetation.

Unfortunately for this appealingly simple hypothesis, it is not enough to say that darkness kills, or even that the repercussions of some killings are felt clear to the top of the food chain. The Cretaceous extinction has a very particular pattern, and if a theory is to explain it, that theory must account both for those organisms that died and for those that survived.

The mystery of the catastrophe at the end of the Cretaceous is not so much why many died off, but why any survived at all. The marine plankton living at the ocean surface were hard hit, while deep-living benthic organisms were spared. Among the plankton, those secreting calcium carbonate skeletons were almost entirely wiped out, but those secreting silica escaped largely unscathed. The swimming ammonites and belemnites became extinct, but the nautiloid mollusks lived through the crisis. Among the benthic, or bottom-dwelling, organisms that lived in shallow water, the casualty rate was also uneven: Echinoids fared better, for example, than brachiopods, and brachiopods inhabiting muddy bottoms survived while those inhabiting chalky bottoms expired. Small freshwater invertebrates, like mollusks in rivers and lakes, did not seem to be affected at all. On land, the larger animals, especially those with an estimated body weight of more than 25 kilograms, were particularly vulnerable. This selectivity of the terminal Cretaceous extinction is its most fascinating aspect, and it can be clarified only by understanding the biology of various organisms, for one creature's demise is another's opportunity—or at least only a temporary crisis—depending on how exactly each one lives.

The Alvarez team, for instance, took it as axiomatic that phytoplankton could not survive very long without light, but total darkness for several months is a normal situation in the polar regions where phytoplankton and their browsers, zooplankton, thrive. Plankton may not multiply in polar winters, but they do get through the dark months and bloom again each spring. I asked my friends in marine biology how this could be.

Phytoplankton, like coccoliths, I was told, have life cycles consisting of a motile and a dormant stage. They reproduce by simple division, or fission, during the motile stage when their rate of division ranges as high as four times a day for certain species. When a phytoplankton goes into a dormant stage, the cell loses its whiplike flagellum and thus no longer moves around. In some phytoplankton, the living cell hides itself inside a cyst, like a bear in a cave. The dormant or encysted organism does not need to photosynthesize and does not care whether it is light or dark outside. Eventually, the non-motile cell divides again to form a number of daughter cells, which, again whipped along by flagella, are released as motile swarmers of the next generation. Polar and temperate nannoplankton can become dormant, and it is this life cycle adaption that allows them to withstand long, cold, and dark winter periods.

We could suppose that a brief global darkening would drive many phytoplankton into a dormant or a cyst stage. Surely when the light returned some of them should produce motile daughters and get on with reproduction.

If phytoplankton could survive a blackout, could zooplankton also be saved? They, too, can alternate between active and dormant stages. My colleague, Hedi Oberhänsli, together with a group of Tübingen scientists, studied living planktonic foraminifers in the tropical seas near Barbados. She told me that the life cycles of her favorite species, *Globorotalia sacculifer*, follows lunar cycles. Juvenile swarmers dive down to deep water. They grow to adult size and return to the surface at the next full moon to reproduce new swarmers. The longevity of an individual is thus one lunar month. If several months of blackout is required for death by starvation, the first generation of the short-lived foraminifers could have reproduced easily and would have died their natural death long before starvation set in. Each succeeding month's generation should, however, have found less and less to eat, because their dormant fodder could not bloom again until light returned. Would they have starved to extinction?

I posed the question to Jerry Lipps of the University of California at Davis. Lipps is a specialist on living foraminifers of the polar regions, where zooplankton have no fodder during the dark winter months.

Lipps told me that as winter comes these creatures cease to reproduce and go into a dormant stage until the following spring when food becomes plentiful again. How long can they remain dormant? Lipps was not certain but thought that they certainly remain so for several months, and some forms may be able to stay inactive for several years.

So much for that axiom: Although it is a fair guess that darkness kills, it is by no means clear that all individuals, especially of polar species already adapted to months of darkness, would fail to come through the ordeal, and reproduce ensuing generations. Clearly, mass killing doesn't necessarily lead to mass extinction. Especially when one evaluates the blackout effect on land plants, one must make a special effort to separate the question of mortality from that of extinction.

A darkness of several months would seriously damage all plants in active growth. They would yellow and drop their foliage en masse. Pollen assemblages in sediments have provided impressive evidence in support of this scenario. Robert Tschudy of the U.S. Geological Survey studied the *Aquilapollenites* flora whose extinction in western North America marks the end of the Cretaceous in the Raton Basin sediments at about the same horizon where the last dinosaur is found, and where Carl Orth and his Los Alamos colleagues found evidence of an extraterrestrial event in the form of an iridium anomaly at the boundary. Tschudy's pollen diagram provides an impressive record of catastrophic environmental change.

The dominant vegetation in the swampy forests of the Raton Basin toward the end of the Cretaceous consisted of flowering plants, or angiosperms, many of them trees. Ferns grew here and there, but the spores by which they reproduce constitute less than 5 percent of the pollen and spore assemblages examined by Tschudy. Suddenly, at the time represented by the horizon where the iridium anomaly was found, the vegetation of the countryside became almost completely different: There is practically no tree pollen, whereas fern spores constitute more than 90 percent of the assemblage. Apparently all the trees of the swampy forests were suddenly destroyed, and only ferns could grow over the devastated landscape. Tschudy compared the castastrophic change to that observed in the volcanic terranes of Indonesia. Hot lava spitting out of volcanoes has on many occasions killed all the trees in its path; ferns have grown between barren lava blocks for decades before reforestation occurred.

The similarly overwhelming floral turnover which Tschudy's pollen diagram recorded took place during the interval of time represented by two samples spaced a mere centimeter apart. A centimeter of ocean ooze normally represents about a thousand years, but the sedimentation rate on land is commonly many times faster than that in the ocean. Judging by the thinness of the pollen-poor sediment, the Raton Basin forest must have disappeared in considerably less than a thousand years. In fact, we can envision the forests dead in less than a year's time after the meteorite hit.

Tschudy found wood fragments carbonized at high temperatures in the sediments immediately above the boundary clay in Raton Basin; he suspected widespread forest fires. Tschudy's guess has since been confirmed by a team of chemists from the University of Chicago. They found carbon soot in the black boundary clay of Stevn's Klint and that from the North Pacific, and identified the soot particles as the product of wildfires on land. So much soot is now buried in the boundary clay of the oceans that the Chicago chemists suspected that one-tenth of all living organisms, animals and plants, were burnt to death in a pyric catastrophe after the meteorite hit.

The landscape after the catastrophe is not hard to imagine: burnt timber and fallen trees piled up on top of one another. There may have been plenty of mushrooms covering dead logs, and everywhere, as the record suggests, a luxuriant growth of ferns. Only here and there, one supposes, could one have found new seedlings of flowering trees, valiantly raising their crown above the mess of organic debris.

Tschudy's pollen diagram told us, however, that recovery was relatively rapid. The layer of sediment rich in fern spores is very thin. A few centimeters above the boundary sediment, the amount of pollen again exceeds the amount of spores. We might imagine that the new generation of second growth made its way back within dozens of years, and that the region was again a forest of flowering trees within a century or two. Except for a few species, such as those of the *Aquilapollenites* flora, that never came back the plant kingdom soon recovered.

Although the story told by spores and pollen is a catastrophe of the first order, with dead forests and clearings no longer decorated by wildflowers when the silent spring came, the events seem insignificant in the long evolutionary history of land vegetation, for the mass mortality of land plants at the end of the Cretaceous resulted in relatively few extinctions. If Tschudy had been concerned only with extinction patterns or diversity changes, he might have concluded that not very much had happened at the end of the Cretaceous. Another noted paleobotanist, Leo Hickey of the Smithsonian Institution, did just that. Hickey, in a statistical analysis of the survival of plant species across the Cretaceous-Tertiary boundary, computed the percentages of late Cretaceous species which are also present in early Tertiary floras.

In an article in *Nature* entitled "Land Plant Evidence Compatible with Gradual, Not Catastrophic, Change at the End of the Cretaceous," Hickey claimed that the pattern of survival was too random to be in keeping with one awesome episode of world-enclosing darkness. For example, he found that about 90 percent of plants at high southern latitudes (above 60 degrees south) had survived, and that 60 percent had survived at middle southern latitudes. The record of the tropics showed a variation ranging from 100 percent survival in some locations to a minimum of about 20 percent in other locations. The record from middle and high northern latitudes revealed even more variation, ranging from 95 to 5 percent. Among the *Aquilapollenites* flora of Siberia and western North America, 75 percent of the Cretaceous species became extinct. The only pattern Hickey's analysis seemed to reveal was an apparent increase in destruction toward the north, but he saw no dramatic significance in that.

In fact, Hickey's data on selective extinction are quite compatible with a scenario of an extraterrestrial catastrophe, if one thinks in terms of seasons. Plants, like plankton, have evolved dormancy as an adaptation to harsh times, but preparation for winter dormancy precedes by several months the actual arrival of winter. A months-long blackout starting in April would have done little harm to plant communities at high southern latitude, where winter is then closing in and plants have completed their preparations for dormancy by such means as storing starches and shedding leaves. When the southern spring returned in September, the sky would have been clear again, and plants as well as their seeds would be ready to sprout. As far as those floras were concerned, nothing had happened to disturb their annual rhythm.

On the other hand an April blackout would have been

devastating for flora in the north, where that month is early spring. They would already have broken dormancy and resumed the active, growing stage of their annual cycle, for which photosynthesis is necessary. Once committed, there would have been no retreat back into dormancy; they would have died. Seeds unable to hold their dormancy any longer would have germinated into seedlings. But the seedlings would have died without light for photosynthesis. There would have been mass mortality, and extinction on a scale much greater than in the southern hemisphere, as Hickey found in his paleobotanical data. Hickey's pattern of increasingly more severe damage northward could mean that the giant meteor hit the earth during a northern spring.

The variation in extinction percentages that Hickey thought were random can be explained by a number of other considerations. The duration of dormancy in seeds, for example, is critical. A study of the germination patterns of 180 species of Malaysian trees was cited by David Jarzen as an illustration. In those tropical forest 65 percent of the species germinate within an average of twelve weeks. If the meteorite fell during spring and the dust cleared in three or four months, the most rapidly germinating species, those which can hold dormancy for only six weeks or so, would have had little chance for survival. It would be a matter of touch and go for the majority whose seeds could remain dormant for only three months or so. Regions forested by trees which had seeds that could remain dormant for more than six months, however, would show a high survival rate.

Of those species that survived by holding their dormancy long enough, some may have become extinct over the ensuing years because of a failure to reproduce. David Dilcher of the University of Indiana noted that the Cretaceous flowering plants have been generally assumed to be insect-pollinated. Yet there was a rapid radiation of wind-pollinated plants during the early Tertiary. Is that an indication of catastrophic insect mortality during the terminal Cretaceous event? Plants requiring insect pollination would be in reproductive trouble if insects had died en masse, but wind would have blown as hard as ever, giving wind-pollinated species an advantage during the first years of recovery.

ALTHOUGH THE DARKNESS AT NOON SCENARIO MAY PROvide an explanation of the floral changes at the end of Cretaceous, the attempt to link dinosaur extinction to darkness carries little conviction. If the blackout lasted only a few months, as the computations lead us to believe, there should have been enough fodder around to maintain some vegetarians and enough carcasses to maintain some carnivores. One can hardly believe that all dinosaurs, great and small, died of starvation. Some have suggested that dinosaurs may have starved during the dark months because they located food by vision alone, but not only is there no evidence that they had poorly developed senses of smell and hearing, there is also no evidence that nocturnal animals were favored during a struggle for existence in darkness.

The darkness at noon scenario is furthermore weak, not because a massive meteorite could not kick up enough dust to darken the sky, but because smaller meteorites which hit earth every million or every 10 million years could also do the trick. As Gene Shoemaker, who knows how often the earth is bombarded by meteorites, commented in a workshop discussion, we should have evidence of many more mass extinctions if darkness alone were responsible for them.

The final test of the hypothesis is the chronology of the catastrophe. If a blackout was responsible for the Cretaceous extinction, the deed had to be accomplished before the light returned in a few months, or, according to even the most extreme estimates, in a few years. But did all ammonites, all belemnites, all rudistids, all dinosaurs, and all but a few species of nannoplankton and foraminifers become extinct quite *that* fast?

10

The Doomed Survivors

THE OCEAN FLOOR IS A GRAVEYARD FOR PLANKTON. The soft tissues in dead cells are oxidized and changed into carbon dioxide and water; only traces are preserved in sediments. Those plankton which secrete hard parts, however, leave fossils. Foraminiferal and nannoplankton skeletons consist, in most cases, of calcium carbonate, the stuff that forms limestone. Less common are fossil remains of radiolarian and diatoms, which secrete silica, the compound that makes flint rock. In polar waters, where diatoms or radiolaria are most productive, ocean oozes are mainly composed of siliceous skeletons. In most other areas, calcareous oozes are the rule. Seawater is undersaturated with respect to calcium carbonate at depths below a few hundred meters, so some of the lime from foraminifer and nannoplankton skeletons dissolves. The rate of dissolution is very slow, however, and the steady accumulation of new skeletons tends to prevent the old from being completely dissolved. Only in regions where the production of plankton is meager, or in the deepest parts of the ocean where dissolution is rapid, are all skeletal parts dissolved. The only sediment left then is an insoluble residue of very fine particles—dust from land or from outer space. The dust forms clays that are commonly red because bottom waters in the very deep parts of oceans are often richly oxygenated and turn the iron in sediments to its red ferric, or rusty, state.

Red clays begin at depths of 4 kilometers where plankton fertility is low, and at 5 kilometers even where plankton are abundant. The line separating the white, calcareous oozes from the red clays is called the calcite compensation depth (CCD). *Compensation* refers to the balance between arriving and dissolving skeletons. Above the calcite compensation depth, calcareous oozes are deposited because more limy skeletons are arriving than are being dissolved away. Below the CCD, only red clays accumulate because the supply of plankton skeletons is not sufficient to compensate for their dissolution. The calcite compensation depth varies from place to place, both because of variations in plankton fertility and because of the differing corrosiveness of seawater.

Wolf Berger of Scripps used an analogy to explain the concept of calcite compensation depth. He asked us to imagine an ocean without water: The underwater elevations would be peaks and ridges with a white cap like snow. The lower slopes, the abyssal plains, and the deep-sea trenches would be covered with dark sediments of red and brown clays. The calcite compensation depth separates the white from the dark, as the snowline on land demarcates regions of permanent snow. The snowline, like the CCD, is not at the same height everywhere; it is a *compensation* elevation, the elevation at which annual melting of snow is exactly compensated by annual supply of snow. The snowline is low where there is plenty of precipitation or where the temperature is too cold for much melting. The snowline is high in deserts, where there is scant precipitation, or in the tropics, where the temperature is high. The calcite compensation depth behaves likewise: The CCD is low in the equatorial zone, where the precipitation of plankton skeletons is plenty, or in regions where the bottom water is not too corrosive. The CCD is high in the middle-latitude ocean "deserts" where plankton production is scanty, or in regions of active bottom currents, which tend to be very corrosive.

All this had been well established for some time when I joined the DSDP Leg 3 cruise of the South Atlantic in 1968. Therefore I was startled to find a red clay where it did not belong. Our drilling vessel was exploring the Mid-Atlantic Ridge. This underwater mountain chain has a ridge top about 2.5 kilometers below sea level and, because the calcite compensation depth of the region is deeper than 4.5 kilometers, it is covered by white oozes. Red clays are found in the more central parts of the Atlantic abyssal plains, where water depths are more than 5 kilometers. Yet we ran into red clays below recent lime oozes in several boreholes on the flank of the Mid-Atlantic Ridge well above the present calcite compensation depth.

Prejudiced by my Lyellian upbringing, I chose a dogmatic uniformitarian approach when I offered an explanation in my report: I assumed that the CCD in the South Atlantic had remained constant at 4.5 kilometers throughout the past, but that the Mid-Atlantic Ridge had not stood as high in previous times as it does now. According to this interpretation, the older sediments are red clays because the crest of the Mid-Atlantic Ridge was then more than 4.5 kilometers below the surface so that all fossil foraminifers and nannoplankton were dissolved.

Looking back, I see my naïveté. Nobody assumes that the snowline should remain always at the same elevation. The whole of Switzerland, valleys as well as peaks, stood above the snowline during the last Ice Age, not because the country was any higher, but because, when melting was negligible and snow abundant, the snowline was much lower. There was no reason to assume that the lime-white "snowline" of the oceans should remain the same during the great reaches of the geological past. My mistake was soon corrected by other scientists on subsequent deep-sea drilling cruises. They presented convincing arguments that the crest of the Mid-Atlantic Ridge has not changed height, but that the calcite compensation depth has gone up and down as a result of both changing fertility at the surface and changing chemistry at the bottom. Red clays are present on top of the ridge in sediment dating to 10 million years ago because the CCD was unusually high at that time. Bill Hay, who was a shipboard scientist on Leg 4, constructed a diagram to illustrate the ups and downs of the calcite compensation depth during the last 100 million years.

Hay was teaching at the University of Illinois then. One of his graduate students, Tom Worsley, selected the Cretaceous-Tertiary boundary as the theme of his dissertation. Marine sediments of late Cretaceous and early Tertiary age have been uplifted and are exposed on roadsides in various southern states. Worsely collected his samples from a place near Braggs, Alabama, because the sequence there is continuous and the fossils are well preserved. He found at the Cretaceous-Tertiary boundary horizon a hard layer of a kind of rock that is deficient in calcium carbonate. Recalling the limeless boundary clay of Gubbio and other places, Worsley made the startling proposal that the CCD had risen at the end of the Cretaceous all the way from the normal oceanic depth of 4.5 kilometers to the zone where light penetrates, a few hundred meters deep at most. He went on to speculate that the changing chemistry of the oceans which caused the rise of the compensation depth could also have caused the mass extinction of phytoplankton.

Few experts took Worsley's speculative idea seriously. Yet the changing CCD was a fact, and we needed critical information concerning the causes of its rise and fall. In the meantime, I had had reason not only to reject my own naive interpretation of the South Atlantic red clays, but to question my whole philosophy of geology because of my experiences at sea.

The Deep Sea Drilling Project, originally funded for eighteen months of drilling only, had enjoyed such spectacular successes in its first few cruises that the continu-

ation of financial support by the United States Congress
was assured. The second phase of DSDP sent the *Glomar Challenger* to the Indian Ocean, and the third phase
explored the Antarctic. I was then involved in uncovering the geological history of the Mediterranean, and I
persuaded my friends in the JOIDES organization that
some boreholes should be sunk there, as well. That drilling led to the sensational discovery that the Mediterranean had 6 million years ago been a vast salt desert
3 kilometers below present sea level.

The Mediterranean venture made a deep impression
on me. I began to question, for the first time, uniformitarianism, the fundamental premise of our science. Lyell
cannot have been right. Conditions on the surface of the
earth have not always remained uniform; a sea could become a desert, the calcite compensation depth in the
ocean could change, and the reasons could be more
drastic and exciting than anything Lyell had imagined.

The Mediterranean expedition also made a deep impression on the National Science Foundation, because
the shipboard scientific staff were 90 percent Europeans.
Uncle Sam had been picking up the tab till then. If foreigners were that much interested in deep-sea drilling
they should also contribute funding. A press conference
was called in Paris at the conclusion of the Mediterranean cruise. After I gave my report of the latest discovery, the chairman of the JOIDES Executive Committee
made a speech inviting foreign governments to join this
greatest, most expensive experiment in Earth science.
France, Germany, the United Kingdom, Japan, and the
Soviet Union took the bait. The JOIDES organization
became international, and the International Phase of
Ocean Drilling (IPOD) began in 1975.

I made a valiant effort to secure an associate membership status for Switzerland, but international science
politics fouled my attempt. I did manage, however, to
submit a drill proposal to explore the calcite compensation depth at the site where we had unexpectedly found
red clays beneath the white oozes of the modern seafloor.

In 1975, at the start of the International Phase of Ocean Drilling, I wrote to the Planning Committee of the JOIDES organization proposing that a series of boreholes be drilled on the east flank of the Mid-Atlantic Ridge along latitude 30 degrees south to investigate the apparent rise of the CCD during the Miocene, some 10 million years ago. Two alternative hypotheses had been suggested: The "supply-siders" insisted that the plankton production in that part of the Atlantic was drastically reduced during the Miocene. Their opponents the "demand-siders" proposed a sudden intrusion of cold, corrosive bottom water as the cause of more intensive and extensive dissolution of calcareous oozes, a loss too great to be compensated by the supply. We needed production figures, and we needed chemical indicators to resolve the controversy. The South Atlantic was the best region for obtaining such data.

The problem was significant to the scientific community, and the place was well chosen. Based on my 1975 proposal, a seven-week drilling expedition was scheduled for 1978 but was then postponed until 1980. We had, therefore, plenty of time to plan for this and two other cruises to the South Atlantic.

DELAYS ARE A SOURCE OF FRUSTRATION FOR SCIENTISTS, but delays also bring forth unexpected dividends. One advantage was the opportunity to make use of the most advanced technology.

Although the "standard product code" of remnant magnetism had been worked out by using the stripes of ocean crust that originate at the axis of seafloor spreading, magnetostratigraphy had never been applied to the sequence of sediments which can be sampled in the ocean only by drilling. Deep-sea drilling cores taken during the first decade of the project were not suitable because they were almost invariably disturbed by rotary drills. Also the recovery was rarely 100 percent, and a perfect recovery is indispensable for a complete register of polarity reversals. So be it, we thought.

We scientists are often ignorant of the potential of

engineering developments. While we were resigned to
imperfect cores, development engineers employed by the
Deep Sea Drilling Project were unaware that we considered that a problem. Stan Serucki, a colleague during my
days with Shell, had worked for the project almost a decade before he learned by chance that we needed undisturbed cores for precise dating. The engineering problem
turned out to be quite easy to resolve. Instead of the
conventional practice of cutting a long core with a rotary
drill bit, Serucki developed the hydraulic piston corer. A
steel barrel, driven by hydraulic pressure, is sent
through the rotary drill collar to take a core. This piston-
coring technique does not disturb the sample and assures
complete recovery with no samples lost.

In the summer of 1979, when I was in China, a letter
came from Jim Hays of Lamont. He was ecstatic after
the successful first trial of the piston corer during a drilling cruise to the Gulf of California. "Next to the dynamically positioned drill vessel," he wrote, "the
hydraulic-piston-corer is the greatest gift to students of
ocean history." We could now attain the precision to describe happenings of short duration. Instead of having to
reckon with million-year averages obtained from
smashed and incomplete cores, we would be able to
identify an event recorded by an ocean sediment deposited in a century or a millennium. Hays wanted support
from his colleagues to interrupt the normal drilling
schedule with a special cruise to try out the new gadget.
This meant a further delay of my South Atlantic cruise.
Nevertheless, he was right; I would rather do my job
later if I could do it better. We should give the new corer
a chance.

The invention of the new coring apparatus also gave
impetus to the Deep Sea Drilling Project; the international phase was extended until 1983. Thus I found during the first planning session after I came back from
China that our mandate was enlarged. We now planned
for five, instead of three, drilling expeditions to the
South Atlantic. One whole cruise was to be devoted to
the Mid-Atlantic Ridge sites. For precise determination

of sediment ages, the hydraulic piston corer was to be used if possible. Seven drill sites of first priority were chosen for Leg 73 of the Deep Sea Drilling Project.

I joined *Glomar Challenger* at Santos, Brazil, for my fifth tour of service. A young specialist on seafloor magnetic anomalies, John LaBrecque of Lamont, was my co-chief scientist. Three old friends, Max Carman of the University of Houston, Steve Percival of Mobil Oil Company, and Ray Wright of Florida University, as well as two former students, Judy McKenzie and Helmut Weissert, came along as shipboard scientists. The American-Swiss contingent was reinforced by colleagues from Britain, France, and Germany.

The drill vessel sailed on April 13, 1980, just before my article on the terminal Cretaceous catastrophe was to appear in *Nature*. Ten days of steaming time before we were due to arrive at our first drill site gave plenty of opportunity to discuss our latest project. I had brought along a copy of the galley proof of my article. On our long journey toward the first drill site, I endeavored to convey to my colleagues my enthusiasm and my interest in the question of mass extinction, and why the subject was relevant to the project at hand.

Not that my original proposal in 1975 included an investigation of the Cretaceous boundary: I had not appreciated its significance then and focused only on the ups and downs of the Miocene calcite compensation depth, not the startling rise of the CCD that Tom Worsely proposed, and which coincided with the end of the Cretaceous. After our mandate was expanded, we had formulated a proposal to investigate the whole Cenozoic, that is, right down to the boundary with the Cretaceous, but still the boundary itself did not figure in the drilling plan. A proposal to study the boundary by Isabella Premoli-Silva had been all but ignored.

The lack of enthusiasm could be traced to the fact that deep-sea drilling efforts had never been able to core a continuous and undisturbed sequence across the Cretaceous-Tertiary boundary. True, we had twice during Leg 3 drilled *through* the boundary, but our paleontologists told us that where the actual boundary should have been there was nothing. The same story was repeated over and over again during subsequent deep-sea drilling expeditions. For one reason or another, either the youngest Cretaceous, or the oldest Tertiary, or both, were missing —disturbed, incompletely recovered, or not available for study because we neglected to core the critical section.

The invention of the hydraulic piston corer did not fuel optimism, because the corer cannot punch through very hard sediments or penetrate much below 250 meters. The last Cretaceous sediments, deposited 65 million years ago, are commonly buried 0.5 or 1 kilometer (500 to 1,000 meters) below the seafloor. They are, as a rule, too compacted and too deep to be reached by the hydraulic piston corer.

My own optimism had been boosted, however, shortly before I boarded the *Glomar Challenger* by a colleague's offhand remark during the very last planning session in February. Dieter Fütterer of Kiel gave a short report of some research his team had done the previous summer aboard the R/S *Jean Charrot*. He mentioned, more or less in passing, that a sediment of Paleocene age had been obtained just below the seafloor by conventional piston coring at a place not far from one of our proposed sites in Cape Basin, west of Capetown.

The Paleocene is the earliest epoch of the 65-million-year Cenozoic era, spanning its first 10 million years. Sediments of this age are normally buried under hundreds of meters of younger deposits. Now Fütterer told us that the Paleocene sediment at that site directly underlies the modern seafloor. Its contact with the Cretaceous could not be very far below, perhaps at a depth of 100 or 200 meters below the present floor, well within the reach of the hydraulic piston corer. It would be a bonanza indeed if we could obtain samples across the boundary by this new coring method.

My shipboard colleagues were impressed by my reasoning, but the Cape Basin site had been assigned third priority, and first had to come first. From April 23 to May 19, we drilled five transect holes on the east flank of the Mid-Atlantic Ridge, as originally planned. We had good luck. The weather was fine, the operations went smoothly, and few time-consuming mistakes were made. Our work was almost done, and we were now more than halfway across the South Atlantic. We had originally planned seven holes on the transect. The first drilling results indicated to us that the holes had been too densely spaced. After we completed the first four we skipped the fifth hole on the transect and were now finishing the sixth. The schedule dictated that we had to dock in Capetown on June 1. We had only enough time to drill one more hole.

We could go to the seventh site, but it could be omitted without great harm to our transect project. Or we could go to the Cape Basin site, where the Cretaceous-Tertiary boundary might be penetrated by hydraulic piston coring.

I called a staff meeting in the morning of May 19. We stood around the work table and a straw vote was taken. Everyone wanted to go for broke. It was a gamble, to be sure, to leave a first-priority hole undrilled for a third-priority objective. Yet it was allowable to make tactical decisions during a voyage. We drafted a telegram to the chief scientist of the project, asking permission to drill the Cape Basin site, and steamed the drill vessel in that direction while awaiting formal approval.

The target site, number 524 of the Deep Sea Drilling Project, was located about 1,000 kilometers west of Capetown. We arrived there on the evening of May 21 and promptly ran into a string of bad luck. The start of drilling was delayed because the engineering department wanted to test a new piece of equipment. It was a total failure. The designer of the test package forgot to check with the drilling department and made a casing with an outer diameter exactly the same as the inner diameter of the hollow drill bit. The package in its casing was pumped down and got stuck inside the bit. No test was possible, and no drilling was possible. The roughnecks had to raise all 4,000 meters of pipe up again to remove the blocked drill bit before they could assemble a new string of pipes. The delay cost us twenty-four hours and $50,000 worth of science.

The hydraulic piston coring operation began finally at noon on May 23. The sediment we quickly encountered was Paleocene as we had expected on the basis of Fütterer's report, but we were soon to meet another disappointment. At a depth of about 30 meters, we hit flint, the hard rock composed of cemented skeletal debris of radiolaria, and the piston corer could not punch through. We were stuck in the Paleocene. With our hope of using this corer to sample the boundary dashed, we had to start all over again, using only the rotary driller to penetrate the hard layer in a second hole, but now the samples were merely conventional rotary cores, subject to discontinuity and damage. Still we had a chance and we pushed on.

Meanwhile the captain showed up in the Core Laboratory. He had bad news for us. After we had foolishly squandered precious hours of calm sea on a stupid mistake in instrument design, Neptune was to manifest his waves of anger. We were threatened by an invading storm front due to arrive at 6 o'clock the next morning. The captain would like us to drill a little faster. The lower end of a drill string is most delicate and easily broken. We would have a better chance to avoid damage if this delicate segment were well buried in ocean sediments when the storm came. We would have liked to drill faster too, but there were technical limitations. Fortunately the storm never came; the front turned abruptly east after reaching a spot 100 kilometers south of the vessel.

We had good weather on the following day, May 24. Cores were hauled up at a rate of one every two hours. We drilled deeper and deeper. The cores were not much disturbed, even though we were using the conventional technique. Recovery was also good; we were getting a nearly full barrel of sample material each time our sampling device was hauled up.

The samples were studied on board ship immediately. The paleontologists investigated the foraminifers and nannofossils. The geophysicists spun a magnetometer to determine the polarity of remnant magnetism of each sample.

Nannoplankton assemblages in ocean sediments differ with age and on that basis are divided into dynasties called *zones*. There are about fifty nannofossil zones in the Cenozoic, of which most at our site had been removed by erosion. Like the dynasties of Egyptian pharaohs, the nannofossil zones are given consecutive numbers. The first zone we cored was of the Paleogene zone, a reference to the first half of the Cenozoic, and its number was 13, or Nannofossil Paleogene 13, abbreviated NP 13. Our goal was NP 1, the very first sediment of the Paleogene zone that would be found directly on top of the boundary with the Cretaceous. We drilled quickly through NP 12, 11, 10, 9, 8, 7, 6, 5, 4 and were in Zone NP 3 at midday of May 24, when Core 13 from the new hole came up. We all waited eagerly for the sample across the Cretaceous-Tertiary boundary below the sediments of NP 1.

Meanwhile, the magnetometer spinners were confirming the ages of the samples as determined by the paleontologists. We had gone past Chrons C-24-N, C-24-R, C-25-N, C-25-R, C-26-N, C-26-R and had hit Chron C-27-N, which correlates with the paleontological age of NP 3. The boundary would lie within the infamous Chron C-29-R.

The sediments of Zone NP 3 turned out to be very thick. All afternoon, nannoplankton specialist Percival found nothing new. Every hour after a new core came up, he would chalk up *N*annofossil *P*aleogene 3 on the inventory blackboard in our lab. After he had repeated the exercise four or five times, we began to tease him and wrote "*N*othing-new *P*ercival 3" for his inventory. Percival did not identify any fossils in Zone NP 2 until 9 o'clock in the evening. Then the captain showed up again. The weather forecast was discouraging. Another storm was due next morning. We might, the captain warned, have to pull the pipes out of the borehole if the front should come. It was now a race between the slowly grinding drill and the fast-moving front. Could we reach through NP 1 and into C-29-R before the storm came? Would we be lucky enough to recover a core sample across the boundary?

We waited impatiently and anxiously. At 1 o'clock in the morning on May 25, Percival told me that Core 19, hauled up some hours before, contained Cretaceous nannofossils.

"But how about nannofossil Zone NP 1? We have not reached Zone NP 1 yet."

"There are no NP 1 fossils," Percival answered.

We were all very disappointed. It was well past midnight, and the storm was coming. Too discouraged to face the coming crisis, I asked my co-chief John LaBrecque to take over my supervising duties. I went to bed.

When I woke up, I was greeted by a glorious morning, sunshine and blue sky. The storm had not materialized. Like its predecessor, it also had turned east, this time after coming within 50 kilometers of our drill site.

I went to the Core Laboratory. Percival told me to look for myself at the contact between Nannofossil Zone NP 2 and the uppermost Cretaceous in Core 19. He had not found any of the earliest Tertiary nannoplankton species. There had to be a gap in the sequence, Percival thought, an erosion surface where the boundary should have been.

I stood in front of the core and examined the cut surface with a magnifying glass. Pelagic sediments falling from above onto sea bottom are comparable to snowfall accumulations on ground. Where the air is dirty, one can often see laminations where layers of snow alternate with layers of dirt. The oldest Tertiary sediment in our core showed the same laminated structure, and I could discern an alteration of paper-thin layers of slightly different compositions. If there had been erosion, the very regular laminations would have been interrupted by an irregular surface that cut through and truncated the pattern. But I could find no such surface of interrupted sedimentation. Besides, a gap just did not make sense to me. The Cape Basin where we were drilling is called that because it is a depression. Sediments on shallow shelves or on submarine ridges might be removed by the flow of bottom currents, but where could the sediments in a basin go? Instead of a missing interval we should have the unusually thick and complete sample known as an expanded sedimentary section. Indeed, the other Paleocene sediments, like the very thick NP 3 one, had all been expanded. Now Percival was telling me that the earliest Paleocene sediments were missing altogether.

Percival had been up all night as three more cores following core 19 had been hauled aboard; now he took to his cabin for a rest. Alone in his laboratory, I went through his notes. Core 20 had come up at 3:30, 21 at 5:30, and 22 at 7:30 A.M. Percival had taken a quick look at them. He found abundant nannofossils of Cretaceous age in all but the upper half of Core 20. Samples taken from the top 3 meters of that core seemed to contain no nannofossils. Percival had written on his work sheet the remark, "Barren of nannofossils after cursory examination."

This was strange indeed. Everywhere else in the world, fossil organisms had flourished until the very end of the Cretaceous; only the first Paleogene sediments, those laid on the boundary itself, are ever barren of fossils. The boundary clay is, furthermore, usually only a few millimeters or, at most, a few centimeters thick. It did not make sense to have a barren interval 3 meters thick just below the youngest Cretaceous sediments. Had Percival committed an error in his haste and fatigue during the wee hours of the morning?

Percival had always been the old reliable. We had sailed together during Leg 3, our first cruise. When I had planned for a drilling expedition to the Black Sea, I requested that he be appointed the shipboard micropaleontologist, and we had spent some time together again on *Glomar Challenger* after she sailed through the Bosporus in 1975. He impressed me with his hard work, his cooperative spirit, and his cheerful manner; he would often stay on duty for thirty-six or forty-eight hours with little sleep. So when we discussed the staffing for the Leg 73 drilling, I had asked for the third time for the services of Percival. I had absolute trust in him.

While I puzzled over the matter, Percival showed up at the lab again after his brief nap. Core 23 came up at 9:30 A.M. I approached him after he had made his routine examination of the new samples and asked him about the barren interval.

No, he was not certain it was barren. It had been late, or more exactly very early in the morning, and he had not tried very hard to search for tiny nannofossils in the clayey sediments. Now that he had slept almost two hours, he felt able to reexamine those samples again.

Leaving Percival to work in peace, I went up to the bridge to chat with the weatherman, the meteorologist whose computer-printed satellite pictures gave us advance warning of the late May storms that usher in the austral winter.

Our conversation was interrupted by a message through the intercom system; I was wanted at Percival's lab. I hopped and skipped my way downstairs and found Percival all smiles. He had found fossils in the apparently barren interval, and he had identified the earliest Tertiary nannofossil among them. He now believed that the Cretaceous nannofossils in Core 19 were "reworked" fossils, ones that had been unearthed from a Cretaceous sediment and reburied higher up in an early Tertiary sediment. The boundary was not in Core 19; it was in Core 20. The succession was not interrupted by erosion. The sequence was one of continuous deposition, passing from the latest Cretaceous to the earliest Tertiary.

We had hit paydirt. The first three segments of Core 20 at DSDP Site 524 were eventually to become one of the most thoroughly investigated sections of deep-sea drilling cores.

The Paleocene sediments at the Cape Basin site had been deposited at an unusually high rate of about 3 centimeters per thousand years. The boundary clay, less than a centimeter thick at Gubbio, is several times thicker here. The earliest Paleogene nannofossil zone, NP 1, is more than 3 meters thick and thus provides an excellent opportunity to investigate biological changes across the boundary.

Percival determined the nannoplankton assemblages in samples spaced only centimeters apart, representing intervals of one thousand years or less. My colleague at Zurich, Käthi Perch-Nielsen, did the same. Dick Poore of the U.S. Geological Survey and Jan Smit of Amsterdam examined the foraminifers. The extinction seemed, at first glance, the same as elsewhere: mass extinction of Cretaceous nannoplankton and foraminiferal species, suddenly and without forewarning. The extinction horizon was overlain by a boundary clay almost devoid of all fossils. Then came the Tertiary species. Phytoplankton and zooplankton appear at first as a few species represented by rare individuals. This general scarcity of fossils had been the reason Percival had failed to see any in the upper half of Core 20 when he had first peered into the microscope during the dark hours before dawn.

BEFORE I HAD A CHANCE TO DELVE INTO THE NEW DATA, I had had a simplistic picture of the change in fossil content across the boundary. I had been told when examining the boundary clay at Gubbio that one could put a knife edge at the contact, and that was true of those samples. All fossils found below the contact belonged to the Cretaceous, and all those above belonged to the Tertiary. But what had been a razor-thin boundary at Gubbio and in the Danish Fish Clay was in Core 20 stretched to a multimeter-thick transition zone. That gave the first detailed record of what had happened there 65 million years before. Percival had come upon the first Cretaceous nannofossils at the bottom of Core 19, which was not Cretaceous at all. He had not made a mistake: Those fossils were there. But he had also identified Tertiary species in the same sample. Now if the very highest occurrence of a Cretaceous species were to have marked the boundary, it would have been somewhere in Core 19, as Percival had thought initially. The common practice is, however, to draw the boundary where the first Tertiary forms appear. This horizon, as Percival and Perch-

Nielsen eventually determined, is way down, at 4.05 meters below the top of Core 20. There is an interval of about 4 meters above the Cretaceous-Tertiary boundary in which Cretaceous and Tertiary fossils are found together, although the percentage of old species decreases steadily upward in this transition zone. Could they have been descendants of the survivors of the months-long blackout, evidence that darkness alone was not enough to cause the extinction of Cretaceous plankton?

Talking to Percival and, later, to other experts, I found that they were not surprised that such a transition zone existed, except that the zone was unusually thick at the Cape Basin site. The experts had discerned a similar transition zone everywhere. It was news to me, however, and I asked for clarification.

Nannofossils are so small, Percival explained, that they are moved around by any slight movement of bottom water. Much to my disappointment, he felt that the Cretaceous fossils were probably skeletons of organisms that had lived before the beginning of the Tertiary but had later become mixed with Tertiary fossils in the sediments of this transitional zone.

Hans Thierstein of Scripps blamed the movement on burrowing organisms that inhabit the seafloor. He had studied sediments above the boundary at a West Atlantic deep-sea drilling site where the boundary had been disturbed by worms and other creatures burrowing through the sediments. Mixing of the earliest Tertiary and the latest Cretaceous sediments was, in Thierstein's view, unavoidable.

Although we found little evidence of disturbance by burrowing organisms here at Site 524—the delicately layered structure of the fine sediments above the boundary had been well preserved—the possibility of reburial by bottom currents remained. How could we distinguish the skeletons of organisms that had died in a terminal Cretaceous holocaust from those that had possibly lived in the earliest Tertiary oceans, descendants of the survivors? To resolve this question, we needed help from chemistry again.

* * *

THE CHEMISTRY OF MARINE FOSSILS CHANGES IF OCEAN chemistry has changed. When you go to the beach to collect shells, those that lived before and after 1945 may all look alike. Yet the shells of the atomic era are characterized by their content of strontium 90, the radioactive isotope that contaminated oceans during the dropping and testing of nuclear bombs after 1945. Shells, bones, and teeth of organisms living since that time are now all imprinted with this isotopic signal in contrast to the nonradioactive skeletons of the prebomb era.

"Precatastrophe" plankton fossils also have a different isotope imprint than those that lived after the end of the Cretaceous. That 5-degree temperature rise Shackleton had discovered at the boundary, for instance, altered the ratios of oxygen 18 and oxygen 16 in such fossils for several millennia after the catastrophe. Two other geochemists, J. C. Brennecke and Tom Anderson, found in 1977 that carbon-isotope ratios were also distinctly different in latest Cretaceous and earliest Tertiary fossils. Isotope analyses could, therefore, discriminate pre- from postcatastrophe fossil skeletons.

OUR SOUTH ATLANTIC EXPEDITION ENDED ON JUNE 1, 1980, when *Glomar Challenger* docked at Capetown. Three boxes of samples were air-freighted to Zurich. I had then a hardworking trainee, Qixiang He from the People's Republic of China. He unpacked the parcels and, after sending portions of several samples near the Cretaceous-Tertiary boundary to Urs Krähenbühl at the University of Bern for neutron-activation analysis, went right to work.

After a month Krähenbühl told us that there was an iridium anomaly exactly at the horizon where Percival had placed the boundary; the first Tertiary nannoplankton species appeared at the very horizon where the iridium concentration suddenly leaped from the background value of 0.1 part per billion to a peak of 3.6 parts per billion. This horizon lies within C-29-R, as magnetostratigraphic work by our shipmates Lisa Tauxe, Nikolai Peterson, and Peter Tucker had already shown. The pieces were so far falling into place, except for the presence of supposedly Cretaceous fossils in the earliest Tertiary sediments. Isotope analysis would decide whether they were skeletons of Cretaceous nannoplankton already dead or killed when the comet hit, or fossil remains of the descendants of survivors of species, which, although doomed for imminent extinction—as we know from the geological record—had struggled on for several millennia.

I did not stay in Zurich to wait for the answer. The People's Republic invited me on an excursion to Tibet. I was at the Government Guest House of Lhasa, after a sight-seeing tour to the Portola, when I opened a letter from my colleague Judy McKenzie. Our trainee Qixiang He had analyzed hundreds of our samples from the South Atlantic in our isotope laboratory. Both the oxygen and carbon isotope anomalies had been found, and exactly at the boundary where the iridium anomaly occurred. We had assumed the boundary clay was deposited in the early years of the Tertiary, because it contained key species from that period, and now isotope analysis had confirmed that observation. Yet Perch-Nielsen, examining the nannofossil assemblages in the boundary clay, found that the bulk of them, 90 percent, are taxonomically the same as those in the underlying Cretaceous sediments. Perch-Nielsen made systematic counts and found that the percentage of fossils belonging to Cretaceous taxa decreases to a negligible amount only at a level some 2 meters above the boundary, or perhaps as many as fifty thousand years after the catastrophe that caused the iridium anomaly.

Their isotope chemistry is the fingerprint that identified these "Cretaceous" fossils in the transition zone as the remnants of populations that continued for a while to live in the earliest postcatastrophe ocean. If this interpretation is correct, we have to conclude that the three or four months of blackout did not do the trick; many Cretaceous nannoplankton groups must have revived after the sunlight returned. But somehow the damage had been done; the descendants of the survivors were headed toward oblivion.

IF NANNOPLANKTON HAD OUTLIVED THE BLACKOUT, how did foraminifers fare? Jan Smit of Utrecht made a survey of the global micropaleontological records across the Cretaceous-Tertiary boundary. Although he agreed with our conclusion that nannoplankton extinction was accomplished within tens of thousands of years, he found evidence of a more sudden extinction of zooplankton. At Caravaca, Spain, for example, the foraminiferal transition zone is only a few centimeters thick, in contrast to the meter-thick nannoplankton transition. The more robust Cretaceous Globotruncanas and Ruboglobigerinids disappear, but small and very small forms which occurred only rarely in the uppermost Cretaceous suddenly became more numerous. Those species had lived through the catastrophe but faced "imminent" extinction: The last of even the tiniest Cretaceous species were to disappear from the scene 10 centimeters above the boundary, some three thousand or four thousand years after the event that produced the iridium anomaly. The last Cretaceous foraminifers were then replaced by the typically Tertiary eugubinas.

How long did it take before the dinosaurs became extinct? Leigh Van Valen of the University of Chicago thought he had found the last dinosaurs and the first Cenozoic mammals together in the Bug Creek formation of Montana. He estimated that the Cretaceous-Tertiary transition had a time span of fifty thousand years. The Berkeley paleontologist Bill Clemens also held this view. Jan Smit disagreed, however, after he and his students investigated the depositional history of the Bug Creek formation. They found an earlier flood plain deposit and a later river channel sand. All dinosaur bones were found in the flood plain deposit, which includes an iridium-rich horizon. The river channel was later cut into the older flood plain, and all mammal bones were buried in the river channel. The Dutch scientists believed, therefore, that the dinosaurs died out before these mammals invaded Montana.

Heinrich Erben, an expert on dinosaur eggs at Bonn University, maintained that some dinosaurs survived the "final event" at the end of the Cretaceous. In a talk at Strasbourg in 1983, he claimed that dinosaur eggs found in the uppermost Cretaceous sediments are all normal, but that five "horizons containing pathological dinosaur eggshells" can be dated as Paleocene. Erben has not yet published his detailed results, and no doubt the work of many others is still to be completed before we will have the last word on whether those giant monsters died on doomsday when Earth was covered by darkness, or whether they survived the shock only to suffer the fate of eventual extinction more slowly.

Opinions have nevertheless converged during the last few years that although the terminal Cretaceous event caused mass mortality, it did not cause immediate extinction. There is irony in this. For decades scientists who suspected that a global catastrophe had caused the great dying were challenged to prove that the extinctions had been sudden and rapid. Now that a global catastrophe is largely accepted, it turns out that extinction was probably not so rapid after all. We are now challenged to explain how it could have been so slow.

11

A Strangelove Ocean

I HAD KNOWN JUDY MCKENZIE SINCE 1972 WHEN, ON sabbatical from my university in Zürich, I was a guest professor at the Scripps Institution of Oceanography at La Jolla, California. I gave one course, on the geology of the Swiss Alps. The subject did not have much relevance to students of oceanography. Some graduate students and young instructors attended my classes, attracted more by scenic photographs of the Alps than by my lectures. Judy McKenzie was one of those who came. She was always very helpful, hanging up a map, looking for a slide projector, or reproducing handouts as the occasion required. Judy McKenzie was a student of isotope geochemistry. One day she came to visit.

"What are you doing for a thesis?" I asked.

"I work on geo-secs."

"Geo-sex?"

"Not s-e-x, s-e-c-s. It's a big project to study the chemistry of ocean waters along certain cross s-e-c-tions."

"What do you have to do, then?"

"I am building an extraction line for nitrogen to be fed to a mass spectrometer."

I could not understand why anyone should be interested in the isotopic composition of dissolved gases in seawater, nor could McKenzie exactly. She had, in fact, come to ask me whether I had some more "visible" project, something in which she could see what she was doing. Yes, I had one. A group of us in Zürich were doing research on the recent sediments of the Persian Gulf, and our team needed an isotope geochemist. McKenzie eventually came to Zürich and did her Ph.D. dissertation with us in the Persian Gulf area.

Little did I know that a decade later geo-secs were to provide our first understanding of how a meteorite collision could cause extinction over millennia.

THERE IS AN ANALOGY BETWEEN WARS, THE CATAStrophes we bring on ourselves, and natural catastrophes. We have many examples in human history of the rapid recovery of the population of war-devastated lands. Rapid recovery of species after natural catastrophes is also typical. David Raup has estimated that even if a catastrophe were to kill all the organisms on one-quarter of the earth's surface, only 2 percent of the species would become extinct. The reason is that most species have what is called a cosmopolitan distribution: They live widely scattered over the face of the earth. Total annihilation at one region may wipe out the population there, but not exterminate a race. In the aftermath of a catastrophe immigrants repopulate the devastated area and begin to multiply.

There can be, however, some unforeseen consequences of a very great catastrophe. Take the hypothetical case of a global nuclear war. Many may survive such a holocaust; more than a few Maoris or Patagonian Indians might live through the disaster in their isolated corners of the world. But they and their descendants could not repeople a world made unviable for their kind by environmental destruction. In a study conducted by the International Council of Scientific Unions a committee of experts came up with a "nuclear winter" scenario. They soberly concluded that in the aftermath of a nuclear war, the species *Homo sapiens* could well be doomed to eventual extinction. Could the impact at the end of the Cretaceous similarly have destroyed environments, dooming survivors of the dark months to extinction even tens of thousands of years after the holocaust?

Luckily for us who seek the answer to that question not all students ask for the more visible. Students like Peter Kropnick, McKenzie's classmate, persisted with geo-secs and did very valuable research for his dissertation. Data from the geo-secs research, and data McKenzie later gathered by isotope analysis of lake sediments, ultimately clarified what may have happened 65 million years ago to make the oceans an unviable environment for the plankton of that time.

WE TEND TO THINK OF THE OCEAN AS A VERY HOMOGENeous body of water with a certain chemical composition, an average salinity, and a mean annual temperature. Yet there are differences from one portion to another, and the differences are what make the ocean run.

The ocean is not static. Winds and tides generate surface currents, knowledge quite useful to ancient mariners. There is also dynamic movement of intermediate and bottom ocean waters. German submarine commanders were quite aware of that and during World War II used these currents to evade detection. When entering and leaving the Mediterranean where the British Naval Command at Gibraltar had a listening station, they shut off their motors. To enter, the submarine dived to a shallow depth and rode the surface current which carries Atlantic waters into the Mediterranean; to leave, it dove deeper to move out with the bottom current.

The Mediterranean water returns to the Atlantic as a bottom current because it is heavier than water entering from the ocean. It is heavier because it has suffered much evaporative loss, and because it has been chilled by the cold wind that blows over it from Europe. Underwater streams similar to the Mediterranean bottom current have been detected deep in the Atlantic, Pacific, and Indian oceans, too. Where does the saltier, colder, and denser water come from?

Two major sources of ocean bottom waters are the Weddell Sea in the Antarctic and the Norwegian Sea in the Atlantic. Cold polar waters there become saltier than usual when sea ice is formed, and the density increase makes enough of a hydraulic head to drive the bottom-current circulation of the oceans. The polar seas have been considered the lungs of the oceans because they are the primary sites of oxygen intake. Bottom circulation can therefore be compared to blood circulation, for within those currents oxygen is circulated to all parts of the ocean bottom to be consumed by the metabolism of organisms while they live, and by their decay when they are dead.

The atmosphere is the ultimate source of oxygen, and surface waters in general are rich in it. But they are especially rich in polar regions because more gas can be dissolved in colder water. As this oxygen-rich water descends to the abyss, it oxygenates the ocean bottom. That is why ocean clays have rusted to a bright color in many places, for iron in its more oxidized state is a red compound.

Between the surface and the abyss, at intermediate depth, water is relatively stagnant in many regions and is not rich in oxygen. The sediments at that level are commonly gray, or even colored black by minute particles of organic matter not quite oxidized in this oxygen-minimum zone. Numbers illustrating this pattern of oxygen distribution have been ground out by workers like Kropnick in the geo-secs project, under the supervision of Wallace Broecker of Lamont and Harmon Craig of Scripps.

Carbon dioxide is a crucial compound for life processes, for it is the basic "food" for all organisms. Plants photosynthesize from carbon dioxide and water the sugar from which they build cell tissues. Vegetables and grains feed us, either directly or indirectly, through their conversion by herbivorous animals into the meat we eat.

When we die, our dead bodies decay, releasing again the carbon dioxide and water. Both eventually find their way back to the ocean and the atmosphere.

Carbon dioxide, despite its importance, is a quantitatively insignificant component of the atmosphere, making up only 0.03 percent of air, compared to 20 percent oxygen. Although far more soluble than other atmospheric gases, the total dissolved carbon dioxide in ocean water is still less than 1 gram per liter at the surface. The amounts of carbon dioxide in the atmosphere and in the ocean are related to one another: The more carbon dioxide is in the air, the more is dissolved in the ocean, and vice versa. The amount of the gas dissolved in water is also modulated by the changing productivity of marine phytoplankton. A fertile ocean with frequent plankton blooms uses up a lot of carbon dioxide, and the ocean surface water is depleted in the dissolved gas. A sterile ocean, one in which for any reason plankton fail to thrive, is enriched in carbon dioxide.

Carbon dioxide depletion is a near-surface phenomenon because phytoplanktons live only in the very shallow depth where enough light penetrates for photosynthesis, commonly not more than 50 meters. Deeper ocean water is not depleted in carbon dioxide but instead is enriched in it. That is because decay of the dead organisms that drift down produces the gas, and it is readily dissolved in cold bottom waters.

Exchange of carbon dioxide from ocean to atmosphere is, like the exchange of oxygen, a result of circulation. Deep ocean water wells up from the bottom in coastal and other regions. The dissolved carbon dioxide gas can then bubble out again and replenish atmospheric carbon dioxide. Atmospheric gas is in turn dissolved in surface water, consumed by phytoplankton, and sunk with their corpses to the bottom. This recycling of carbon dioxide is going on all the time. Wallace Broecker, using radioactive carbon 14 as a tracer, found that about half a trillion tons of atmospheric carbon dioxide goes annually into ocean surface water to be picked up by phytoplankton, released to the deep after their death, distributed by ocean-bottom currents, and returned to the surface after some two thousand years.

This two-thousand-year recycling is a dynamically steady state. In the thin surface layer of light penetration where plankton grow, the seawater is always depleted in carbon dioxide. The bulk of the ocean, homogenized by current circulation, remains relatively enriched by the carbon dioxide derived from organic decay, especially in the stagnant intermediate depths where oxygen is at a minimum. This pattern of dissolved carbon dioxide distribution in the ocean has also been charted by geo-secs scientists.

Dissolved carbon dioxide is carbonic acid, a weak acid, but an acid nevertheless. This is one reason why soda pop is bad for your teeth; the dissolved carbon dioxide that, as it reenters the atmosphere is the bubbles that pop at the surface, corrodes tooth enamel. In the oceans, carbon dioxide-rich water attacks dead shells and bones, which commonly consist of calcium carbonate. That we should have any lime ooze deposited on the sea bottom at all is due to the fact that skeletons from dead nannoplankton and foraminifers accumulate above the calcite compensation depth at a faster rate than the weak carbonic acid in the bottom water can dissolve them away. Only where the rate of dissolving is greater than the rate of accumulation is the bottom sediment a clay like that at the Cretaceous-Tertiary boundary.

At Gubbio and at many other localities late Cretaceous and early Tertiary sediments are chalks or limestones, accumulations of the minute skeletons of foraminifers and nannoplankton that thrived before and after the catastrophe. In between, just above the boundary event marked by the iridium anomaly, is a thin layer of clay. In other places the boundary sediment, although a limestone, has a higher proportion of clay than immediately underlying and overlying sediments. When Thomas Worsley noticed this depletion in calcium carbonate in the boundary sediments he studied in 1970, he suggested that the ocean water had been unusually corrosive, unusually rich in dissolved carbon dioxide at the end of the

Cretaceous. Unusual seawater chemistry would have dissolved plankton skeletons, leaving only the insoluble residue that is the boundary clay.

On the other hand, the boundary clay could just as easily be the result of a failing supply of skeletons, and we can go a step further and say that the supply of dead plankton failed because there were very few living ones. The sediment of a sterile ocean, like that of a corrosive one, would be a lime-free clay. How do we resolve this question?

The geo-secs project and our own studies of lake sediments led to a suggestion: we can use carbon isotopes as a monitor of ancient plankton productivity.

In making mass spectrometer analysis of calcium carbonate, a rock sample is dissolved and produces carbon dioxide gas, which is fed into the instrument. Harold Urey, in his work on a paleothermometer, measured the oxygen-isotope ratio of his samples. At the same time, he obtained values of their carbon-isotope composition. He could not understand those results. He was sure that the carbon-isotope composition could not be influenced very much by the temperature of the environment in which an organism secretes its skeleton. He found various carbon-isotope values, but he could find no correlation between them and any other variable, either in fossil specimens or in present-day ones.

Carbon-isotope data for ocean sediments were in fact gathered for decades, but they were not always published because scientists could not understand the results. The problem was discussed in a forum during an international conference on marine planktons at Kiel in 1973. Nobody had a very good idea then. Oxygen-isotope analyses could give useful data on ancient ocean temperature, but carbon-isotope analyses yielded only numbers, seemingly meaningless.

In the mass of data produced by the geo-secs project, a pattern finally emerged. At station after station, scientists saw the same systematic variation of carbon-isotope composition: Surface waters always have a higher ratio of carbon 13 to carbon 12 (or relatively more carbon 13 atoms) than the intermediate and bottom waters.

Once the trend was recognized, the explanation of carbon-isotope data from sediments came easily. Lime oozes are fossil skeletons which organisms build by removing calcium and dissolved carbon dioxide from seawater. The calcium carbonate skeletons contain thus both carbon 13 and carbon 12 atoms originated from the carbon dioxide, and the relative abundance of the two isotopes is chemically determined by the original abundance in the raw material. The more carbon 13 is dissolved, the more carbon 13 is taken up. The carbon-isotope composition of the carbonate in shells thus simply reflects that of the dissolved carbon dioxide in the water where they lived, and the same is true of fossils or the calcareous sediments they become.

The same is not true of the living soft tissues or cells of organisms. They take up a substantially lesser proportion of carbon 13 from the surrounding water no matter what its isotopic composition. Because the soft tissues of organisms, unlike their shells, incorporate carbon 12 preferentially, they can have an effect on the isotopic composition of the water in which the organisms live.

Living phytoplankton and zooplankton are present only in surface waters. Because their cell tissues prefer carbon 12 to carbon 13 atoms, surface seawater becomes enriched with unused carbon 13 atoms wherever plankton flourish. Bottom dwellers also shy away from carbon 13, but they are too few to have much effect, so that bottom water has a proportion of carbon 13 not much different from that of average ocean water.

IF BOTH THE DEPLETION OF CARBON DIOXIDE AND THE relative enrichment of carbon 13 atoms in surface waters of the ocean are the work of living plankton, what would happen if there were no living plankton in the oceans? I posed the question to Wally Broecker in 1981, when he came to our institute to deliver a lecture on the carbon isotopes of the oceans.

I had known Broecker for some time through his reputation and through mutual friends. He is a respected expert on marine geochemistry, the field of specialization of my young colleague, Judy McKenzie. When she applied for a fellowship in the Geological Society of America, I nominated Broecker as one of the three sponsors she required. Fellowship in professional societies is like membership in a union; all senior researchers in the Earth sciences in North America are fellows of the Geological Society, I assumed. I was rudely surprised by a curt letter from the headquarters of the society. Broecker could not sponsor McKenzie's application for a fellowship, I was informed, because he himself was no longer a fellow of the society. The busy scientist had forgotten to pay his annual dues.

Broecker is best known for his work on carbon dioxide cycling in the oceans. Ideas are always bubbling out of him like the gas out of soda pop. After several years of administrative duties at Lamont, he had taken a sabbatical leave at Heidelberg. A Swiss friend from our pollution-control research center heard of it and called me to ask whether we could bring him over to Zurich for a lecture series. I was indeed pleased to have him visit, even though he was no longer a member of our "union."

One of the most exciting scientific discoveries in the early 1980s was made by chemists analyzing the composition of air trapped many thousands of years ago as bubbles in ancient, still frozen ice: They found a substantially lower concentration of carbon dioxide in "fossil" air trapped during the Ice Age. Broecker, ever quick on the draw, had immediately come up with an explanation of why the Ice Age atmosphere was depleted in carbon dioxide.

During the Ice Age, when the upwelling of nutrient-rich bottom waters was augmented, the ocean surface was more fertile than it is today. Plankton must have been unusually productive at that time. The more plankton there are, the more carbon dioxide they consume, and the more the atmosphere becomes depleted in this gas. Ocean sediments provide some evidence that plankton fertility was indeed greater during the Ice Age than it is now; Broecker suggested to us a way to double-check their productivity. We could use carbon isotopes.

We knew from geo-secs data that surface waters are relatively depleted in carbon 12 because of phytoplankton's preferential utilization of that isotope. If Ice Age plankton had been more numerous than now, the depletion of carbon 12 and the enrichment of carbon 13 in surface waters should have been more extreme than today's values. Ice-age values should be evident in fossil plankton of that age, because fossil skeletons accurately record the carbon-isotope ratio of the water in which they were formed. Furthermore, because bottom dwellers are at no time numerous enough to have much effect on the carbon-isotope ratio in the deep waters where they live, there should be a greater difference between the proportion of carbon 13 in their fossils and those of surface dwellers than there is in modern specimens. Using what little carbon-isotope data had then been published Broecker was able to detect a greater difference between the carbon 13 content of the surface- and bottom-dwelling foraminifers of the Ice Age than in their modern counterparts, signifying greater plankton productivity during that cold epoch.

His explanation intrigued me. If extraordinarily high plankton productivity results in an exaggerated difference between the carbon 13 content in the shells of surface and bottom dwellers, what would happen if the opposite had occurred, if there had been no plankton production at all?

"Oh, you are asking me about the Strangelove effect," Broecker answered in high spirits when I posed the question after his talk. "An ocean without plankton would have no gradient of carbon isotopes. There would be the same carbon-isotope composition from top to bottom. The ocean would be a Strangelove ocean!"

I had never seen the movie, but I understood that the fictional Dr. Strangelove wanted to wipe out with a nuclear holocaust all living beings on Earth save for an elite including, of course, himself, who would eventually repopulate the planet. Half in jest, Broecker had picked a very picturesque term, and I did not miss the chance to formalize the concept and the term in my next publication.

BROECKER WAS THEORIZING, OF COURSE. WE CANNOT kill off all the living creatures in the oceans to verify the prediction that the carbon-isotope composition of the water would then be the same from top to bottom. But lakes are smaller bodies of water, and nature has there conducted for us many experiments in plankton productivity. In the course of her research into the origin of chalk in Swiss lakes, Judy McKenzie unwittingly found evidence of the Strangelove effect.

Greifensee in northwestern Switzerland is what is called a eutrophic lake: Agricultural and industrial activities during the last century have augmented the normal flow of nutrients by dumping excess phosphates and nitrates into the water so that the organic productivity in the lake has been much enhanced. The peak season of algal growth falls in July and August. Algae's selective rejection of carbon 13 atoms leads to a maximum vertical gradient of carbon isotopes during the summer, when surface water has 4.5 more carbon 13 atoms per thousand than bottom water has. As autumn sets in, biological productivity is reduced. The surface water samples McKenzie collected in late September have only about three more carbon 13 atoms per thousand than that of the bottom. Algae become dormant in deep winter and growth stops. Mid-December water samples have the same isotopic composition from top to bottom. When spring comes and the growing season starts, the first algal bloom in early May creates a slight gradient again, which then increases over the summer. The carbon 13 cycle of Greifensee is thus repeated annually.

McKenzie plotted these seasonal variations by analyzing the carbon-isotope ratios of carbonates in her samples. Oceans have a much higher reservoir of dissolved carbonates than do lakes, so short-term fertility cycles have little influence on their isotopic gradient

over the seasons. Long-term, sustained increases or decreases in productivity should, however, have an effect.

The hypothetical Strangelove ocean of zero productivity can be compared to the dormant winter season at
Greifensee. If carbon-isotope fractionation is no longer
conducted by plankton, ocean chemistry should gradually be homogenized by upwelling bottom waters and de-
scending surface waters. The turnover rate is the same
as that for carbon dioxide in general—from top to bottom and up again in two thousand years. If the ocean
plankton were to be exterminated, the carbon 13 values
in the resulting Strangelove ocean should two thousand
years later be the same from top to bottom, just as they
are during the winter in Greifensee.

Was there a Strangelove ocean after the Cretaceous
catastrophe?

AFTER PUZZLING MANY YEARS OVER CARBON-ISOTOPE
analyses of fossil skeletons I conclude that the answer is
yes. Clues that were not understood at the time have a
way of falling into place once more evidence has
sketched out the picture of an event. Way back in 1978,
in his inspiring talk to us in Zürich, Nick Shackleton
mentioned the carbon-isotope data he had compiled on
foraminifers from the earliest Cenozoic sediments. Contrary to his expectations, the planktonic skeletons in
those samples were not enriched in carbon 13 as they are
in normal oceans. Shackleton was puzzled; he offered
four or five explanations, but he was happy with none of
them.

At that time I, too, had no idea what his carbon-
isotope data might mean. After being enlightened by
Broecker, and after McKenzie told me of her work at
Greifensee, the significance of Shackleton's data became
clear: There was no enrichment of carbon 13 in the
shelly fossils of plankton that had lived in surface waters
after the end of the Cretaceous because there were too
few phytoplankton living in the oceans to do the frac-
tionating job. There was a Strangelove ocean then!

As is often the case, data indicative of an anomalous

carbon-isotope ratio at the end of the Cretaceous had in fact been staring us in the face for years. Two University of Illinois geochemists, Tom Anderson and his graduate student J. C. Brennecke, had discovered in 1977 that the earliest Tertiary marine sediments are always depleted in carbon 13 atoms as compared to those of the latest Cretaceous.

The precipitous fall in carbon 13 at the boundary is about ten times the background variation. No changes in the carbon-isotope composition of ocean sediments were as rapid as that which occurred during the few millennia across the boundary. The carbon-isotope anomaly was a perturbation, not a shift, for the isotope composition then returned after those few millennia to what it had been during the late Cretaceous, and stayed there.

What was the meaning of this perturbation?

Like Shackleton, Anderson and Brennecke were baffled by their own findings, and the significance of their discovery remained obscure. Only a thorough analysis of samples from Core 20 hauled up in the final hours of drilling at the Cape Basin site five years later was to give us the final piece to the puzzle.

Anderson and Brennecke had done their analysis on bulk samples that contained mostly planktonic skeletons plus some bottom dwellers. They had noted the total drop in carbon 13, but because they had not separated out surface from seafloor dwellers, they had no idea whether a gradient existed from top to bottom. Isotopic measurements of our South Atlantic bulk samples confirmed their discovery; the boundary clay has a carbon 13 value smaller than that of the last Cretaceous sediment immediately below the boundary. But we wanted to know more exactly what had happened to the ocean environment. Traces of bottom-dwelling foraminifers were therefore removed, and samples consisting exclusively of surface-dwelling nannoplankton skeletons were analyzed. The results showed the same anomaly as the bulk samples, indicating that the change in isotope ratio had occurred at the surface. Still not satisfied we asked Ramil Wright of Florida to pick out from our samples the rare specimens of benthic foraminifers so that we could carry out isotopic measurements on those. The benthic skeletons show no anomaly at or across the Cretaceous-Tertiary boundary, confirming to us that the anomalous drop in carbon 13 had taken place only in the surface waters where plankton grew—or, more properly, no longer grew.

In progressively later sediments the few remaining plankton repopulated surface waters, again began to use up their preferred carbon 12 isotope, and, as leftover carbon 13 accumulated, the gradient from top to bottom was gradually restored.

Carbon-isotope data therefore turned out to be an excellent monitor of fertility in the ocean.

Like the iridium anomaly, the carbon-isotope anomaly has been found in boundary sediments everywhere. There was a global biotic crisis after the catastrophe in which the ocean became almost sterile. The normal process of carbon-isotope fractionation by plankton was halted. Over the next two thousand years waters from various depths homogenized, resulting in a nearly identical carbon-isotope composition from the top of the ocean to the bottom.

A closer look at our data showed, in fact, that the planktonic skeletons have an even lower value for carbon 13 than their benthic contemporaries. We attributed this relative depletion of carbon 13 atoms to the presence of "Strangelove continents" after the terminal Cretaceous catastrophe.

Land plants, like oceanic plankton, prefer to take in from the atmosphere carbon 12 atoms rather than carbon 13 atoms for their cell tissues. When they die and decay, their organic matter is oxidized, releasing their carbon dioxide, which is dissolved in groundwater and eventually transported by rivers to the ocean. Strangelove continents burdened with decaying plants would deliver a large excess of organic carbon debris as well as an excess of dissolved carbon dioxide to the ocean, and both would be depleted in carbon 13 atoms. Consequently the surface water of the oceans could become even more depleted in carbon 13 than is accounted for by the death of plankton alone.

Although the biomass of the ocean was sufficiently reduced to prevent carbon-isotope fractionation, the first Tertiary ocean after the terminal Cretaceous catastrophe was not an absolute "Strangelove ocean." Plankton reproduction did not stop completely, so that the boundary sediments are lime oozes, albeit clayey ones, that at several deep-sea drilling sites show a carbon-isotope anomaly indicative of disturbance, but not a halting of, ocean life. Apparently enough foraminiferal and nannoplankton skeletons were produced at such sites to escape complete dissolution and to accumulate as whitish oozes on some parts of the ocean floor.

After years of investigation, we finally noted an unusual distribution pattern in the various kinds of boundary sediments. A carbonate ooze, containing more or less clay, was laid down at intermediate depths of 2,000 to 3,000 meters. Clay devoid of any carbonate was deposited below the calcite compensation depth on abyssal plains. But the deposition in coastal waters turned out to be an exceptional case. On continental margins plankton production is usually substantial, and where the water is not corrosive, the normal sediment is a carbonate ooze. But the first Tertiary sediments on continental shelves are not oozes. They are clays—the boundary clay at Gubbio, the Fish Clay at Stevn's Klint. The absence of plankton skeletons in those clays can only be explained by an assumption that the seawater of the coastal regions was unusually corrosive at that time. Perhaps the oxidation of abnormal amounts of organic debris washed off the Strangelove continents of that time produced an excess of carbonic acid that made the coastal water corrosive.

If unusual quantities of organic carbon were oxidized to produce carbon dioxide, oxygen must have been consumed in equally unusual quantities. Moreover, photosynthesis is the only source of oxygen in the atmosphere. With both terrestrial and marine photosynthesizers decimated, one could imagine that the atmosphere at that time was not exactly plentiful in oxygen anyhow. Between short supply and excessive consumption, coastal waters should have been noticeably oxygen-deficient. Do we have evidence of that in our sedimentary record?

Yes, indeed.

I visited the famous Stevn's Klint locality of Denmark in 1982. The boundary clay was easily located. The Cretaceous chalk is white, and the Tertiary limestone is white, but the boundary clay is black. One also sees paper-thin laminations in the clay. Both the color and the laminations are excellent indications that the bottom water was deficient in oxygen at the time the boundary clay was deposited. The delicate laminations are preserved because few or no animals were alive to disturb them. There were no bottom animals because there was no oxygen in the water for them to breathe, and there was no oxygen because it had been all used up in the decay of organic matter washed from the dead landscape to the sea. The unoxidized leftovers, and the unoxidized carbon soot from forest fires, colored the sediment black.

The influx of excess carbon from devastated continents could not have continued very long. Within a few thousands of years much of the dead organic debris would either have been washed away or buried under new sediments, and recovering plant populations would have covered the land again with forests, retaining carbon in the soil and minimizing erosion. Evidence from studying the boundary transition confirms that the oxygen depletion of coastal waters did not persist for more than several thousand years. Walter Alvarez described, for example, two colorations in the boundary clay at Gubbio; the lower half-centimeter is gray and the upper red. Because the total time span of boundary clay sedimentation was about five thousand years, the episode of gray-sediment deposition under oxygen-poor conditions seems to have lasted no longer than twenty-five hundred years, after which time ocean water was again rich enough in oxygen to color the clay red with rusty iron pigment.

Unlike in the oxygen-poor coastal waters there is evidence of much less severely anoxic bottom water in the open oceans of that time. The boundary clay at Cape Basin has a darker shade than sediments above and below it, but the clay is still somewhat reddish with iron pigment, indicating at least some oxygen. On the abyssal plains of the Pacific one can detect no color change at all across the boundary, but two minerals formed typically under oxygen-depleted conditions, pyrite and glauconite, have been found in the boundary sediments at many localities of the Pacific, even in the red boundary clay of the Central Pacific. Unusual concentrations of arsenic and antimony sulfides have also been detected there, and those metals could only have been precipitated from oxygen-poor bottom waters. Slight as these effects seem, they do indicate that the chemical disruption of ocean water that followed the catastrophe reached to the very abyss.

IF ONE WERE LOOKING AT THESE EVIDENCES OF CHEMIcal disruption in a lake, one might interpret them as a bad year or so in the lives of the organisms that lived there. But in the vast ocean, which covers three-quarters of the globe to a mean depth of 4 kilometers, the record must be read differently. The ocean's depth and extent tend to swamp brief chemical events, wiping them out in grander, millennia-long cycles. If a few months of darkness were the worst of the disaster 65 million years ago, one would therefore either not catch a glimpse of it at all or see evidence of a quick recovery. When the sun emerged from clouds of dust, whatever plankton had survived would resume their prodigious rate of reproduction. Nannoplankton can divide at least once daily, doubling their number with each division. Spring and summer plankton blooms produce 10 million individuals per liter of water, or some 300 billion photosynthesizing organisms thronging each square meter of surface. The total area of such blooms can cover many thousands of square kilometers.

The finding of a Strangelove ocean in the sedimentary

record tells us that mortality was high or reproduction low for a much longer period than darkness can explain, and that recovery was slower and extinction greater than can be accounted for by mass mortality. In fact, the topsy-turvy seas should have speeded recovery and saved even species represented by few survivors. Plankton blooms are usually limited only by the amount of nutrients available. Nutrients would have been conserved during the nonproductive months of a blackout, and an excess of fertilizer—phosphates and nitrates—would have enriched surface waters with the flood of organic matter from deforested continents for a thousand years. Well-fed and brightly lit, blooms of all kinds of surviving plankton would be ubiquitous.

Yet, although Core 20 and other samples from boundary sediments have shown that quite a few species did survive beyond the Cretaceous, the only blooms common in the earliest Tertiary ocean are those of a very few species of two genera, *Thoracosphaera* and *Braarudosphaera*. All other plankton simply dwindled into oblivion over the next few thousand years.

Investigations of living nannoplankton descended from those that recovered show that they bloom even under conditions of unusual temperature, salinity, and chemistry. That just those species flourished while others gradually became extinct implies a severely stressed environment. The mass mortality of plankton may have caused a Strangelove ocean, but the failure of nearly all of them to recover has led to the conclusion that the Strangelove ocean at the beginning of the Tertiary was also polluted, and therefore not conducive to the growth and reproduction of plankton.

As it happens, the nature, although not the cause, of the pollution may be the same as that which is killing our forests now.

12

Acid Rain And No$_x$

THERE WAS A SAYING IN OLD CHINA: ACCIDENTS HAP-
pen to the neighbors; catastrophes come in one's own
backyard. My twelve-year-old son, Peter, was to appreciate literally the truth of this Chinese wisdom.

Peter has been a passionate fisherman, and he has had
a lot of practice, especially during the year when he did
not have to go to school because I took my family on an
extended lecture tour to China. The autumn after our
return Peter caught two large perch—a prize catch for a
freshwater fisherman. Sportsmen rarely consume their
victims. They prefer trophies, and Peter was no exception. Big game fishermen mount their marlin as the conversation piece in their living room. Peter had a better
idea; he wanted his trophy alive. We had to sacrifice the
lily pond in our backyard to make room for a fishery.

Winter soon came. Peter acquired an aquarium in
which his older brother Martin had kept aquatic plants.
So the two perch, one docile and the other aggressive,
and fondly called Ralph and Niki, respectively, in honor

238

of two comrades at school, had a luxurious winter refuge.

Feeding was a problem. Ralph and Niki had cavernous appetites. They could each gobble down six or eight worms a day. Peter had to use ice picks and hack away at the frozen ground to find enough daily rations for his pets.

When spring came, the perch went back to their summer residence. To ameliorate the shock of the sudden temperature change, many buckets of hot water were hauled to the lily pond during the day of the big move. Peter even left last-minute instructions before he went to bed that his father was to conduct a midnight run of the hot water express so that Ralph and Niki would not be chilled to death.

The pond was regularly cleaned and scrubbed. Perch, like trout, need clean and oxygenated water for their healthy development. Not happy with the chlorinated stuff from a faucet, Peter designed and constructed an elaborate collecting system: Rainwater from the eaves of the roof was guided to a plastic tank, which was in turn connected to a garden hose and emptied into the lily pond.

We had a wet spring that year. It rained off and on for almost two weeks in a row. Peter announced proudly one day that his engineering feat had been successful; the original tap water had been completely replaced by rainwater in his fishery. I was invited to an inspection tour and was duly impressed: Ralph and Niki were happily making their way through the crystal-clear water.

Alas, this blissful state of affairs was not to last long! The day after the completion of the water-replacement campaign, Peter came home from school and found both Ralph and Niki dead.

What could have happened? Had the neighbor's cat or the naughty boy down the street killed his pets? No, that couldn't be. We had seen neither cats nor kids in the garden.

"It was your damned polluted water," suggested

young Iones, a neighbor and a fellow fisherman, who joined us at the lily pond.

"But it was not polluted. There is nothing purer than rainwater, and it is so clear that you can see to the bottom of the pond."

Indeed, the water was clear, a beauty of liquid transparency. Yet the fish were dead.

Peter left no stone unturned in his search for the culprit. A water sample was taken to his sister Elisabeth, who was studying biology at the university. She was not able to make a chemical analysis, but she did look up perch in her textbooks and found that they can't survive in water with a pH of 5 or less.

The expression pH denotes a scale to express hydrogen-ion concentration, or the acidity of a solution. A neutral solution has a pH of 7. A solution with a pH of 6 has ten times as great a concentration of hydrogen ions and is, therefore, acidic. A liquid with a pH of 5 has a hydrogen-ion concentration one hundred times that of a neutral solution and is very acidic indeed.

Was it possible that we had acid rain?

"Oh, yes," my wife Christine replied. "Only last month, the city council was debating the problem. The heating plant of the Technical University down the street from us is burning sulfurous oil. With its low chimney, much pollutant has been spilled over our neighborhood. The situation was particularly bad during the cold winter months when all the oil furnaces were at full blast."

I had read articles in *Nature* about acid rain. Scandinavian governments complained that pollutants from the industrial regions of the British Isles make acid rain. Water in lakes in northern Scandinavia have water with a pH more acidic than 5. No fish are left, a tragic situation for fishermen. The same problem besets the lakes of the Adirondacks: The high chimneys of factories in the Midwest send pollutants as far as the Northeast and into Canada. More than a hundred lakes in the Adirondacks are now devoid of fish as a result of the acidity of the water, and many rivers in Nova Scotia are acidified to such an extent that salmon can no longer spawn there.

I decided to call my friend Werner Stumm, the director of the Swiss Federal Water Protection Agency. He should know whether we had acid rain in our backyard.

"Oh, yes," Stumm replied. "You've come to the right person. I just published an article last year on acid rain. I shall send you a reprint." I sidestepped the reprint and got to the point. Could he just tell me offhand the pH of rainwater in Zürich?

Stumm explained that we have acid rain all over Switzerland, not only in Zürich but in Tessin, Geneva, and St. Gall. The pH of typical Swiss rainwater was then 4.3. The acid components were 50 percent sulfuric acid, 30 percent hydrochloric acid, and 20 percent nitric acid. Fortunately, the many limestone formations in Switzerland quickly neutralize excess acid, but the latest figure for lakes in the granite terranes of Canton Tessin were down to a pH of 4.5 or less because of acid rain pollution.

That was all Peter wanted to know. His engineering skill had accelerated the process of acidification; he had accomplished in a couple of days what it had taken two decades to do to the lakes of Tessin. Our tap water comes from Lake Zürich, the home of Ralph and Niki, where the pH value is about 8, pretty much on the alkaline side. Peter, with all his kindness and good intentions, had killed his own pets by making his fishery a cistern of acid rain.

NOT ONLY FISH, BUT ALL AQUATIC ORGANISMS ARE AFfected by excess acid. Mollusks rarely survive in acidity below pH 6. Many species of insects, and even zooplankton, perish in waters with pH less than 5. An aquatic environment becomes almost sterile if pH drops below 4.

Acid rain has also been implicated in Central Europe's tragic *Waldsterben*, the death of forests. Pattering through the foliage of a fir or a spruce, acid rain of pH 4 picks up organic and mineral acids that render it even more sour by the time it hits the ground. Such high acidity dissolves away potassium, calcium, and other mineral salts, depriving trees of essential nutrients. Trees, I had read, might thus become sick and die. My daughter Elisabeth did not agree, however, that the withering of forests has much to do with acid rain. She was working on a paper on the subject and had done a great deal of reading. The culprit, according to Elisabeth and many experts, is NO_x.

Earth's atmosphere consists mainly of nitrogen and oxygen. Under normal atmospheric temperatures, these gases are chemically inert; that is, they do not react to form other chemical compounds. At very high temperatures, however, nitrogen will combine with x number of oxygen atoms to form the group of compounds called NO_x, which might be NO, NO_2, or another nitrogen-oxygen combination. Temperature high enough to form NO_x in the atmosphere occurs seldom and for brief moments when lightning strikes. Natural production of NO_x is therefore normally negligible. But sustained very high air temperature results from industrial combustion and from internal combustion of automobile engines. Some 30 million tons of NO_x, Elisabeth informed me, were produced in 1980, of which almost half was catalyzed by motor vehicles.

NO_x compounds are eventually oxidized to produce nitric acid, which contributes to the problem of acid rain. But even before that happens the various gases may seriously damage trees directly. Nitric oxide (NO), for example, is an effective defoliant that was used extensively by America during the Vietnam War. Now, unwittingly, we are destroying our own forests with our fast automobiles, in peace.

So acid rain kills and NO_x pollutes. But they are the by-products of industrial revolution, the making of human intellect. Could there have been acid rain and NO_x pollution 65 million years go when the most advanced animals were dinosaurs? I was to learn the answer at the Snowbird Conference of 1981, a few months after we had buried Peter's fish. The idea of chemical pollution was of course on my mind.

* * *

As a physicist, Luis Alvarez had a quick appreciation of the physical consequences of the fall of a trillion-ton meteor. The ascent of the ejecta dust to the stratosphere is a physical phenomenon; so is a "blackout." Reasonable as Alvarez's "darkness at noon" scenario for the great dying had seemed at first glance, it did not hold up to close scrutiny. The problem of timing would not go away: If, after the catastrophe, tens of thousands of years went by before the last doomed species had died out, the mass extinction could not have been caused by a temporary blackout or by any other brief effect. There must have been some other long-sustained result of the meteorite impact. In contrast to Alvarez, I have been active in geochemistry; I saw a chemical consequence of cometary collision and had postulated cyanide poisoning at the previous conference in Ottawa where many others had also been attracted by the idea of chemical pollution as the major cause of mass extinction. Besides the possibility of cyanide poisoning, several heavy metals found in the Cretaceous-Tertiary boundary clay are very poisonous. Osmium and ruthenium, for example, are harmful at concentrations of a few parts per billion, and arsenic, selenium, antimony, and other elements are toxic too. Because the concentrations of those metals in the boundary clay are so high and the possibility of their derivation from terrestrial sources could be excluded, Paul Feldman of the Herberg Institute in Canada suggested that we might "come to some kind of consensus that there is evidence for a cometary object that brought volatile poisons into the terrestrial environment."

First stabs at an explanation by scientists in any field tend, however, to be off the mark. The problem with the "poison scenario" is that the extraterrestrial input was too small to cause global pollution. Calculations revealed that concentrations of cyanides, carbon monoxide, or poisonous heavy metals that might have been dumped into the oceans by a trillion-ton comet could not have been anything even close to lethal doses. I had dodged that problem in my paper published the previous spring by assuming that toxic materials were restricted to surface water. With only "local" contamination, concentrations of poisons might have been just high enough to cause selective extinction of marine plankton in surface currents. The theory neatly explained why benthic organisms escaped the catastrophe: Not much of the extraterrestrial poison had gotten into the deep bottom waters.

I was rather smug that I might have chanced upon the right answer with a cyanide-poisoning story until the Snowbird Conference. On the morning after my arrival, I met Tom Ahrens of Cal Tech. He congratulated me on that brilliant idea but persuaded me that it would not work: "The high shock pressure and the high temperature after the impact would destroy any cyanides that might have been brought in," he assured me.

He is probably right. The temperature would rise to hundreds of thousands of degrees, high enough to deionize cyanide compounds or other toxic gases as the poisonous comet turned into a column of fire rising tens of kilometers vertically above the target site and spread outward in a mushroom cloud. That very scenario, however, opens up the possibility of creating new toxic materials.

John Lewis of Arizona University gave a very significant talk at Snowbird, "Chemical Consequences of Major Impact Events on Earth." He confirmed what Ahrens had told me: The fireball temperature for any large impact is so high that there cannot be any survival of toxic molecular species carried by a comet nucleus. His second point emphasized the consequence of a shock heating of the earth's atmosphere. From investigations of lightning discharges, of large nuclear explosions, and of the Tunguska event, we are now certain that a large quantity of NO_x, especially the defoliant nitric oxide, would be produced.

Lewis and his associates made computations on the basis of various assumptions. Assuming a trillion-ton stony meteorite impacting at a speed of 14 kilometers per second, the production of NO molecules is 1 billion tons. That was a conservative estimate. A comet is likely to travel much faster. Assuming the impact of a trillion-ton comet at 40 kilometers per second, the production is a hundred times more, or 100 billion tons of nitric oxide. This compound is quickly oxidized by ozone in the stratosphere and by oxygen in the atmosphere to produce NO_2, N_2O_4, and other species of NO_x. In less than an hour, Lewis told us, the earth's atmosphere would be polluted by a disastrous quantity of NO_x.

Lewis figured that the impact-produced NO_x would be spread around a latitudinal circle in a matter of weeks, but it would take a few years for the toxic product to be distributed globally. Meanwhile, the atmospheric NO_x would be removed as nitrous and nitric acids by atmospheric moisture and fall as acid rain. Consequently, Lewis suggested that NO_x pollution may not have been global, but was located at middle latitude. The pollution could devastate an east-west strip of the earth at least 2,000 kilometers wide by 35,000 kilometers long. That is 14 percent of the globe.

The damage pattern to terminal Cretaceous floras is consistent with an assumption of a cometary fall at a middle or high northern latitude. Such a hypothesis would explain the deforestation of North America revealed by pollen analyses, and the almost total extinction of the floras in the *Aquilapollenites* province, which extended from Siberia all the way to Alaska.

Although immediate damage to the floras may have been along such an east-west belt, some long-lasting effects to faunas could have been global. A most serious consequence is the depletion of stratospheric ozone, because it is consumed in its reaction with NO_x. Brian Toon and his coworkers investigated the chemical consequences of the Tunguska event. Their computations predicted a 35 to 45 percent ozone depletion in the northern hemisphere through the production of 30 million tons of nitric oxide in the stratosphere. They then checked that prediction against actual data collected by the Smithsonian Astrophysical Observatory at Mount Wilson in the years following the explosion at Tunguska. Ozone had indeed been depleted by 30 percent during the first four years after the meteor fall. Such damage is self-repairing. When ozone is depleted, more of the sun's ultraviolet rays penetrate the atmosphere, and enhanced ultraviolet radiation in turn increases the rate of production of ozone (O_3) from oxygen (O_2). But repair takes longer the greater the damage has been. Toon calculated the minimum effect of a trillion-ton meteor impact and estimated a global ozone reduction in excess of 90 percent for the first year, and more than 50 percent for several years thereafter. More alarming estimates by O'Keefe and Ahrens indicated complete destruction of the ozone layer for at least a decade.

THE EARTH'S OZONE LAYER PROTECTS ORGANISMS FROM the lethal effects of the very intense solar ultraviolet radiation known as *UV*-B. Studies by the biologists of the committee constituted by the U.S. National Academy of Science to study the consequences of a major nuclear war came to the startling conclusion in 1975 that the destruction of the ozone layer by nuclear detonations might have more serious consequences than the immediate radioactive fallout. The present level of exposure to UV-B is almost as high as organisms can tolerate. The present level of ultraviolet radiation causes in us the skin damage of sunburn and, after long exposure, skin cancer. Exposure to unshielded UV-B radiation can cause multiple cancerous growth, mutate reproductive cells, or even kill outright. Abnormal reproductive cells in turn can result in sterility, abortion, stillbirth, birth defects, and inheritable changes to chromosomes that are deleterious or lethal. A most sensational discovery in connection with a research project on "Nuclear Winter," or the aftereffects of large-scale nuclear war, was announced by the U.S. National Academy of Sciences, in September 1985. Two Brown University physicians had discovered that exposure to intense UV-B, after stratospheric ozone is eliminated by reaction with NO_x, would result in the destruction of the immune system's thymus-derived cells

(T cells) in animals. Ultraviolet radiation, like the acquired immune deficiency syndrome (AIDS) virus HTL-3, can thus cause an immunity deficiency that reduces resistance to a host of other diseases.

It is quite possible that many of the terminal Cretaceous extinctions were caused by the biocidal action of unshielded sunlight, that survivors tended to be those organisms that could tolerate the unusually high level of UV-B, or that were protected from it by sufficient depth of water, or that lived a burrowing or nocturnal life. Of those survivors, some few individuals may have experienced beneficial mutations, thus enhancing the rate of speciation. But that, of course, cannot be the whole story.

The blackout, the air pollution, and the ozone depletion did their work quick and dirty. The dust must have settled and the pollutants have vanished in a year, and the ozone layer was very likely repaired within a decade. The survivors should then enjoy a quick recovery, but they did not. Instead, many species continued their decline toward extinction. The reason is probably that the water was by then polluted. A trillion tons of nitric oxide had been removed from the air, but more than a trillion tons of nitric acid had been added to the soil and the oceans.

I had first thought that acid rain would do more damage to plants and animals on land than in the oceans because such pollutants become concentrated in ponds and in local drainage basins. It is not difficult to imagine a small lake so acidified that all the animals in it were killed like Peter's pet fish. But the ocean is immense, and a trillion tons of nitric acid cannot significantly change its chemistry. Even if all that acid were confined to the top 75 meters of the ocean, as Lewis, the NO$_x$ expert, had assumed, the surface water would change its pH by only about half a unit, or a threefold increase of acidity. That change seemed to me not enough to exterminate many, if any, organisms. Yet the paleontological record shows that freshwater animals and land plants underwent little evolutionary change, although marine plankton became almost entirely extinct over the years of the earliest Tertiary. If acid rain was the culprit, why should marine communities suffer the most damage?

One answer is that although a small system is easier to pollute than one the size of an ocean it is also faster to recover. After Ralph and Niki died in our lily pond, the acid rain was drained, to be replaced by tap water to accommodate newcomers. We can imagine the same for terrestrial environments. Some forests might have been completely defoliated. Some lakes and rivers might have been polluted to such an extent as to cause mass mortality. But rain, acid or not, cleanses the air, and fresh precipitation from the cleaned air flushes polluted water to the ocean. Land, lakes, and rivers might have been more severely polluted in the beginning, but they would again become viable environments for new immigrants from less polluted refuges, such as larger lakes where acidity had been less affected.

A second answer is more to the point. Evolution guarantees that no organism shall actively develop a harmful trait for those individuals that do have few progeny or do not live long enough to have any at all. But nothing decrees that a once-useful trait will continue to be useful as circumstances change. The North American moose, for example, requires a certain minimum of cold days in order to become fertile. That is a clever adaptation: In its native land, a moose that became fertile too early in the season would bear young while the weather was too cold and fodder too scarce to support offspring. But in England, where noblemen for several centuries made valiant efforts to breed moose to populate their parks, the animals were unable to breed at all. There were not enough cold days in the year to bring them to fertility. Were climate to change gradually, there might well be a number of individuals in each generation whose "clock" was slightly off, and who became fertile after fewer days of chilling. The population would gradually shift toward animals on the new schedule; we would say they had adapted to the changed climate. But had moose in their native land been subjected to so rapid a change as those transported between continents, they would have become extinct.

Plankton are admirably adapted to the temperature and chemistry of the ocean just as it is now. But any researcher whose work involves cultivating plankton can tell you that their fertility is easily impaired. One of my classmates in graduate school started a dissertation on environmental factors detrimental to the cultivation of foraminifers in the laboratory. He gave up after a year because he could not get them to reproduce at all. He could capture living specimens, and he could make them survive in his laboratory, but they would not breed. That was more than thirty years ago. Experts have had some success since then in cultivating some species of marine plankton in the laboratory, but even with these the temperature has to be just right, and the chemistry of the artificial seawater has to be exactly so. Plankton culture is still an art; a successful breeder shares his secret recipe with his friends, as a gourmet chef passes on his latest culinary invention.

Several modern nannoplankton species cease reproducing when the water pH drops below 7.5. Today, and presumably also before the catastrophe, ocean water becomes this acidic only below 1,000 meters, or lower than where plankton live. Foraminifers are also sensitive to chemical change: Both too much nitrate and too much acid inhibit their reproduction.

So picture the scenario: First, there is darkness, and mass mortality. By the time light returns, the ocean surface is already abnormally acidic because the missing biomass of plankton is no longer consuming dissolved carbon dioxide, resulting in an unusual accumulation of carbonic acid. To this is added a trillion tons of nitric acid from acid rain precipitation and from continental run-off. The pH value would have dropped then considerably below 7.5, inhibiting the reproduction of all but the toughest of plankton. This drastically altered chemistry is likely to have persisted for thousands of years because plankton productivity remained low, and also because as the water homogenized into a Strangelove ocean, corrosive bottom water would have become mixed with surface water.

EVENTUALLY THE OCEAN WOULD HAVE RIGHTED ITSELF by natural processes. Lime neutralizes acid. The chalk on Charles Lyell's estate was mined and sold as an agricultural buffer to neutralize the acid soil in the marsh country of northern England, and lime is routinely used on lawns today wherever soils are acidic. Erosion of limestone on land and the dissolution of calcium carbonate skeletons on the sea bottom were finally to provide enough lime to neutralize the excess acid in the Strangelove ocean. After thousands, or perhaps tens of thousands, of years the surface would again favor plankton productivity, but the damage would have been done. Not even a dormant cyst can retain its potency for a millennium. Mass extinction of nannoplankton and foraminifers was plausibly the inevitable result of chemical pollution.

Interestingly, floating diatoms, which secrete skeletons of silica can multiply in seawater with a pH as acid at 6.4. They did not suffer extinction to the same drastic degree that foraminifers and nannoplankton did.

If only we knew as much about dinosaurs as we know about plankton, we might be able to put a finger on an environmental change that disrupted their fertility or, as Heinrich Erben's work with fossil dinosaur eggs suggests, caused some other pathology in their reproduction. Alas, they have left no descendants that we might breed in a laboratory. Therefore, the best strategy may be to look for the obvious, the subject everybody talks about—the weather.

TEMPERATURE CHANGES FOLLOWING A GIANT METEORite hit are a complicated matter. Cesare Emiliani and his colleagues proposed a scenario of three stages.

The immediate effect following the meteorite collision would have been the scene described vividly by de Laubenfels. He erred, however, when he envisioned a global heat wave. There would have been a "Sodom and Gomorrah" in the target area, where a gigantic fireball rose into a column of smoke and superheated air to form a vast mushroom cloud. If the impact occurred on land, there would certainly have been scorching winds and forest fires running out of control. But that temperature disturbance would have been temporary and regionally limited.

Not so the ensuing cold wave, the second stage known as nuclear winter. Physicists from the United States, the Soviet Union, the Federal Republic of Germany, and other countries have recently confronted the world with the freezing consequences of a nuclear war. If many bombs were dropped, smoke and dust carried into the stratosphere by mushroom clouds would then form a thick envelope of suspended particles. Deprived of solar energy for months, global temperature would fall by dozens of degrees. The ground and water would freeze, no crop would grow, and most survivors would perish in the resulting cold and famine. The world has quite recently had a very mild foretaste of dust-caused temperature drop after several large volcanic eruptions during the last century.

Stratospheric dust in the months after a giant meteorite hit would have completely banished summer. Brian Toon reported at Snowbird that the temperature on earth in some areas could have dropped by as many as 40 degrees Celsius, and certainly to below freezing. Again, there might have been less mortality where the artificial winter coincided with actual winter than in places where it should have been summer then. Animals used to basking in tropical sunshine would have had to shiver in bitter cold, if they survived at all.

A nuclear winter cannot have lasted very long because as ejecta dust settled, returning sunlight would have again given warmth to the earth. Therefore, we do not anticipate finding evidence for such a brief event in the geological record. Nevertheless, the oxygen-isotope data of our cores from the South Atlantic did indicate a centuries-long cooling episode after the event marked by the iridium anomaly. Though not the nuclear winter itself, this continuing chill was probably its aftermath. Considering the likelihood that the meteorite hit the ocean, there might have been 200 inches of precipitation each day for weeks. Recalling the drop in temperature during just that period, this incredible precipitation would have fallen not as rain, but as snow in the chilly darkness. Every inch of rain is the equivalent of 10 inches of snow. The globe would have been a giant snowball when the sun shone again. Scientists from the U.S. Weather Bureau have noted that early snowfall in a year tends to create a colder than normal winter because the reflective surface bounces back into space more solar energy than does snow-free land. The effect from an early snowfall lingers only through that winter, but the heat loss from a very large snow-covered area of the globe, melting only slowly in the cooled climate, could linger for the several hundred years our data seem to register.

The final climatic change, a global warming, is registered in the data Shackleton reported in his 1978 talk. His data indicated a 5-degree warming even at the ocean bottom. We found evidence of an 8-degree warming in our Atlantic samples.

Emiliani invoked the greenhouse effect to explain the warming. Carbon dioxide in the atmosphere acts much like glass in a greenhouse. Both the glass and the gas are transparent to sunlight, but they are opaque to the heat that normally radiates back into space from the earth's surface. Trapped heat inside a greenhouse heats up the room. Heat trapped inside the atmosphere heats the whole globe. Ordinarily, the variation of atmospheric carbon dioxide is too small to have much effect, but recently climatologists have noted with concern that the carbon dioxide content in the atmosphere has increased some 20 percent during the last century because of the burning of fossil fuels for human consumption. The trend is continuing, and the increase has been exponential during the last few decades. In the not too distant future, the atmospheric carbon dioxide content could double, causing a global warming of perhaps 2 degrees. Eventually, heat trapped by the greenhouse effect could melt the polar ice caps, causing a rise in sea level that would drown every coastal city in the world.

DINOSAURS, OF COURSE, HAD NEITHER SMOKESTACKS nor exhaust pipes. It is plankton that during the hundreds of millions of years of the preindustrial world controlled the amount of carbon dioxide in the atmosphere. The more of the gas plankton consume in the ocean, the less of the gas bubbles into the atmosphere. The fewer plankton there are to consume carbon dioxide —and there certainly were few in the early millennia of the Tertiary—the more carbon dioxide builds up in the atmosphere. Broecker estimated that atmospheric carbon dioxide could have increased threefold as a result of the mass dying of plankton and their continued low productivity. Such a tripling would have increased global temperature by between 2 and 5 degrees according to various computer estimates. A return to normal temperature was possible only as the ocean became gradually fertile again, and plankton survivors could repopulate it. Our core samples indicate that the transition from a devastated remnant of Cretaceous species to a normally dense population of Tertiary species took perhaps fifty thousand years.

Sudden temperature changes could have wreaked havoc in the community of terrestrial animals. A third of North American mammalian species became extinct during the millennia after the Ice Age, although we are not certain that the temperature rise was the only culprit. Dewey McLean, who had always believed that warming was the decisive factor in dinosaur extinction, discussed the effect of abnormally high temperature on reproductive cells: A rise of a few degrees in air temperature may not have killed any dinosaurs, but it may have rendered many sterile. Mass mortality was not directly responsible for their extinction, but mass sterility could be. An even more intriguing possibility was suggested by zoologists studying incubation of reptilian eggs. The sex of the individuals in many reptilian species is not determined by their chromosomes, but by incubation temperature. One might imagine that the last dinosaurs all belonged to the same sex; they became extinct because they could have no offspring. Unfortunately, we will never know.

We are able to develop speculations about both the plankton's effect on environment and the environment's effect on them because we know a good deal about living plankton. Such is not the case with ammonites, belemnites, and rudistids, or with the dramatic dinosaurs and giant reptiles that, nearly since their discovery in the eighteenth and nineteenth centuries, have been the very symbol of extinction. None is left to whom we might address our inquiries; we cannot test their tolerance of heat, cold, acidity, or pollution or observe the even more subtle interactions that are the more likely sources of their disappearance.

In June 1985, I joined a group of ecologists and paleobiologists in a forum discussion on mass extinction at a Dahlem Conference in Berlin. As the discussions progressed, the idea crystallized that the problem must be viewed from two levels: There are immediate causes of extinction, which may be unique to each species, and there are ultimate causes, which may underline the extinction of many species. We are well warned not to trap ourselves in the labyrinth of immediate causes. Recently, the year's only pair of California condor eggs laid in the wild was found to have been devoured by ravens. Ravens may indeed close the book on the last generation of these magnificent birds, but habitat destruction, not ravenous appetites, is the ultimate cause of their and many modern species' endangerment. Basing their opinion on studies of recently extinct species, the ecologists at Berlin concurred that habitat destruction and other disturbances that lead to reduction of population size, narrowing of genetic variability, and impairment of fecundity are the ultimate causes of extinction.

Ultimate causes do not necessarily elucidate immediate causes. It is well known that passenger pigeons became extinct through gross overhunting, but theirs was a particular vulnerability. Crowding in huge flocks was a necessary condition of their courtship; small remnant bands were unable to maintain an adequate reproductive rate. Some plants, as city gardeners know, are so vulnerable to pollution that they can't be grown in urban environments. Other plants, as researchers have just discovered, are not only inured to pollution, but actively decontaminate the atmosphere of such toxins as carbon monoxide, formaldehyde fumes, and cigarette smoke. Knowing the ultimate cause of the Cretaceous catastrophe, the severe and prolonged disruption of habitats that followed in the meteorite's wake cannot explain any particular group's demise unless its particular vulnerabilities become known.

SO, YES, THE AMMONITES MIGHT HAVE BEEN THE VICTIMS of a collapse in the food chain. On the other hand, they might have been rendered sterile by chemical pollution. Tropical reef builders—corals and rudistids—might have vanished abruptly during the long winter that followed the brief darkness, or more slowly by suffocation as shallow waters became depleted of oxygen. Perhaps brachiopods were poisoned; perhaps the "carpet" was pulled out from under them as their clean, chalky habitat became a muddy bottom.

Extinction scenarios become all but impossible to choose among when we consider the dinosaurs. "The" dinosaurs were as much alike as mammals are today, which is to say not at all. Researchers studying one group of dinosaurs may well discover overly fragile eggs or unfertilized ones and diagnose reproductive failure caused by excessive heat. But others studying a different group may discover no eggs at all, either at the end of the Cretaceous or at any time, and might guess that group was capable of live birth. To explain the extinction of any species of dinosaur we would have to know innumerable facts about its physiology and behavior, for there is no telling where its vulnerability lay. Speculation in ignorance loses its pleasure.

Though we are ignorant of details, however, our understanding of the dinosaurs' end is not an anticlimax.

Only a few years ago any possible scenario of their extinction violated reason. All failed to take into account the multitude of organisms that perished with them, and that can only have done so had there been a global derangement that, in those days, was beyond the imaginings of science.

We have come now to a more telling and a more powerful view of mass extinction. Cruelly, the way to this revelation has been paved by our own depredations. Our own biotic interactions with other species as we have overkilled, deforested, acidified, polluted, threatened the ozone layer with aerosols; started our own greenhouse effect; and even considered unleashing a nuclear winter of our own making have brought home to us the possibility of global disaster that previous generations could blissfully ignore.

We have brought our living planet to such a brink in the course of pursuing competitive rights which we thought reflected our species' natural superiority, and which we believed were derived from nature's law of survival of the fittest. The ultimate cause of extinction before man was, however, distinctly different. Mass extinction was the consequence of drastic physical changes that no living creature brought about.

Therefore we have to ask at the conclusion of this tale, as we asked at the beginning, is Darwinism science? As we appreciate the full significance of death from the sky, does our new perception destroy the scientific validity of social Darwinism and give us reason to shun it?

13

The Race Is Not to the Swift

WHEN I LEARNED PALEONTOLOGY, I WAS TAUGHT Darwin's theory of the survival of the fittest through the case history of South America. Prior to a few million years ago, the North and South American continents had been separated from one another for a very long time. On each, a diverse and numerous fauna had evolved, each quite different from the other. When the Isthmus of Panama was raised from the sea, North American animals invaded South America.

The newcomers, tempered by the harshness of the northern climate, were superior to the slower, less advanced native animals, who had long stagnated in their insular homeland. Unsurprisingly, the story concluded, the inferior fauna was largely exterminated by the superior invaders. Many groups of modern animals now considered natives of South America, such as llamas, jaguars, and tapirs, are in fact descended from the northern hordes, whereas only a few primitive mammals, such as the armadillo and the opossum, successfully achieved a foothold on the northern continent.

It was Darwin's opinion that natural selection is a creative process. He well understood that were nature to act only as executioner, preserving the fit by killing off all those that deviated from the form most suitable in its niche, the law of natural selection would result in a history of life no different from that proposed by creationists: That is, had each form been created perfect, and natural law acted to preserve perfection, species would indeed have been immutable, and the facts of evolution as he had observed them in his studies of extinct and extant forms would not be explained.

He therefore proposed that natural selection improves the fitness of an organism, with each change, however slightly different, approaching more closely to the form that would most efficiently and most productively utilize earth's resources for its own benefit at the expense of its competitors. The history of life, then, is one of gradual improvement; were all of today's flora and fauna to be transported back in time to the days of the dinosaurs, they would dispossess the older inhabitants as had the superior northerners supplanted the inferior southerners when North and South America were rejoined.

This view of evolution as improvement was inescapable to Darwin because of his commitment to the analogy of population pressure. He conceived of the competition among organisms as the controlling principle in evolution, so that the improvement of a predator's speed in catching prey, for example, would cause similar predators either to speed up themselves and therefore successfully compete, or, if they remained unchanged, to become extinct.

Even very prominent biologists today see no alternative. In an issue of *Nature* published in 1984, John Maynard Smith, a population geneticist whose work has been central to the development of the modern synthesis of Darwinian theory with genetic mechanisms, expressed surprise that "paleontologists read the fossil record differently. The dinosaurs, they believe, became extinct for reasons that had little to do with competition from the mammals. Only subsequently did the mammals, which had been around for as long as the dinosaurs, radiate to fill the empty space. The same general pattern, they think, has held for other major taxonomic replacement." He, in contrast, had "expected a major cause of extinction to be competition from other taxa."

I NEVER HAD OCCASION TO QUESTION THE IDEOLOGY OF orderly progress through competition until I finally became interested in the problem of mass extinction. When I came back from my South Atlantic expedition in 1980, I began to feel restive, even rebellious, about the doctrine of evolution toward higher and higher perfection. The evidence for a wanton catastrophe was impressive. Was that natural selection, and if it was, by what criteria could one judge the superiority of the survivors? I decided to ask for clarification from my paleontologist friend Steven Gould.

I first met Gould in 1972. I was at Oxford for a meeting, and he was taking his sabbatical leave there. We were introduced during a coffee hour. We had known each other by name, and by our work: I for my Mediterranean researches that had shattered my faith in Lyellian uniformitarianism, and he for his critique of the same dogma. He differed with Darwin on the tempo of evolution. Darwin the gradualist had quoted in terms no less uncertain than Einstein's "God does not play dice" the dictum "Naturum non facit saltum"—Nature does not take leaps. Gould found evidence that nature does take leaps. He noted that a species seems to remain unchanged in the fossil record for millions of years before abruptly disappearing, to be replaced as rapidly with a species that is clearly related, but substantially different. "Gradualism," he pronounced, "is a culturally conditioned prejudice, not a fact of nature." With a colleague, Niles Eldridge, he invented the term punctuated equilibrium to describe this jumpier tempo he perceived.

Gould also, much to my satisfaction, challenged the parable of the South American mammals as it had been taught to me during my student days. In an article called "O Grave, Where Is Thy Victory?" he publicized the recent revelation by scientists of Chicago University that the interchange between continents had not been so one-sided after all.

Although it is true that members of fourteen North American mammalian families eventually made their home south of Panama and represent 40 percent of the total number of families on the southern continent, twelve South American families migrated north over the isthmus and now represent 36 percent of the mammalian families of North America. Extinction rates were also balanced: About the same proportion of North American genera as South American genera became extinct. As Gould remarked, "the old story of 'hail the conquering hero comes'—waves of differential migration and subsequent carnage—can no longer be maintained."

However, the new study did indicate that the North Americans produced many new genera in their adopted land, and that the immigrants from South America evolved very few new genera in the north. Gould suggested that this difference may have resulted from an incidental change of climate in South America. The recent rise of the Andean Mountains created a rain shadow over much of South America, changing the damp forest to which indigenous fauna had been adapted to drier woodland, grassland, and desert. Many of these forest-adapted mammals were already extinct or on the decline at the time of the invasion, and those that migrated northward were as stymied by the dry climate north of the isthmus as they had been by the drying climate to the south.

On the other hand, the northern families may already have been preadapted in their former home to conditions similar to those they were to find in their new home. Physical change in climate, not competition among species, better explains the fossil record of extinction and speciation there.

Such refreshing thoughts had been the tenor of Gould's work since we had first met at Oxford, and we had maintained our friendship over the ensuing eight years through occasional correspondence. Now that I saw not only the "punctuation" Gould had pointed out, but the wholly new paragraph that opened the Cenozoic, I thought I should let him know. Perhaps he would agree that Darwin had erred when he proposed that survival of the fittest explained the course of evolution.

I wrote to Gould in August after my return from the South Atlantic, asking, among other questions, the meaning of the sudden extinction of all those wonderful creatures of the Cretaceous: Against whom had they struggled? Why weren't they fit?

I was amazed at Gould's reply. In a long and thoughtful letter, he vehemently affirmed his faith in natural selection, told me it was Darwin's greatest contribution to the science of evolutionary biology, and said that he saw no reason to deny its role even during environmental crises.

He backed up the letter with the gift of his book containing an essay warning of "Darwin's Untimely Burial." The essay was a critique of an article titled "Darwin's Mistake" written by Tom Bethell for *Harper's* magazine in 1976. Bethell had claimed that Darwin's theory was on the verge of collapse ("natural selection was quietly abandoned, even by his most ardent supporters, some years ago") because it was no more than a tautology.

Gould disagreed on both counts. A tautology is a statement in which the object of the sentence contains no information that is not already present in the subject. "My father is a man," Gould pointed out, is a tautology because one's father is inherently a man; no new information is given by stating the obvious. "The fit survive" seemed to Bethell to be just such a tautology, because we define survivors as those that are fit (or, in a population geneticist's version, "the genotype with the largest survival rate is defined as the fittest"). The criterion of an organism's fitness is the fact of its survival.

Bethell blamed this "mistake" of Darwin's on a faulty analogy. The first chapter of *Origin of Species* is about pigeon breeding. In the artificial selection by which pigeon breeders have shaped from the single wild species of rock pigeon the very different traits of fantails, tumblers, pouters, and carrier pigeons, Darwin saw an analogy with how nature shapes by selection improved species of organisms from a single ancestral species. The fault in the analogy is that whereas pigeon fanciers imagine in advance the goal they aim to achieve through selection, and thus have independent criteria by which to measure their progress, nature is without goals, there are no independent criteria, and species, however much they may change, cannot be said to improve.

Gould argued that there is an independent criterion. Given a change in physical conditions, such as the one that followed the raising of the Andes and the more minor changes that occur continually everywhere on the globe, one can imagine organisms worse or better engineered to survive under the changed conditions. He did not argue, as I believe Darwin did, that there is such a thing as cosmic superiority, but he found in the idea of superior design to cope with new local conditions the "pearl" of Darwin's wisdom. "These traits," he wrote, "confer fitness by an engineer's criterion of good design, not by the empirical fact of their survival and spread. It got colder before the woolly mammoth evolved its shaggy coat."

By that standard, the idea of fitness seemed to him testable. If we knew that climate was cooling, we could predict that those organisms capable of improving the design of their insulation would survive. However, how could one have chosen among the numerous species of elephant that existed prior to the Ice Age that one which could grow a shaggy coat? And if the Ice Age were to have descended on the world with the speed of a comet, who would have had time to don furs? I was not convinced.

I HAVE SINCE HAD REASON, HOWEVER, TO BE CONVINCED that Gould was right when he objected to Bethell's second claim: that Darwin's theory is on the verge of collapse, that "natural selection has been quietly abandoned." The advocates of natural selection are vigorous and vocal, as Gould pointed out. Noting statements by the architects of neo-Darwinism, Gould concurred that natural selection had been "compared to a composer by Dobzhansky; to a poet by Simpson; to a sculptor by Mayr; and to, of all people, Mr. Shakespeare by Julian Huxley" because these most prominent of evolutionary biologists—and Gould himself—intend by such metaphors to "illustrate the essence of Darwinism —the creativity of natural selection." That such passionate avowals of belief penetrate to the rank and file of biologists was recently brought home to me when I was invited to Berlin to help select speakers for a conference on evolution. I was surprised to hear a young and brilliant geneticist argue against the participation by another because of the latter's lack of faith in natural selection. I had breakfast with the young professor and asked him why he had been so very righteous, as though there were no alternative to the theory of natural selection except the doctrine of divine creation.

He cited evidence both from artificial selection experiments performed in genetics laboratories and from a natural experiment that had recently taken place, appropriately enough, among the finches Darwin had studied in the Galápagos Islands.

The results of the natural experiment were published in *Nature* under the title "Intense Natural Selection in a Population of Darwin's Finches *(Geospizinae)* in the Galápagos." The event had been a perfect illustration that "survival of Darwin's finches through a drought on Daphne Major Island was nonrandom. Large birds, especially males with large beaks, survived best because they were best able to crack the large and hard seeds that predominated in the drought."

I complained that I did not understand what had been proved by the survival of big-beaked birds. Random means haphazardly, without aim, purpose, or principle. By nonrandom, the author seemed to me to have implied that selection on the island was purposeful and governed by principle. I could easily agree that the survival of powerful beaks had been nonrandom—certainly they were a superior design for cracking hard nuts—but what was nonrandom about the drought? Is drought not a vagary of nature, I asked? Is adaptation to survive through a drought a definition of fitness? What would be the fitness of big-beaked birds if the climate were to change in the opposite direction, so there would be no more droughts? Is such selection creative, as when a sculptor imagines in a block of Naxos marble the image of Venus, and by slow chipping brings her forth?

Being a Chinese fatalist, I could see only chance. By chance there was a drought on Daphne Major. By chance there were big-beaked birds who survived on big hard seeds. What is creative in the selection of a trait that may be as transient as the weather? On other islands, other finches survived because a different set of chances was at play.

Indulging in a game of semantics and tautology, I suggested that we could, of course, define chance as the caprice of nature, and chance selection would therefore be natural selection. Those that survive are then by definition the luckiest. But they are not necessarily the fittest (what if it should rain?).

My neo-Darwinist friend was not amused. Since Mendel's work on the patterns of inheritance was rediscovered in the twentieth century, and the language of genes themselves decoded in the 1950s, the mechanism of evolution has been opened both to laboratory experiments and to field investigations that are far more precise than anything Darwin could have imagined. Geneticists have found that because traits are inherited through genes, and the variations within a population are an expression of different combinations of genes, a large population with a large gene pool has the potential for very large variations. In addition, genes can be changed suddenly and radically by mutations caused, in the laboratory at least, by everything from irradiation to chemical pollutants. The results have been heady.

Through artificial selection in the laboratory—he mentioned fruit fly labs—individuals carrying a particular genetic trait or a particular mutation can be separated and bred among themselves. When such a breeding group is isolated from the rest of the population long enough, a new species can theoretically be created. Scientists, my young friend earnestly explained, have as yet bred such isolated groups only for long enough periods to produce novel varieties, not new species, but nature has, and recently enough that their evolution can be documented beyond doubt.

He gave me this example: The ancestors of many plants and animals now indigenous to the Hawaiian Islands became isolated there only a few million years ago. Because they were unable to interbreed with their mainland relatives, they evolved into new species which exist nowhere else. He added, for good measure, other mechanisms of "apartheid" that have also resulted in reproductive isolation and, consequently, in speciation.

All this he explained to me patiently, as a youngster caught up in the "real world" explains life to his elders, and as, for a long time now, evolutionary biologists have explained living phenomena to paleontologists, who live with the dead, with cases of bones, drawers of shells, and fossil collections. The present is the key to the past, and experiments in the fruit fly lab simulate nature so exactly that he questioned whether an evolutionary biologist has any need at all to know anything about the history of life as recorded by fossils.

EARTH SCIENTISTS PROBABLY HAVE THEMSELVES TO blame for being so roundly ignored. Paleontology, which added the dimension of time to the study of the Earth, took center stage during the nineteenth century as the link between ancient history and the ongoing processes that might elucidate it. The chair of paleontology was the first chair of numerous geological institutes in Europe, and of the first thirty recipients of geology's prestigious prize, the Wollastan Medal, more than half, from William Smith in 1830 to Charles Darwin in 1859, did major work in paleontology. Of the last thirty recipients, however, only one was a paleontologist.

The field went into a steep decline after the turn of the century. Students were taught to classify and identify petrefacts which proved useful in assigning relative ages to geological formations, and though the task was well done, paleontologists were still arguing whether a particular boundary between formations should be 10 meters higher or 5 meters lower while geologists turned their attention to the drama of geophysics, geochemistry, oceanography, and plate tectonics. Paleontology ceased to be taught in some universities, and the subject of evolution was dropped from the curriculum for geology students. As John Maynard Smith remarked, "the attidude of population geneticists to any paleontologist rash enough to offer a contribution to evolutionary theory has been to tell him to go away and find another fossil, and not to bother the grown-ups."

YET AN ATTEMPT TO UNDERSTAND THE ORIGIN OF SPEcies by the purely rational insights of genetics is paramount to trying to elucidate the origin of nations by applying the disciplines of ethnology, sociology, physical anthropology, and mass psychology. The origin of national states is history. No amount of social science research can explain why the northwestern boundary between Switzerland and France is drawn right through the middle of the Jura Mountains, separating people who speak the same language and who go to the same church. Only the study of history reveals that the acquisition of Bernese Jura by Switzerland was a chance decision by a group of politicians at the Vienna Congress of 1815, a historical fact understandable only in terms of the politics of the Napoleonic War.

The survival of national states is also explained only by their unique history. No theory could have predicted that Liechtenstein was to remain a sovereign state while dozens of other German or Austrian feudal lands were to lose their independence. Certainly it would be tautological to claim that the survivor was the fittest.

If we are to explain the evolution of species as we now know them, a knowledge of mechanisms is helpful, but a knowledge of history is indispensable. The nations as we know them have certainly evolved, and various

disciplines suggest mechanisms by which we can understand some aspects of their evolution, but each has a
unique history—plagues, wars, economic or ideological
crises—without knowledge of which our theorizing will
be utterly confounded. Similarly, we cannot understand
the origin and extinction of species if we ignore the fossil
record and deny the reality of biotic crises.

WHAT DOES THE GEOLOGICAL RECORD TELL US ABOUT
extinction in the history of life? In his 1982 presidential
address to the Geological Society of America, Digby
McLaren summed up the consensus among paleontologists. There have been a number of mass extinctions in
the history of life on earth, of which the terminal Cretaceous event was the most recent.

The patterns are similar for all the events. Large communities of diverse organisms are wiped out and are replaced by new communities low in diversity but rich in
numbers. McLaren emphasized the tempo of mass extinctions: They come suddenly, without warning, after
long periods in which nothing dramatic seems to have
happened in the evolution of the organisms living at that
time. The large, abruptly extinguished population is replaced "immediately"—to a geologist such as McLaren
that means within a few thousand years—by a population as large as the original one, but only after a few
million years has that new population again become spe-
ciated to the degree of diversity it had before the extinction. To a geologist or paleontologist, that degree of
speciation within a few million years is also very rapid.

This pattern of speciation and extinction is quite different from the pattern Darwin proposed, and that he
based on the Malthusian pattern of population growth
and check. We see no increase in species until after the
extinction event, as we see no evidence of an escalating
struggle for existence prior to it. Unlike the Malthusian
world where reproductive success leads to clashes and
calamities, the history of life has been characterized by
episodes of wholesale slaughter followed by explosive
radiation of new forms. Reproductive success does not

precede calamity; it follows it. Like the baby boom after World War II, increased fertility is the consequence, not the cause, of catastrophe.

MANY PALEONTOLOGISTS SUBSCRIBE TO THE NICHE theory of evolution: There are only so many niches on earth, and they are occupied by a finite number of species. When all niches are filled, evolution slows or nearly halts. But when a catastrophe comes and kills off the occupants of many niches, a new scramble for living space begins. This scenario is somewhat analogous to that of a neutron bomb, which kills people but leaves buildings intact. After a mass extinction, the area the former species occupied—prairie, desert, woodland, shore, and so on—is left empty for habitation. The explosive speciation that follows refills these empty "buildings" with newcomers.

In actuality, the scenario is not quite so simple. Many of the niches inhabited before the catastrophe cease to exist. For example, the niche inhabited by parasites adapted to dinosaur hosts vanished with the extinction of dinosaurs, and so did countless other niches that had been occupied within the complex web of relationships among organisms. Interrelationship among organisms is the condition that allows diversity in the first place. The niche of a predator includes the peculiarities of its prey, just as the niche of a dandelion includes the humans that bare the ground for its germination. However, such "occupational addresses," too, are put on the market in the wake of a catastrophe, though more slowly than the raw space of habitats. As habitats refill with pioneer species, the increasing complexity of their interrelationships eventually makes available again the tremendous variety of "jobs" there had been before.

After a catastrophe the rapidly increasing populations descended from the survivors are in no way comparable to the species whose physical habitats they refill. They are not more fit; they are simply first. These pioneers are followed by descendants of the same lineage who, as they speciate, begin to fill a variety of previously vacated occupational addresses. Again, they are not necessarily the most fit for those niches, but again they are first. Thus it is as impossible to say that the brand-new species of foraminifers that appeared where the Cretaceous species had once lived were more fit as it is outrageous to claim that whales are superior to mosasaurs. When mosasaurs became extinct in the Cretaceous catastrophe, they vacated both their space in the seas and their role of oceangoing fisheater. When whales evolved 10 million years later, they did so on an empty stage.

Evolution may be creative, but nature, the creator, does not seem to work according to Darwin, slowly but unerringly chipping from each block of marble the shape that will most perfectly fill a preexisting scheme. I think of this creation more like that of an impulsive writer let loose with a Macintosh computer. She pounds the keys furiously, nearly filling the memory of her MacWrite disk. Then, for a long time, she fiddles with this and that, deleting a word here, substituting another of similar meaning. Then, one day, she finds her disk has been accidentally wiped out, and the draft must be begun again almost from scratch.

The new draft may or may not be better than the first, but it is different. Nor is it really a revision of the first, for, constrained only by the limits of her knowledge and her vocabulary, which might be compared to the constraints of genetics, developmental pathways, and the "grammar" of relationships among organisms and to their habitats, she has completely rewritten her text.

Scientists attempting to decipher the fossil record of such manuscripts have of course been puzzled. We find successive drafts with almost completely different contents. Darwin solved the puzzle to his satisfaction by assuming that intermediate versions, the evolution of, for example, late Mesozoic to early Cenozoic life forms, were missing from the record. But although the record is certainly fragmentary, in that paragraphs and whole pages may never be recovered, our new evidence tells us that chapters are not missing. There never was a transition. There is no chasm at Gubbio.

As McLaren declared in his speech, few paleontologists now dispute that mass extinctions have occurred, although scientists still argue about the rates and about the causes. Certainly few seriously consider the cause of extinction to be competition among organisms in the struggle for life or propose that mammals battled with dinosaurs or even fought for their niches. Yet a dyed-in-the-wool Darwinist might still try to rescue his master's thesis with the argument that survival of the fittest applies to the ability to survive a crisis.

I am reminded of the "little water bears" that Gould described in one of his essays. They are tiny creatures, less than a millimeter, and look something like insects. Their appealing name was given them by the German naturalist Goeze, who discovered them in 1773 and, puzzled about their classification, called them *Kleiner Wasserbär*. More than four hundred species of these crustaceans have since been discovered inhabiting an amazing diversity of niches from the Arctic to the Antarctic, and from high mountains to the ocean abyss. Little water bears survive extremes by going into a profound dormancy. In that state they are oblivious to hunger; they can live through temperatures exceeding that of boiling water, and dropping to 0.0008 Kelvin, or nearly absolute zero. They can withstand radiation a thousand times more intense than the lethal dose for humans. And, Gould wrote, they can awaken like Sleeping Beauty after a dormancy of a hundred years, as one curator discovered when he moistened a specimen of dried moss in his museum's collection.

If the ability to survive a crisis is the bedrock criterion of fitness, then little water bears are the fittest of us all, and that is the direction, the purpose, and the perfection to which natural selection should have tended. Luckily, it has not.

What is then fit? Being adapted. Adapted to what? To one's niche. What if the niche is disrupted? Then one becomes a misfit.

The dinosaurs may have been superbly fit, each to its way of life in relationship to the organisms that affected it and in the physical environment which it inhabited. Then the meteor hit, the dinosaurs became misfits, and they perished. The fitness of the Irish elk and the woolly mammoth to the environments of the Ice Age is beyond question, but they vanished when the climate ameliorated. There is no meaning to fitness if the conditions on which it is based are capricious.

WE CAN RETURN NOW TO THE QUESTION OF WHETHER natural selection is a law of science or a statement of ideology. By Popper's test of falsifiability, and by the test of its power to predict, it fails. Its powers of prediction are less even than those of history, for if we studied the records of Rome before its fall and knew the nature, the condition, and the aspirations of the peoples that surrounded it, we might predict its fall without knowing that that had happened. But were we to know everything of the last days of the Maastrichtian flora and fauna, were actually to watch movies of dinosaurs and ammonites, study in the greatest detail their ways of life on the earth of that time, we could not predict their demise. There was no warning; no theory can encompass what happened. We also cannot falsify the notion of inferiority in those that expired, or superiority in those that survived, because, in the words of the creationists, "it is impossible to describe a scientific experiment" that would duplicate the event that ended the Cretaceous era.

Indeed, we cannot prove that an organism is unfit unless it has become extinct; neither can we prove that an organism is fit save by observing that it is alive. We may believe that *Mosasaurus* was not fit to keep its job preying on fish in the open ocean, and we may believe that the mammal that became a whale preying on fish in the open ocean was more suitable for that job, but such interpretations are not science. Were mosasaurs here today, perhaps their flesh would be less palatable, their oil less valuable to humans, and they would fare much better than overhunted, endangered whales. Such is the caprice of evolution.

Probably all extinction, even the background extinction that goes on all the time, is no less accidental, no more predictable, and every bit as unrelated to fitness as catastrophic mass extinction. After all, everything is always changing, and a proportion of the fit are continually transformed into misfits too rapidly for chance variation to discover in time a revised niche. But mass extinctions arrest our attention, particularly as they have happened quite a few times in Earth's history.

Almost every major division of geological time, as between the Ordovician period and the Silurian, marks the extinction of previously flourishing suites of organisms and the arising of equally flourishing new suites. The abrupt transition from the Paleozoic era to the Mesozoic era has about the same pattern as that from the Mesozoic to the Cenozoic, but was even more severe. Fully 95 percent of Paleozoic species vanished 250 million years ago. Very early in the Paleozoic, at the beginning of the Cambrian period 560 million years ago, the fossil record shows an astonishing burst of shelled forms of life. Either because too few fossil-bearing strata are preserved from Precambrian times, or because the organisms that flourished then were soft-bodied and therefore seldom preserved, we have little record of what happened then. Judging from the pattern at other times, however, the dramatically explosive speciation followed an equally dramatic extinction.

When I was still a university student, Steve Stanley of Johns Hopkins University interpreted the Precambrian disaster according to the niche theory as it was understood at that time, when the word niche meant more habitat than way of life. He visualized a Precambrian world covered with algae which obstructed the evolution of other groups of organisms that might have put the space to better use. He then imagined a unicellular grazer that ate up the algae, sweeping clean new niches for occupation by multicellular animals. The basis for Stanley's imaginings is the cropping principle well known to ecologists. A well-cropped ecosystem, whether it is a tidal pool or the African plains, permits a greater diversity of life than is possible in one overgrown, for example, with mussels or a single species of grass. The tiny grazer, Stanley supposed, made the Cambrian explosion of life forms possible. Steven Gould dubbed this creature "the unsung hero in the history of life."

The trouble with this brilliant idea is that the hero left no bones behind and was therefore unlikely ever to be found. Only a few primitive shells had at that time been discovered in rock older than the Cambrian. However, in 1947 an Australian geologist made a spectacular discovery in the late Precambrian sandstones of the Ediacara Hills in South Australia. Because of a particularly favorable mode of preservation, many 600-million-year-old fossils of soft-bodied organisms were found: some medusalike and possibly jellyfish, others apparently worms and algae, and still others strange animals that bear no resemblance to any known organisms, living or dead. Since then similar assemblages of soft-bodied creatures have been found at other sites in Australia, and in South Africa, England, the Soviet Union, and Newfoundland.

If these are the creatures we must look to either to give rise to the dizzying array of new organisms that followed them in the Cambrian, or to be disposed of to make way for the new forms, a unicellular hero will not do. Such tiny things, no matter how voracious, do not eat jellyfish. What did happen to the Ediacarian fauna, and why is it so difficult to assign them to later categories of life?

WHEN I WENT TO CHINA IN 1981 TO JOIN THE SIXTIETH anniversary celebration of the Geological Society of China, I met an old friend, C. C. Wu. Wu told me that Frank Asaro of Berkeley had found a very large iridium anomaly in a sample from a horizon just below the first appearance of trilobites, an ancient arthropod that became tremendously abundant in the Cambrian and that heralded the explosion of other shelled creatures. It was exciting news.

An iridium anomaly, as we by then knew, is a good indicator that a meteorite might have hit the earth. Perhaps we could make a carbon isotope study of this Precambrian-Cambrian boundary. My Chinese hosts were very helpful, taking me to the cliffs on the side of the Yangtze Gorge in central China where the boundary is well exposed. I collected six samples for preliminary study. I sent a portion of this little collection to Urs Krähenbühl at Bern for iridium analysis; Hedi Oberhänsli, my assistant, helped me with the mass spectrometry.

The results delighted us. We found the iridium spike indicative of a meteorite impact, and also the negative carbon-isotope anomaly suggestive of a nearly sterile ocean, both right at a boundary analogous to that between the Cretaceous and the Tertiary—that is, just before a fantastic episode of speciation.

Unwilling to rely on the results of analyzing only six rock chips, we asked our Chinese colleagues for more systematic sampling. Sun Shu, the director of the Geological Institute of the Chinese Academy of Sciences, sent us two suites of samples across the boundary, one from the Yangtze location where I had obtained the first six chips, and another from a site in Yunnan Province, more than 1,000 kilometers to the south.

Oberhansli analyzed the samples in our mass spectrometry lab. There was no mistake about it. The carbon-isotope anomaly is there, and at exactly the boundary horizon at both localities.

The "unsung hero of the history of life" was not, we are now convinced, a little cropper. It was a very big visitor from outer space. The Ediacarian fauna, the dinosaurs of their day, were probably among its victims.

Our Chinese colleagues had meanwhile communicated to us the results of their work on still another era boundary, the one between the Paleozoic and Mesozoic, which, with 95 percent of species wiped out, may rank as the most devastating biotic crisis there has ever been. Using neutrons as detectives, the Chinese scientists were able to flush out the suspect: An iridium anomaly was found in a boundary clay that separates the Permian, the last period of the Paleozoic era, from the Triassic, the first period of the Mesozoic era. There was also a negative carbon-isotope anomaly at that horizon. We now have the same pattern of geochemical changes for all three era boundaries that mark the most drastic turns in evolution in the history of life on Earth.

The word catastrophe comes from the Greek *kata strophe*, "to turn around thoroughly." Each of these major impacts has turned evolution in a different direction, from the strangely flat, soft Ediacarans to the shelled and shapely organisms of the Cambrian, or from a dinosaurian fauna to a mammalian one. It is hard to think of the most crucial turnarounds in life's history as wayward happenings. If our planet's collisions with meteorites seem capricious—and the disruption such catastrophes cause to life chaotic—is there nevertheless some pattern to them? If history repeats itself, does it do so with regularity?

DAVE RAUP AND JOHN SEPKOSKI BELIEVE THAT MASS extinctions come in cycles. There have been, in addition to those major mass extinctions by which we separate geological eras, quite a few lesser episodes of extinction that are nevertheless of a great enough magnitude to make them visible in the fossil record. Looking at such identifiable episodes over the last 250 million years, University of Chicago scientists charted a rhythm of one catastrophe every 26 million years; the most recent occurred 14 million years ago.

Walter Alvarez and Richard Muller then compared that temporal pattern with the record of impact cratering on earth during the same 250-million-year period. Very few are well dated, but they came up with an approximate fit. There seems to have been a 28.4-million-year rhythm to major impacts; the most recent episode of mass extinction identified by Raup and Sepkoski coincided with a meteorite hit near the town of Ries in southern Germany 14 million years ago.

The inaccuracy of geological dating so far precludes any perfect matching, for the radiometric dating of fossil strata as well as the dating of impact debris can still be off by a couple of million years in either direction. However, Raup, Alvarez, and others have become convinced that there has been regularity in these events, and that the rhythm is controlled by the laws of celestial motion.

There are many such rhythms. One is the 50-million-year rhythm Clube and Napier described as being a possible cause of periodic cometary impact in the 1979 *Nature* article that encouraged me to throw my hat into the ring of controversy surrounding the Cretaceous extinction. That interval obviously failed to correspond to Raup and Sepkoski's 26-million-year cycle of mass extinctions. Another periodicity involves our sun's bobbing motion up and down through the plane of the Milky Way galaxy, but it bobs in a 33-million-year rhythm. The greatest publicity has been accorded the most far-out theory: the sensational idea that a hidden companion star of the sun, ominously named *Nemesis,* could explain the periodic disruptions to heavenly bodies that cause earthly catastrophes. When I visited the Alvarezes in Berkeley in the fall of 1985, they told me that their colleagues had combed through thousands of pictures of the sky without finding a trace of the phantom star.

There are obviously too many unknowns that would have to be fathomed before we could correlate evolution with celestial motion. The cyclicity of mass extinction could be a misreading of the geological record, the periodicity of impact cratering has been charted on the basis of too few data, and we do not have the slightest evidence that Nemesis exists. I share, therefore, the judgment of Gene Shoemaker, who gave the idea less than a 1 percent chance of being correct, and perhaps would go so far as to concur with Dewey McLean's opinion that "It's science gone absolutely bonkers."

Besides, it is beside the point.

Even if we were to discover that earth is regularly bombarded by comets, we could still make no prediction about evolutionary trends. What would happen after an impact depends on the meteorite's size, where it hit, at what time of year, and—most crucial, and in complexity way beyond what even the latest supercomputer could analyze—what the consequences would be for the whole fabric of the living world, in which all organisms depend in one way or another on all other organisms.

IT IS TIME TO AWAKEN TO THE ABSURDITY OF THE IDEA OF natural selection. Ernst Chain, a Nobel laureate in biology, spoke bravely: "To postulate...the development and survival of the fittest...seems to me a hypothesis based on no evidence and irreconcilable with the facts....It amazes me that [it is] swallowed so uncritically and readily, and for such a long time, by so many scientists without a murmur of protest."

The hypothesis based on no evidence and irreconcilable with the facts was swallowed so readily, I think, because we would like to believe it. The only natural thing about the "natural law" of the survival of the fittest is that it corresponds in some degree with human nature. We have been competitive; we have exterminated others, both our own and other species, whom we perceive to be inferior, or at least of no account; and we would like to feel justified in such endeavors. But the history of life can provide a scientific basis neither for capitalism nor for socialism, neither for Marxism nor for racism nor for the Maoism of ceaseless revolution. The opinion that "favored races" are preserved in a struggle for existence was a speculation that has become a dangerous ideology. We should cease to lend it a cloak of scientific respectability.

But I can imagine that the loss of that ideology will leave many feeling bereft. The concept of rational causes and ultimate purposes may be built into our root perception of the world, an artifact of our own unique evolution. If the great happenings of life's history, even the fact that we are here at all, is happenstance (for would the mammals from which we are descended have had a chance unless the dinosaurs had been knocked out by a stray comet?), then how are we to bear the apparent accident of our existence?

It is not easy merely to be lucky. I know that well. Some people told me that I was lucky that I survived a car crash that killed my wife, Ruth. Was I lucky that I lived, or was she lucky to die, and to be spared the sorrow of bereavement? A minister from a Protestant church visited me and told me to read in the Bible the Epistles of Paul the Apostle to the Corinthians. I found consolation in the thought that life is but a mission, and death the reward. Perhaps Ruth's mission had been completed; she had given birth to three lovely children. With luck, although it felt then like misfortune, I was to survive to complete my mission before my own death.

With my advancing years I have been increasingly attracted to the philosophy of Taoism, taught to me so long ago by my mother in an environment where the struggle for existence, first under foreign domination and then in the midst of global strife, was not only a daily reality, but the overriding goal in life. We are all children of our time and see the world with the colored glasses of our own experience. When I went to America as a student after the war, I became what my daughter calls a *Funfziger*, an achiever. That was the 1950s; we were all achievers then. I was already too old to join the hippies and flower children as they gathered in the 1960s, but their turning away from the spirit of social Darwinism seemed to me a hopeful beginning of a new era, a new outlook on life, and one more in keeping with the Taoist traditions I still harbored, still nascent, from my childhood.

Tao is the Chinese word for "way," and as it is used in Taoism, it means the way, the principle, the truth. This truth, however, is of a more elusive sort than the Western brand, which may mean only "factual." Karl Popper liked to quote the German humorist Wilhelm Bush of Max and Moritz fame:

> *Twice two equals four 'tis true*
> *But too empty and too trite*
> *What I look for is a clue*
> *To some matter not so light.*

In Taoism, any "matter not so light" is also a matter inherently elusive. The first sentence of the *Tao Te Chin*, the scripture of Taoism, is: "The Tao that can be talked about is not the true Tao." Popper said something similar about truth; it is what one can never find. He said we know of its existence, however, because falsehood is easy to detect. The existence of lies proves the reality of truth, no matter how elusive, just as the existence of misfortune proves the reality of luck, although luck, too, is elusive. I think the survival of the luckiest can be grasped, can be accepted, by this sort of thinking. There is a way, a principle, a truth in what has happened on this earth of ours that can't be found, and can't be talked about, but that nevertheless exists.

I am not so arrogant as to pretend to know the Tao of evolution. I shall not attempt to define luck. Corinthians did not offer the meaning of mission as it applies to the dinosaurs, although I can appreciate that my existence may be owing to their timely demise. There must be a Tao in evolution, but if it is something we can talk about, it is not the true Tao. I prefer to leave it that way, to take heart in the presence of truth through the revealing of falsehood. The subtitle of Darwin's book, *The Preservation of Favored Races in the Struggle for Life*, is a false-hood, and so are all the ideologies it spawned or that grew anyhow but used it for a justification.

I also prefer to look differently on life than Darwin did.

IN A RECENT DAHLEM CONFERENCE IN BERLIN, KARL Niklas of Cornell reviewed for us the history of evolution as revealed in fossil communities. His depiction empha-sized the evolutionary relationships within which inven-tion, diversity, and new opportunities arise. The first organisms on earth lived in the sea. The aquatic arthro-pods that evolved into terrestrial insects were enabled to do so by the algae on which they browsed and that be-came able to green the damp shores. The insects were food for their predators, who evolved into spiders, and the former evolved wings while the latter evolved webs as plants grew upward, forest high. Insects that ate pol-len and nectar enabled plants to exploit them for pollina-tion, and the resulting increased diversity of flowering plants created new niches for insects that invented new ways to use them, and the insects in turn created new niches for insectivores—not only spiders, but amphibians, reptiles, and the earliest mammals.

That is only the smallest slice of the record. In the countless such stories that can be read from fossil or from living communities, the interdependence of life forms is the thread of their evolution, each change in one form effecting changes in a web of forms that, altogether, participate in the phenomenon called life. There is in this story little evidence that new groups ride over the dead bodies of the old. Rather, extinction of any form causes a crisis for other forms, for there is no such thing as an organism that lives without dependence on others. An organism may ultimately benefit from crisis, as one might say the *Globigerina eugubina* plankton did, or it might be decimated, as all the other floaters were at the end of the Cretaceous. But one cannot say that the new species of foraminifer survived at the expense of the old, and one must admit that *G. eugubina*'s survival is of great account in the speciation of even mammalian survivors, since it was its descendents that cleared the air.

If such a perception offers a glimpse of the Tao of evolution—of its way, its truth—then it is to be valued for its humility. We cannot say whether misfortune is luck in disguise, or whether luck is really misfortune, because for all our intelligence, it has not been given to us to make such judgments. There have been leaps in evolution; perhaps God does play dice.

The century after the publication of *Origin of Species* has been an age of intense strife and anxiety. We have had two world wars and the tyranny of many totalitarian regimes. It seems to me that the more we try to assert superiority, or judge the worth of others, or channel our destiny into one or another's concept of perfection, the more harm we do. With my mother's old-fashioned wisdom, and with the far more ancient wisdom we can learn from the history of life on earth, I believe we must live without pretending to know who or what is fit and not fit. Instead, we should embrace the diversity of forms and ways that nourish life itself. Looking back over the several billion years of our evolution, that is the closest I can come to the Tao of our existence.

For a Westerner, perhaps the essence of my perception can best be expressed by a quote from the Bible:

> I returned and saw under the sun that the race is not to the swift, nor the battle to the strong, neither yet bread to the wise, nor yet riches to men of understanding, nor yet favor to men of skill; but time and chance happeneth to them all.

Index

About the Author

Kenneth J. Hsü's venturesome curiosity has led him from the oil fields of the American West to some of the most gripping—and controversial—geological discoveries of our time. In addition to confirming the global catastrophe at the end of the Cretaceous, Hsü's deep sea drilling of the Mediterranean sea has uncovered the startling fact that during one period in its history it had dried up entirely. Hsü is a winner of the Wollastan Medal, geology's most prestigious award, and has been elected Honorary Fellow of the Geological Society of America, Honorary Professor of the Chinese Academy of Sciences, and foreign member of the U.S. Academy of Sciences.